MENZIES
& CHURCHILL
AT WAR

Robert Menzies and Winston Churchill
London, 1941
(AUSTRALIAN WAR MEMORIAL)

A CONTROVERSIAL NEW ACCOUNT
OF THE 1941 STRUGGLE FOR POWER

MENZIES
& CHURCHILL
AT WAR

DAVID DAY

PARAGON HOUSE PUBLISHERS
New York

First United States edition

Published in the United States by

Paragon House Publishers
90 Fifth Avenue
New York, New York 10011

Library of Congress Cataloging-in-Publication Data

Day, David, 1949-
   Menzies and Churchill at war.

   Bibliography:
   Includes index.
   1. World War, 1939–1945—Diplomatic history.
2. Churchill, Winston, Sir, 1874–1965—Military leadership.   3. Menzies, Robert Gordon, Sir, 1894–1978.
4. Great Britain—Foreign relations—Australia.
5. Australia—Foreign relations—Great Britain.
6. World War, 1939–1945—Campaigns.   I. Title.
D750.D39   1987   940.53'22   87–9044
ISBN 0-913729-93-0

To Tsila

CONTENTS

Acknowledgements

*I*n any work of this nature, the historian inevitably accumulates a long list of people who helped in varying ways and degrees to produce the final work. In my case I am principally indebted to my wife, Silvia, who put up with the chaos created by my writing and cheerfully accepted the extra burden produced by my absence on research trips.

My friend and supervisor, Professor David Fieldhouse, was important in sustaining my enthusiasm and for ensuring that I approached the subject with a wider perspective than I might otherwise have adopted.

I was fortunate in that my arrival in Cambridge coincided with a decision by the Australian Government to establish an Australian Studies Centre at the University of London under the able direction of Professor Geoffrey Bolton. The centre quickly became a lively focus for discussion of Australian topics and provided the initial opportunity for me to put forward the ideas and research contained in this book. Despite a heavy workload, Professor Bolton was always ready to read and comment on drafts of this work.

The following people also were helpful at various times with advice and encouragement: my parents, Alan and Judy Day; Dr W. J. Hudson; Professor A. Low; Dr John McCarthy; Dr David Reynolds; Dr C. Wischik.

I would particularly like to thank the Master, Fellows and Scholars of Churchill College, Cambridge, for providing me with a pleasant environment in which to live and work. For six months in 1982, I lived in London where the Warden and staff of William Goodenough House provided a similarly pleasant working environment. In March 1985 I began a research fellowship at Clare College which has enabled me to remain in Cambridge to complete this book.

The financial burden of research and of writing was relieved by various grants from the Managers of the Smuts Fund, together with

ix

the Holland Rose Studentship which I held from 1982 to 1984.

In making research trips to Australia, I was tremendously assisted by those people who generously provided accommodation and thereby allowed me to stretch my limited research funds—in Canberra, Don and Marg Wright; in Adelaide, Malcolm and Pauline Day; in Sydney, Sharon Laura; in Melbourne, Brian and Khris Sanstrom.

My thanks are also due to the many archivists in Britain and Australia who coped with my demand for documents and did their best to produce them, and to Avril Symonds who typed the various drafts, often at short notice but always with good humour.

This book might never have appeared without initial support from David Williamson and later Richard Walsh of Angus and Robertson Publishers. Richard Walsh's enthusiasm and financial support was important in initiating this project, and he and my editor, Norman Rowe, have done much to guide the shape of this book and make it more readable than it might otherwise have been.

Despite the generous contribution from all of the above people and organisations, the responsibility for the work must necessarily be mine alone.

For permission to quote from their books, I would like to thank the following publishers: Sidgwick and Jackson Ltd for Cecil King's *With Malice Toward None*; Anthony Sheil Associates Ltd for R. R. James' *Victor Cazalet*; David Higham Associates Ltd for David Dilks' *The Diaries of Sir Alexander Cadogan*; A. D. Peters and Co. Ltd for Kingsley Martin's *Editor*; Cassell Ltd for Winston Churchill's *The Second World War* iii; Collins Publishers for Captain Stephen Roskill's *Hankey, Man of Secrets* iii and Sir H. Nicolson's *Diaries and Letters* ii; Hutchinson Publishing Group Ltd for Major-General Sir John Kennedy's *The Business of War*; Hamish Hamilton for A. J. P. Taylor's *A Personal History*; Weidenfeld (Publishers) Ltd for R. R. James's *Chips: The Diaries of Sir Henry Channon*; Macmillan Ltd for K. Young's *The Diaries of Sir Robert Bruce Lockhart* ii and Vincent Massey's *What's Past is Prologue*; and Oxford University Press for Tom Jones's *A Diary with Letters, 1931–1950*.

For permission to quote from private papers I would like to thank the following people: Mrs Heather Henderson for the papers of her father, Sir Robert Menzies; the executors of the late Sir Percy James Grigg; the Master, Fellows and Scholars of Churchill College in the University of Cambridge for the Hankey Papers; Frank Strahan for the Robinson Papers; the Trustees of the Liddell Hart Centre for Military

Archives for the papers of Lord Alanbrooke, Lord Ismay and Liddell Hart; Dame Elisabeth Murdoch for the papers of her late husband, Sir Keith Murdoch; Lord Halifax and the Borthwick Institute of Historical Research for the Halifax Papers; Lady Seymour for the papers of her late husband, Sir Horace Seymour; Lord Caldecote for the papers of his father; the Controller of H. M. Stationery Office for Crown-copyright material in the Public Record Office and elsewhere; A. J. P. Taylor for the Beaverbrook Papers; Admiral Sir William Davis; the British Library of Political and Economic Science for Hugh Dalton's diary; the Clerk of the Records, House of Lords Record Office for the papers of Lord Beaverbrook and Lloyd George; C. & T. Publications Ltd for a paper by Sir Winston Churchill.

DAVID DAY

ABBREVIATIONS

AA   Australian Archives, Canberra
BL   British Library, London
CC   Churchill College Archives Centre, Cambridge
CUL   Cambridge University Library
DAFP   *Documents on Australian Foreign Policy 1939–49*,
        R. G. Neale et al, vols 1–6, Canberra
FUL   Flinders University Library, Adelaide
HLRO   House of Lords Record Office, London
IWM   Imperial War Museum, London
KC   Liddell Hart Centre for Military Archives, King's College,
        London
LSE   London School of Economics
Menzies 1941 Trip Diary, MS 4936/13/3, Menzies Papers: NLA
Diary
NLA   National Library of Australia, Canberra
NMM   National Maritime Museum, Greenwich
PRO   Public Record Office, London
SRO   Scottish Record Office, Edinburgh
UMA   University of Melbourne Archives

Introduction

*E*arly on the morning of Friday, 1 September 1939, German armed forces stormed into Poland in the first act of the Second World War. On the other side of the world the young Australian Prime Minister, Robert Gordon Menzies, was being driven to the small Victorian country town of Colac where he was due to address a meeting and later spend the weekend with friends. Hitler's plans overrode those of Menzies who returned to Melbourne to proclaim Australia's entry into the war alongside Great Britain.

In London, Winston Churchill was recalled to office after spending 10 years in the political wilderness denouncing disarmament and appeasement. In eight months, this passed-over politician would be Prime Minister of Great Britain and political leader of the British Empire. The issue of prosecuting the war while protecting the Empire was to bring Menzies and Churchill into sharp conflict. The divisions between these two men became so deep that, in the midst of the military defeats of 1941, Menzies was to make a determined attempt to wrest the British Prime Ministership from Churchill's grasp and rescue the Empire from apparent disaster. It is the object of this work to outline and document that attempt.

By the end of 1940 Menzies was already terribly concerned over the direction in which Churchill was leading the Empire. By insisting on a policy of total victory over Germany, the British Premier seemed to be forcing the Empire into a protracted struggle that could produce only mutual exhaustion and desolation, if not the very defeat of Britain itself. Perhaps more importantly, it was gradually becoming clear that Churchill was determined to sustain his policy of total victory at the expense of the Empire that he was entrusted to protect. Under his stewardship, Britain began to cast aside imperial ties and turn toward the United States. Only America could provide the impetus for the complete defeat of Germany. Churchill was willing to subordinate

Britain in an alliance with America that would supersede the Empire in order to ensure the destruction of the Nazis and preserve Britain's place in a liberated Europe. Menzies, on the other hand, was impelled by sympathy and self-interest to protect the integrity of the Empire in its pre-war form. This set him on a collision course with Churchill that reached its climax in 1941. In January of that year Menzies left for London to co-ordinate and accelerate the despatch of armaments to Australia and the British base at Singapore. Apart from an abiding attachment to the British Empire, Menzies also took to London a continuing commitment to the largely discredited policy of appeasement. In the Imperial capital Menzies looked with horror on the death and destruction that surrounded him and regarded the future with great foreboding.

As luck would have it, his visit to London coincided with important military defeats for Britain in Greece and the Middle East. These defeats raised serious questions in Menzies' mind about Churchill's continued fitness for leadership and on the viability of his policy of total victory. At that time, given what was yet to come, the war was still a relatively minor affair. This was, in fact, the last chance to contain the conflict and achieve a compromise peace. Given the terrible risks of general conflagration, and the likely consequences for the Empire, Menzies tried to seize this chance.

He was far from being alone in adopting a critical stance toward Churchill. In the spring of 1941, increasing numbers of the British elite were posing much the same sort of questions that were so disturbing Menzies. There were politicians who shared his commitment to the Empire and feared that Churchill was causing its dissolution; there were businessmen who were disturbed at the disruption caused to their trade by the war and who feared the consequences of a British defeat; there were military men who were unable to square Britain's military capacity with Churchill's aggressive policies; and there were those who shared some or all of these concerns. To some of these people, Menzies appeared as a possible alternative to Churchill and they actively conspired to promote, both in the mind of Menzies and of the public at large, the possibility that his destiny lay in Downing Street.

Political history is littered with examples of unsuccessful bids for power. By their nature many go unreported and unrecorded by the participants. For different reasons, neither Churchill nor Menzies wished their conflict in 1941 to be the subject of future scrutiny. After the war Churchill carefully constructed a huge historical edifice of himself that allowed little scope for the existence of any real opposition to his leadership. He could hardly claim to have personified Britain at war if he publicised the existence of widespread opposition to his policies and style of leadership. Nor was it in British interests to depict Menzies as a wartime opponent of Churchill and a proponent of peace with Germany. Despite his wartime conflict with Churchill, Menzies remained Britain's best friend in Australia and any discussion of his role in 1941 would clearly detract from his future usefulness to Britain.

For Menzies' part, there was nothing to be gained and much to be lost by placing on the public record the real nature of his relationship with the British Prime Minister. After all, Churchill had been vindicated by victory and was probably revered even more widely in Australia than in Britain. At the same time, it was by then anathema to have had any association with the notion of a compromise peace. Menzies therefore carefully constructed an image of himself as having been a loyal follower of Churchill, albeit a sometimes critical one.

Despite these efforts by Menzies and Churchill, evidence abounds of their wartime conflict. In the darkness of the London blackout and between the shock waves of the German bombs, many members of the British elite used diaries to record their private thoughts and deeds. Many of these accounts portray a picture of British wartime politics that is seriously at variance with Churchill's; one which undermines the image of him as an undisputed national leader. In these diaries of 1941, Menzies' name appears prominently among Churchill's critics.

Menzies wrote on one occasion that he would be pleased if his descendants destroyed his private papers. Happily, they seem to have ignored his wish. These papers have now largely been made available for public scrutiny and they provide a fascinating insight into a particularly private man. There are, unfortunately, few letters written by Menzies that reveal his personal hopes and thoughts, but he did keep a diary during his trips overseas. So, at least for part of 1941, the historian now has the advantage of being able to see events through Menzies' eyes, to plumb the depth of his differences with Churchill and to chart the convolutions of their conflict.

The fairly recent release of the papers of Lord Bruce and Sir Frederick Shedden has helped to illuminate the story. Bruce was Australia's High Commissioner in London throughout the war and his extensive papers provide important confirmation of Menzies' activities and of his ultimate ambitions. Shedden, Secretary of the Department of Defence and of the Australian War Cabinet, accompanied Menzies on his visit to London and was an ardent and active supporter of the Australian Premier's plan to supplant Churchill. The release of his papers has provided crucial details of Menzies' London visit and of his relations with the critics of the British leader.

Another person whose papers figure prominently in this book is the enigmatic Australian businessman W. S. Robinson. An examination of his correspondence has uncovered two important letters which reveal the depth of Menzies' despair following his failure to topple Churchill and his own removal as Australian Prime Minister. They also reveal the amazing duration of Menzies' ambition to carve out a political future for himself in Westminster. It would now seem that it was not until early 1943 that he finally abandoned his attempts to transplant his talents to London and decided instead to resurrect his political fortunes in Australia. Australia's post-war political history was shaped in large measure by this crucial decision.

In the early 1950s, when Churchill and Menzies were both comfortably reinstated as Premiers of their respective countries, they sought to gloss over their previous conflict. This book puts the record straight and sets the conflict in its proper context—that of a disintegrating British Empire.

1

The Conflict Begins

Robert Menzies was a very relieved man as he left Melbourne early on Friday afternoon, 1 September 1939. Ahead of him lay a public meeting in the quiet country town of Colac and the prospect of a relaxing weekend in Victoria's Western District. The forecast promised Menzies balmy spring weather away from the cares of his office as Australian Prime Minister. In the forefront of his mind was the recent news from Europe where the prospects for peace now looked promising. Menzies was confident that Germany and Poland could settle their dispute and a second European war be averted.

On arrival in Colac, Menzies found his audience waiting outside the hall and buzzing with excitement. News had been received over the wireless that German troops had launched a surprise attack on Poland. Menzies led the townspeople inside and made a brief statement on the looming world conflict. In August 1914, Andrew Fisher had also been in Colac when Europe had erupted into war and he had then made his immortal pronouncement that Australia would back Britain to the last man and the last shilling. In 1939 Menzies was not so bellicose.

Rather than pledging all-out support for Britain, Menzies merely informed his anxious audience of the inevitable: "If Great Britain was at war Australia was a belligerent country...." Moreover, in further contrast to Fisher, Menzies deplored the war in strong terms, declaring that "it was hardly possible to think that such lunacy had broken out." Despite the German attack, Menzies did not relinquish hopes for a peaceful settlement. On the one hand he held out the possibility that reports of the German attack might be "only one of the exaggerated children of rumour", while on the other he claimed that the chances for "peaceful negotiation" were not yet extinguished. After a round of applause, Menzies left the meeting to speed back to Melbourne. By then storm clouds had also gathered over Victoria, and it was through pouring rain that the now worried Prime Minister hurried to a hastily assembled Cabinet meeting.[1]

Menzies' reaction to the outbreak of hostilities in Europe was in line with his previous support for the appeasement of Germany. He had been a staunch proponent of peace and his stand had been in stark contrast to the firm, uncompromising policies advocated by Winston Churchill. Instead, Menzies had fully supported the policy of the British Prime Minister, Neville Chamberlain, which had culminated in the settlement at Munich in September 1938.[2]

Menzies played an important role in confirming Australian support for Munich. He had only just returned from a visit to Europe and he spoke with seeming authority of Germany's case over Czechoslovakia.[3] Menzies reassured Australians that he was "disposed to discount the significance of German military demonstrations against Czechoslovakia" and that Europe was "more balanced than it was six months ago".[4] In this, of course, he was in good company as the Munich settlement had been almost universally acclaimed, with people everywhere still anxious for peace.

As the European situation developed in 1939, some people in Australia did mirror the attitude toward Germany that Churchill was advocating in Britain. Menzies, however, was not among them. He used his position to deny that there was any essential conflict of interest between Britain, Germany and Italy,[5] and to express the hope that a European crisis would be averted.[6] In June, he proposed to Chamberlain that Britain should pressure France to make a "generous approach" to Italy to settle outstanding questions with a view to ending the German–Italian alliance.[7] This was a classic appeasement position—proposing that peace be bought from an aggressor at the expense of a third party. Then, in July, Australia was prominent in preventing the appointment of Churchill to the Cabinet. Chamberlain noted Australia's concern that "if Winston got into the Government it would not be too long before it were at war".[8]

Though Menzies remained anxious for peace, European events were moving beyond his effective influence. As Australian Prime Minister one might have expected him to have at least acknowledged the warning signals steadily emanating from Europe and begun to prepare Australians for the possibility of war. This he steadfastly refused to do. In mid-August, just over two weeks before the war did break out, the Australian newspaper magnate Sir Keith Murdoch privately complained of Menzies persistently telling the nation "that peace is a certainty".[9]

Though he never really argued that peace was a certainty as Murdoch alleged, he did repeatedly advise Australians that they must not regard war as inevitable. He told one audience that such an attitude was "all moonshine". Moreover, at this late stage, he still insisted that there were no basic differences dividing Britain and Germany. Instead, he claimed that the present crisis was caused by misunderstandings resulting from the peoples of various countries being "cunningly told that others want to get at them . . . naturally they adopt an attitude of self-defence". This criticism seems as much directed at the activities of Churchill as it does those of Hitler. Not only did Menzies imply that the crisis was an artificial creation of the power-hungry warmongers in Britain and Germany, but he also argued that the British and Germans "have more in common than not, and the things we argue about are mere froth on the surface."[10] Such words were hardly calculated to prepare Australia for the prospect of war.

On 18 August 1939, as war with Germany loomed nearer, Menzies cabled to Chamberlain urging that no efforts at peace be left untried. He had still not lost faith in the Munich formula and was anxious that Poland should make concessions sufficient to appease Hitler. In this cable, Menzies set out the formula for peace that he was to pursue until he left office in August 1941. From a position of seeming strength there should be a willingness to compromise with the totalitarian powers, be they Germany, Italy or Japan.[11] The compromise, though, was generally at the expense of third parties, such as Poland. At almost any cost, war was to be avoided.

While continuing to pressure Chamberlain to push for settlement, Menzies continued to over-emphasise the chances for peace to the Australian people. On 24 August, he urged calmness on the country and a concentration of energies towards obtaining a peaceful solution.[12] The following day he issued a further statement reassuring Australians that "essential precautionary measures by the Government must not be taken as an indication that we are resigned to the idea of war." He went on to claim that there were "powerful influences working for peace" and that Australians should "go about their affairs in a normal fashion".[13]

Just before the German troops stormed across the Polish frontier on 1 September, Menzies despatched a personal message to Chamberlain which pledged Australian support for Britain and noted that he was "greatly pleased" with Chamberlain's replies to Hitler. Despite this apparent unqualified support, Menzies took the opportunity to warn Chamberlain that Australia would not consider the issues dividing Germany and Poland as being "intrinsically worth a war . . ." Moreover, Menzies argued that the German proposals "exhibit much more reasonableness than might have been expected and that any point blank refusal on the part of Poland might very well adversely affect public opinion even here''.[14]

With this cable, Menzies signalled a final plea for peace, apparently hoping to weaken Chamberlain's resolve by suggesting that Australian support could not be relied upon regardless of the issue. It was following the dispatch of this cable that Menzies allowed his Cabinet to disperse for the weekend while he optimistically set out on his abortive visit to Colac.

At 8 pm on Sunday, 3 September, the country learned from a BBC short-wave radio broadcast that Britain was at war with Germany. Just over an hour later, Menzies broadcast to the Australian people with the news that Australia was now also at war. Canada and South Africa took some days before confirming that they too stood with Britain. This seeming readiness to commit Australia to the conflict has tended to hide Menzies' real reaction to the war.

To Menzies, the commitment of Australia was automatic but by no means enthusiastic. It was his "melancholy duty", he said, to inform his fellow Australians of a war that he variously described as a tragedy, a wanton crime and an agony. Apparently feeling that his listeners shared his mystification as to why war had erupted, Menzies then launched on a long recitation of how Australia came to be at war because of a German attack on Poland. Menzies concluded his broadcast with a vain appeal to the Almighty: "May God in His mercy and compassion grant that the world may soon be delivered from this agony."[15]

The extent of the agony that awaited the world was impossible to predict, but a struggle of titanic proportions was clearly on the horizon. This was something that Menzies was still loath to admit and even slower to prepare Australia to meet. Two days after the outbreak of the war, Menzies enjoined Australians to "set themselves the working rule, 'Business as usual'...".[16] Though he may have been aiming partly to stem any public panic, Menzies' advice went too far in the opposite direction. It promoted a sense of complacency from which it was later difficult to rouse the Australian public.

Here it should be recalled that throughout Menzies' first Prime Ministership from 1939 to 1941, he was never secure in his position. He had to govern with a very narrow parliamentary majority that depended on the co-operation of the Country Party. Both the Country Party and his own United Australian Party contained members who openly sought his downfall. Within the opposition Labor Party there were also many members with a personal interest in using the numbers in Parliament to embarrass Menzies and threaten his leadership. All in all, he inspired an intense and widespread enmity that exacerbated his isolation at the political level.

Part of the antipathy aroused by Menzies resulted from his rapid rise to the Prime Ministership at the politically youthful age of 44. He was not noted for his humility; nor was he capable of easily making friends with his intellectual inferiors. Both these traits prevented him from creating a strong personal following among his colleagues. He was Prime Minister because of his undoubted ability and intellect but few loved him for it. In 1941, when the antipathy finally overwhelmed the ability, there were few left to raise their hands in his support. Another problem Menzies faced was that of his Melbourne origins: he was widely seen as the creature of Victorian-based capital and an opponent of the interests of the more populous state of New South Wales.

These domestic pressures profoundly influenced Menzies' actions on the international stage. The effort of forever protecting his rear, of suffering an unending cacophony of carping criticism, was eventually to push him towards planning a political future in London. There his ability could both shine and be admired.

With Australia now ranged alongside Britain, however reluctantly, there would seem to have been no more opportunity to pursue a policy of appeasement. This was not to be the case. Of immediate concern now that Britain was militarily engaged in Europe, was the defence position in the Pacific with regard to Japan. Australia had already been worried on this score before the war with Germany and now urged Britain to reach a settlement with Japan that would remove her as a possible combatant.

In a cable to the new Dominions Secretary, Anthony Eden, Menzies stressed the "extreme urgency" of such a settlement and warned that Australia could only play a defensive role in the war so long as the Japanese threat lay over the Pacific. As yet it was still unclear whether Australia would be better served by keeping Japan embroiled in China or by forcing China to the conference table. Menzies therefore urged that Britain pursue both lines of approach— seeking a settlement, but not yet one at great expense to China. As the position of the Allies worsened in Europe, Menzies came to have less regard for the inviolability of Chinese sovereignty.[17]

While Australia pressed for a settlement with Japan, there also arose the possibility of a settlement with Germany. War had not yet erupted all over Europe. Germany had methodically defeated Poland while Britain fulfilled her guarantee to the latter by bombing Germany with leaflets. It soon appeared that, with Poland's defeat, a further effort could be made to prevent a general conflagration. In pursuit of this aim, Bruce, the Australian High Commissioner, proceeded to pressure British leaders to formulate a statement of their war aims. Ostensibly designed to counter expected peace terms from Hitler,[18] such a statement was also the first step in achieving any settlement. The British Cabinet quickly rejected such a statement. It was no longer politically feasible to talk of peace terms and such talk would have split the War Cabinet wide open, with Chamberlain and Churchill being diametrically opposed on the issue. Not content with this rebuff, Bruce renewed his plea, this time to Sir Samuel Hoare, acting in Chamberlain's absence. Hoare found Bruce "verbose, fatuous, defeatist".[19]

If he was defeatist, then he certainly had a like-minded Prime Minister in Menzies. On 11 September, Menzies addressed a long letter to Bruce in London. The letter was practically bereft of hope regarding the war. Menzies still retained a belief that Hitler's ambition was limited to Danzig and the Polish Corridor, over which he believed Germany had "an almost unanswerable case". Furthermore he foresaw that a full-scale conflict would produce no easy victory and be devastating to both sides. Menzies gloomily informed Bruce that he had a "horrible feeling that by the time we have sustained three years carnage and ruin . . . our last state may be worse than our first". With this prospect before him, Menzies impressed upon Bruce the necessity for Britain to consider seriously any peace offer from Hitler and to have such an offer "broadened out to provide for a re-settlement of the whole map of Europe . . . ".[20]

Still, Menzies was not hopeful that his ideas would be accepted now that the Munich spirit was so firmly in the past and thoroughly renounced. Though he could see no sense in the war, neither could he see any way out of it. He admitted to Bruce:

> there is probably no answer to it all—except just to go on fighting until the other country goes down into a state of starvation and riot in which the seeds of another war, in which my grand-children will fight, are sown. But at the same time I see no sanity in it.[21]

As Menzies was aware, Bruce had considerable misgivings of his own about the war, particularly about the likelihood of victory. In order to allay his pessimism (and that of the Canadian High Commissioner, Vincent Massey), five British Cabinet Ministers discussed the war situation with the two High Commissioners. On 14 September, the Chancellor of the Exchequer, Sir John Simon, reported to the War Cabinet on the discussion in which Bruce and Massey "had taken an unwarrantably gloomy view of the situation, and in particular of relative air strengths".[22]

In fairness to Bruce, it must be remembered that, in 1939, a belief in an ultimate British victory rested more on faith than on any calculation of relative strengths. Indeed, victory in Europe was only ever made possible by the involvement of the Russians and the Americans. Menzies and Bruce, long lacking faith in a British victory, could only foresee a debilitating stalemate. It is important to note here that they were not alone in seeking an early compromise peace.

Just as the Canadian High Commissioner accompanied Bruce on his anxious errand, so too did Massey's Prime Minister, Mackenzie King, share his concern. In early October, Mackenzie King even went so far as to propose to Chamberlain that there be an immediate truce while a committee of neutral countries examined the dispute between Britain and Germany.[23] Menzies and Bruce, however, differed from the Canadians in holding to their views until late 1941.

It was not only Dominion leaders who had reservations about an all-out war against Germany. In Britain there were many who questioned just how a military victory could be achieved. Prominent among them was Britain's First World War leader, David Lloyd George. Though now 76 years old, he remained an active member of the House of Commons and was still well respected in many circles. He also had the advantage of having, like Churchill, actual war leadership experience together with a high public profile. Unlike Churchill, but very much like Menzies, he regarded the war against Germany with great foreboding.

The problem facing men like Lloyd George in 1939 was how to enforce the Allied will upon Germany. The battle for Poland was over within three weeks, after Russia came to Hitler's assistance and destroyed the remnants of Polish resistance. This left Britain and France facing Germany from behind formidable fortifications with little conception of how they could be breached. The awful abyss of the First World War's trenches seemed again to gape before Europe, threatening to swallow its youth and wealth.

On 20 September, Lloyd George met with four other MPs and candidly set out his anxiety about the war. One of his listeners noted in his diary that Lloyd George was "frankly terrified and does not see how we can possibly win the war'' and that, ''if the chances are really against us, then we should certainly make peace at the earliest opportunity.''[24] Though this was all good, sensible talk given Britain's circumstances, it was not likely to be well received by a public as yet unused to the bitter taste of defeat. So, Lloyd George was freely ridiculed and attacked by the British press when his views became known.[25] Churchill was reported to be ''disgusted'' with Lloyd George's open defeatism.[26] And the press magnate Lord Beaverbrook, who had been an ardent supporter of appeasement, now found that Lloyd George's views were too pessimistic to be printed.[27]

While the conflict with Germany was foremost in the minds of those in Britain and Australia, the potential for Japanese expansion was to become a subject of increasing concern to Menzies and Bruce. On 21 September, the latter drew up a short note setting out the lines of a possible general settlement with Japan. Unlike Menzies, who had earlier been reluctant to impose sacrifices on China, Bruce was not inhibited by any such reservations. Under Bruce's proposal Japan would retain Manchuria, be given access to the Chinese and British colonial markets and be guaranteed a supply of raw materials. This settlement was to be jointly guaranteed by Britain and the United States, which would provide finance to develop China and supply the industrial and transport equipment for both China and Japan. Bruce also singled wool out as one of the raw materials to be guaranteed to Japan.[28]

Under this scheme Britain would lose part of her colonial market, but would presumably more than recoup this by the supply of capital goods to China and Japan. Australia was to cede nothing but rather was to gain a secure, expanding market for her major export, wool. China was the only clear loser, ceding sovereignty in Manchuria to Japan and having her potentially huge market carved up between Japan, Britain and the United States. It was a classic appeasement position, designed to buy Australian security at the expense of a third party—China. Fortunately, such a plan was never a realistic proposition—Britain was too committed to her colonial rights, America was too protective of China, and China was properly jealous of her own limited independence. Nevertheless, in various forms, this plan to appease Japan at China's expense was adopted by Menzies and proposed at different times both by him and Bruce.

While a general settlement in the Far East was never a practical proposition, this was not so obviously the case in Europe. During the period of ''phoney war'' prior to the German attack on France in May

1940, there was considerable confusion among British leaders, as has been said, about how the country could fight the war, let alone win it, with no clear idea even as to what the battle cry should be.[29]

Various figures tried to exploit this atmosphere of indecision, not least among them being Menzies and Bruce. On 25 September, Hoare wrote to Lord Lothian in Washington that "some of our Dominion friends...were wondering whether we should not do well to have a peace by negotiation."[30] These Dominion friends continued their pressure on the British Government and demanded another meeting with War Cabinet Ministers to discuss the British attitude to a German peace offensive.[31]

The meeting arose from Bruce's urging and he used it to try and pin down Chamberlain on what Britain's response would be to a possible German peace offensive. He could not have been too impressed with the result. The Foreign Secretary, Lord Halifax, admitted that protecting Poland was no longer a viable aim, but asserted that somehow an end must be put to Hitlerism, perhaps by encouraging an internal overthrow of the Nazi regime. As for peace proposals, he felt they could not be pre-judged and would have to be accompanied by tangible assurances. Bruce saw that this indecisive British attitude would negate any such proposals and he stressed that it was "imperative that immediate consideration should be given to what sort of tangible assurances should be asked for and how we would express ourselves in doing so".[32] With such prior consideration it was much more likely that a German offer could get a ready Anglo–French response and that concrete peace talks could eventuate.

Bruce's efforts were doomed to failure. The consensus holding the War Cabinet together would not allow for such talks. And, on 4 October, his efforts were opposed by a cable from the South African Prime Minister, Jan Smuts. Smuts was highly regarded by British leaders and his cable absolutely rejected any notion of peace talks, arguing that "any German peace offer now will not be sincere but will be simply meant as a peace offensive to weaken us..."[33]

That same day, Bruce came up against the principal opponent to his peace plans—Winston Churchill. Bruce tried in vain to convince Churchill of the need for formulating in advance a reply to any peace offensive and for the declaration of war aims. Churchill dismissed him out of hand, stridently declaring that "Hitler had his hands dripping with the blood of the Poles and their scalps hanging on his belt, and our task was to fight him until he was defeated."[34] It is a wonder that Bruce even tried to convince Churchill—he cannot have been unaware of Churchill's views—and he now wound up firmly painted as an appeaser in Churchill's eyes.

On 20 October, Bruce returned to the fray when he confronted Churchill at an Admiralty House dinner. Even at this early stage of the war, Churchill was adamant that Britain should not accord Germany an easy peace. Rather, she must be punished and partitioned, rendering her innocuous. Bruce again argued vainly against a vindictive victory and was forced to conclude that "Winston's attitude is an extremely dangerous one and if his will is to prevail he will lead us into a most unenviable position."[35] He feared that Churchill and his allies would prevent the possibility of an early peace and ensure another long, drawn-out war in Europe.[36]

While this was occurring in London, Menzies was confronting the Australian War Cabinet with the urgent issue of underwear for the expanding Australian Army. Sealed samples of men's underwear, supplied by the Melbourne merchandiser Norman Myer, were handed round. After careful examination and considerable discussion, the meeting approved the issue of cotton underwear to cover the first three months of 1940, but deferred approval of a later issue of woollen underwear. Apparently hope had still not faded of an early peace being reached prior to the woollen underwear being required and they were mindful of the political consequences of being left with warehouses full of redundant woollens. The decision revealed that, seven weeks into the war, Menzies and his colleagues remained reluctant to undertake that total effort that the war would soon require.[37]

But Menzies' fears of a drawn-out war were reinforced when the French Government adopted a similar position to Churchill's by rejecting any talk of an easy peace for Germany.[38] The French attitude clarified the division on the Allied side. Bruce now urged Menzies to join with the other Dominions and weigh in against the French–Churchillian attitude.[39] He immediately took up Bruce's suggestion and cabled Chamberlain with a strong argument against a repressive peace. Though he opposed a "patched up and premature peace" Menzies was adamant that victory in the field must be followed by a "great and genuine gesture of generosity and of justice" with Germany being guaranteed her part as "a great nation on a footing of freedom and equality".[40] Obviously he still believed that the German cause was not without justice and that the Versailles peace was an unjust imposition that should not be repeated.

Despite the Dominion pressure, the Anglo–French statement on Allied war aims had still not been produced by January 1940. Bruce, though, remained anxious that such a statement be produced and that it be done on the right lines. Accordingly, he despatched a 21-page letter to Menzies on 2 January setting out the position to date, the problems preventing agreement on such a statement and a possible solution to the dilemma. He was well aware that the shaky united front in Britain, and that between Britain and France, would be threatened by any close examination of war aims.[41]

Bruce argued that agreement could eventually be reached on a soft peace that would still ensure that the world was safe from future German expansion. His proposals were extremely idealistic, encompassing such concepts as an International Police Force, general disarmament and the disavowal of exclusive colonial empires. Indeed, much of Bruce's plan found expression in the post-war world. Of interest, however, is the timing of these otherwise far-seeing proposals.[42]

It is one thing to propose a magnanimous peace when one is clearly on top and victory is near; it is quite another to propose it before battle has even been joined. So that while Bruce could pronounce with favour and at considerable length on the sort of peace he hoped for, he was particularly circumspect in outlining the military means by which such a victory could be achieved. In fact, he believed victory was not militarily possible and his proposals for a soft peace were really designed to produce a resolution of the conflict by other means.

Bruce's lack of faith in the possibility of a military victory was shared by some members of the British War Cabinet. On 24 January, Sir Alexander Cadogan, the top civil servant at the Foreign Office, reported in his diary a talk with Halifax on "possible peace terms". He noted that Halifax appeared to be in a "pacifist mood" and agreed himself that he would "like to make peace before war starts".[43] Unfortunately for Bruce, the Australian Cabinet was similarly divided on the question of war aims. His proposal for applying Dominion pressure to achieve a soft Anglo–French statement was rejected. Menzies, though, was still in accord with his High Commissioner, as was shown by a revealing exchange of letters in February 1940.

On 6 February, Bruce wrote to Menzies setting out proposals regarding economic and social aspects of the Allied war aims. Then, for the first time, he addressed the question of how victory could be achieved. He dismissed out of hand any suggestion that victory could be won by a land or air offensive or by sea blockade. Rather, Bruce wrote, it should be a combination of all these pressures, together with the pronouncement that no harsh penalties would be exacted from a defeated Germany. Only by such a combination would the German people feel it was not worth fighting on and that they had something to hope for from the peace.[44]

Apparently before receiving this letter, Menzies replied to Bruce's earlier letter of 2 January in terms that showed an affinity of views. He revealed that he was now practically isolated within his Cabinet on the question of war aims. He claimed that his Cabinet colleagues shared an "almost pathetic belief that the dismemberment of Germany would alter the German spirit and outlook". Menzies described this as a "tragic misconception" and promised to "work upon their minds" but was pessimistic about his prospects of success. Menzies accepted, almost without qualification, Bruce's proposals for a soft victory and suggested that the danger of expansionist, Russian communism might soon align Britain and Germany on the same side.[45]

Though Menzies was emphatic that he agreed with Bruce on war aims, he also made it clear that he had no political room for manoeuvre on this question. Both in the Cabinet and the country at large there was considerable criticism of anything resembling appeasement. He complained that a section of the Australian press was "already quite disposed to criticise me violently for having what they believe to be a philosophic approach to a matter in which they think my proper function is a mixture of swashbuckling and rhetoric". His task in Cabinet was complicated by a "few minds which are heavily indoctrinated by the 'old soldiers' and by the 'Versailles' point of view".[46] So, while Menzies clearly reaffirmed his allegiance to a soft peace and, if possible, a negotiated general settlement, he was also clearly under pressure not to expound on his views publicly except in the most convoluted form.

Menzies was clearly to be placed in the Chamberlain camp, in opposition to the war policies of Winston Churchill. Writing just 11 weeks before Churchill became Prime Minister, he described the future British leader as a "menace" who "stirs up hatreds in a world already seething with them and he is lacking in judgement . . .".[47]

In early 1940 there existed what appeared to be a stalemate. Poland had been overrun by Germany and the Allies were powerless to intervene. Now the massive armies of Europe were standing prepared to strike but there appeared nowhere for them to go. Each seemed effectively boxed in by the border defences of its opponent. In such a situation a negotiated settlement appeared to many to be possible. Churchill threatened to ruin the chances of such a settlement by his ceaseless advocacy for Britain and France to seize the initiative from

Germany and mount an offensive. To Churchill, Norway seemed to offer the perfect opportunity for British forces to come to grips with those of Germany outside of their respective defensive "boxes". By provoking German forces into action there, Churchill hoped to catch them at a disadvantage and end the "phoney war" with a decisive clash of arms.

The debate over the mining of Norwegian waters, to stem the flow of iron ore from Scandinavia to Germany, occupied the British War Cabinet for several months and Bruce kept Menzies informed of its progress and of the fact that Churchill was the principal proponent of the mining.[48] Bruce was personally opposed to the plan and ensured that Menzies weighed in with opposition from Australia at critical points in the debate, much to Churchill's chagrin. To Churchill, Menzies and Bruce were responsible for delaying his plans to expand the war and he wasn't quick to forget it. It was another case of the Australians being soft on the war and Churchill declaimed in exasperation on "the evident necessity to carry the Dominions with us in any direction".[49] For his part, Menzies was confirmed in his view of Churchill as the wild man of Whitehall.

While Churchill was trying to invigorate the "phoney war", Lloyd George was still convinced that things could only drag on inconclusively for a year or two until the demand for a compromise peace became overwhelming.[50] Through his newspapers, Beaverbrook was also carefully pushing this view. He published articles by the influential military writer and adviser to Lloyd George, Basil Liddell Hart, and in early March 1940 tried to encourage him to embark on a speech-making tour of the country in order to propagate his critical ideas on the war. Beaverbrook claimed that Liddell Hart had "an increasingly big following in the country" and that the movement for peace was beginning to capture the popular imagination. Liddell Hart noted that Beaverbrook "expressed emphatic agreement with my view of the war, and of the wisdom of a policy of restraint in regard to taking the offensive". Beaverbrook was also in touch with Lloyd George and with the Labour MP and Leader of the Peace Aims Group, R. R. Stokes, whose ideas he also tried to promote through his newspapers.[51]

Meanwhile, Menzies' hopes received a fillip in mid-March 1940 when he received a report of a talk between Bruce and Sumner Welles, the United States Under-Secretary of State. Welles was exploring the possibilities for a negotiated peace prior to widespread hostilities and quizzed Bruce on the attitude of the Dominions. Bruce pointed out that the Australian Cabinet would not favour a patched-up peace that might easily break down. Germany would have to relinquish her conquests and security would have to be provided against a repetition of such aggression. However, with these two conditions provided for, there should be no punishment exacted from the German people and, he implied, the Allies should not require the end of the Nazi regime. Bruce optimistically reported to Menzies that Welles "regards with such horror the full scale of development of the war that he is endeavouring to formulate proposals on the basis of which . . . he could urge the President to take some definite action".[52] Clearly, Bruce and Menzies were not yet resigned to fighting Hitler to a finish.

With the Germans' lightning occupation of Norway in April 1940 and the failure of the British forces to defeat them, Chamberlain's position as Prime Minister rapidly became untenable. Though his succession is usually portrayed as a contest between Churchill and the Foreign Secretary, Lord Halifax, there was another contender—Lloyd George. Despite his greater age, Lloyd George was favourably compared by some people to Churchill and judged the more vigorous of the two. Prior to the political crisis, the Conservative MP "Chips" Channon made note in his diary of "chats with both Winston Churchill and Lloyd George". Lloyd George, Channon felt, was "the more alert and hale of the two, in his too-blue suits, blue tie, and flowing mane of hair . . . "[53]

Similarly, another Conservative MP, Harold Nicolson, confidently predicted in early May that Lloyd George rather than Churchill would replace Chamberlain.[54] And Lloyd George himself was encouraged by Liddell Hart, who assured him that public opinion was "increasingly turning towards you as the man to deal with the problem of the war".[55] So convinced was Liddell Hart of Lloyd George's chances, that he even went so far as to draw up a list of suggested changes in the top ranks of the army.[56]

Still Lloyd George hesitated. When he was sounded out by the Conservative MP Nancy Astor on 7 May, he left the impression that he "preferred to await his country's summons a little longer, but that he expected to receive it as the peril grew". To Nancy Astor's "Cliveden Set",[57] Lloyd George represented a real leadership option. As one of the group, the *Observer* editor J. L. Garvin, noted, Lloyd George "was still good for six hours a day and it would be six hours of radium".[58]

On 8 May, Liddell Hart talked with Lloyd George prior to the latter taking a decisive part in the House of Commons debate that effectively destroyed Chamberlain as Prime Minister. Liddell Hart found that Lloyd George was "obviously hopeful, and keen to get a chance of directing affairs". The two men discussed how "public opinion had swung rapidly during the last few weeks" in favour of Lloyd George's recall to office. As for the war, Lloyd George's strategy remained clear—to "foil the German aim" but to "work for an honourable peace". He was, so he claimed, the statesman best able to overcome "Russia's suspicion of British policy, while being the only one who could deal with Hitler and Mussolini on equal terms".[59]

In the event, it was Churchill and not Halifax or Lloyd George who received the nation's call on 10 May 1940. The support of the Labour Party was crucial in getting the Premiership for Churchill. There is little doubt that Churchill rather than Lloyd George better expressed the true feeling of the British people at that time. They were not yet ready to admit that Britain's chances of victory were slim and they preferred Churchill's strident rhetoric to the cautious realism of his rival. Still, Churchill was ever mindful of the fact that Lloyd George had presented a real leadership option for Britain in May 1940. By not joining his War Cabinet and instead standing back from the government like some ancient monolith, Lloyd George cast a shadow over Churchill's claim to national leadership and presented a continuing alternative to his policies.

Churchill's accession to the British leadership radically changed the nature of the war with Germany. The conflict was now clearly to be carried on until the final and decisive defeat of Hitler. There was to be no halfway house where the British Empire could replenish its strength. It would be an all or nothing affair in which practically no sacrifice would be withheld to gain victory. To those who gave the matter thought it was obvious that the enormity of this task would inevitably push Britain into a closer alliance with America and begin the disintegration of the British Empire. Australia's value to Britain would be heavily depreciated and the distant Dominion would find herself suddenly alone in an increasingly perilous Pacific. These were the underlying currents that would soon lock Menzies and Churchill in an unpublicised but nonetheless desperate struggle to realise their separate visions for Britain's future.

NOTES

1. *AGE*, Melbourne, 2 September 1939
2. For Menzies' role in pre-war appeasement, see E. M. ANDREWS, *Isolation and Appeasement in Australia*, Canberra, 1970; R. Ovendale, *Appeasement and the English Speaking World*, Cardiff, 1975
3. R. OVENDALE, pp. 154, 180
4. K. PERKINS, *Menzies*, London, 1968, p. 61
5. R. OVENDALE, p. 222
6. LETTER, Menzies to Lord Lothian, 16 May 1939, GD40/17/392, Lothian Papers: Scottish Record Office (hereafter SRO)
7. CABLE, Menzies to Chamberlain, 15 June 1939, PREM 1/324/7: Public Record Office (hereafter PRO)
8. R. OVENDALE, p. 280
9. LETTER, Murdoch to W. S. Robinson, 14 August 1939, MS 2823/27, Murdoch Papers: National Library of Australia (hereafter NLA)
10. *DAILY NEWS*, Sydney, 18 August 1939
11. R. G. NEALE (ED.), *Documents on Australian Foreign Policy, 1939–49*, (hereafter *DAFP*), ii, Doc. 134, Cable No. 81, Menzies to Chamberlain, 18 August 1939
12. *DAILY TELEGRAPH*, Sydney, 25 August 1939
13. *HERALD*, Melbourne, 25 August 1939
14. *DAFP*, ii, Doc. 174, Cable, Menzies to Chamberlain, 1 September 1939
15. *DAFP*, ii, Doc. 189, Broadcast message by Menzies, 3 September 1939
16. *HERALD*, Melbourne, 5 September 1939
17. *DAFP*, ii, Doc. 219, Cable, Menzies to Eden, 11 September 1939
18. WAR CABINET CONCLUSIONS, 9 September 1939, Cab. 65/1, W.M.9(39): PRO
19. DIARY NOTES, 10 September 1939, XI:2, Templewood Papers: Cambridge University Library (hereafter CUL)
20. LETTER, Menzies to Bruce, 11 September 1939, S. M. Bruce Supplementary War Files 1938–1939, CRS M103: Australian Archives (hereafter AA)
21. *IBID*.
22. WAR CABINET CONCLUSIONS, 14 September 1939, Cab. 65/1, W.M.15(39): PRO
23. J. L. GRANATSTEIN, *Canada's War: The Politics of the Mackenzie King Government, 1939–1945*, Toronto, 1975, pp. 27–8
24. SIR H. NICOLSON, *Diaries and Letters*, ii, London, 1967, p. 35
25. H. CUDLIPP, *Walking on the Water*, London, 1976, pp. 104–6
26. LETTER, Victor Cazalet MP to Lord Lothian, 16 October 1939, GD40/17/399, Lothian Papers: SRO
27. LETTER, F. Stevenson to B. Liddell Hart, 29 November 1939, 1/450, Liddell Hart Papers: King's College, London (hereafter KC)
28. *DAFP*, ii, Doc. 239, Note by Bruce for R. A. Butler, Parliamentary Under-Secretary for Foreign Affairs, 21 September 1939
29. D. DILKS (ED.), *The Diaries of Sir Alexander Cadogan, O.M. 1938–1945*, London, 1971, p. 219
30. LETTER, Hoare to Lord Lothian, 25 September 1939, XI:5, Templewood Papers: CUL
31. WAR CABINET CONCLUSIONS, 28 September 1939, Cab. 65/1, W.M.30(39): PRO

32. HIGH COMMISSIONERS MEETING WITH SUB COMMITTEE, 28 September 1939, S. M. Bruce Monthly War Files, CRS M100, September 1939: AA

33. "VIEWS OF GENERAL SMUTS ON POSSIBLE GERMAN PEACE OFFER", 4 October 1939, Cab. 66/2, W.P.(39)71: PRO

34. NOTE OF A TALK WITH CHURCHILL, 4 October 1939, CRS M100, October 1939: AA

35. NOTE OF A TALK WITH CHURCHILL, 20 October 1939, CRS M100, October 1939: AA

36. *DAFP*, ii, Doc. 300, Cable, Bruce to Menzies, 18 October 1939

37. WAR CABINET MINUTES, 20 October 1939, A2673, Vol. 1, Item 35: AA; See also P. Hasluck, *The Government and the People, 1939–42*, i, Canberra, 1952, p. 158

38. *DAFP*, ii, Doc. 307, Cable D52, Eden to Menzies, 24 October 1939

39. *DAFP*, ii, Doc. 308, Cable No. 586, Bruce to Menzies, 26 October 1939

40. *DAFP*, ii, Doc. 311, Cable, Menzies to Chamberlain, 28 October 1939

41. CALDECOTE DIARY, 13 October 1939: CC. As Chamberlain had complained, Dominion pressure for a statement on war aims revealed "a lack of the sense of realism"

42. *DAFP*, iii, Doc. 16, Letter, Bruce to Menzies, 2 January 1940

43. D. DILKS, p. 249

44. *DAFP*, iii, Doc. 62, Letter, Bruce to Menzies, 6 February 1940

45. *DAFP*, iii, Doc. 71, Letter, Menzies to Bruce, 22 February 1940

46. *IBID.*

47. *IBID.*

48. M. GILBERT, *Finest Hour: Winston S. Churchill, 1939–1941*, London, 1983, *passim*; B. Liddell Hart, *History of the Second World War*, London, 1973, ch. 6

49. M. GILBERT, p. 131

50. H. CUDLIPP, p. 111

51. SUNDRY NOTES, March 6, 7 and 8, 11/1940/15, Liddell Hart Papers; Letter, Beaverbrook to Liddell Hart, 13 February 1940, 1/52/8, Liddell Hart Papers: KC

52. *DAFP*, iii, Doc. 102, Cable No. 182, Bruce to Menzies, 14 March 1940

53. CHANNON DIARY, 13 February 1940, R. R. James (ed.), *Chips: The Diaries of Sir Henry Channon*, London, 1967, p. 232

54. NICOLSON DIARY, 30 April, 1 and 3 May 1940, Sir H. Nicolson, pp. 74–5

55. LETTER, Liddell Hart to Lloyd George, 20 April 1940, 1/450, Liddell Hart Papers: KC

56. LETTER, Liddell Hart to Lloyd George, 26 May 1940, 1/450 Liddell Hart Papers: KC

57. Before the war, Nancy Astor's Cliveden home was alleged to be the centre for many discussions on foreign policy between politicians and others and was popularly believed to have done much to promote Chamberlain's policy of appeasement

58. T. JONES, *A Diary with Letters, 1931–1950*, London, 1954, p. 457

59. DIARY NOTE, 8 May 1940, 11/1940/36, Liddell Hart Papers: KC

2

The Empire
Under Threat

*O*n 10 May 1940 Hitler launched his long-awaited attack on France by way of Holland and Belgium. That same day, Churchill succeeded Chamberlain as the Prime Minister of Great Britain. Both events caused Menzies considerable alarm and he began to foresee the defeat of his beloved Empire under the leadership of that "menace", Churchill. Within three weeks, Menzies' foreboding seemed to be coming true. The British and French armies were decisively routed by the "blitzkrieg" and the evacuation of British troops from Dunkirk had begun.

The evacuation from Dunkirk spelt the beginning of the end for France. Within two weeks, Paris had been occupied and the victorious Germans had pursued the scattered and demoralised French army into central France. With the end of France in sight, Mussolini now brought Italy into the war on the side of Hitler and began to attack from the south. The implications for Britain were disastrous.

For centuries, Britain's involvement in European wars had depended on the assistance of a European ally with a numerically strong army to complement Britain's navy and compensate for Britain's relative weakness on land. In 1939–40, the huge French army had been Britain's main hope of defeating the Germans. With the fall of France and the entry of the Italians, Britain was in a position that she had always sought to avoid. Practically all of Europe was now either at war with her or under the control or influence of Germany. Britain's allies of the First World War had joined her enemies. Italy and Japan now stood with Germany and soon formalised their alliance in the Tripartite Pact of September 1940. Russia had signed a non-aggression pact with Germany and seemed content to watch Europe tear itself apart.

Only America offered any solace to an embattled Britain. But even the United States was firmly isolationist in temperament and its assistance to Britain was limited to the supply of munitions. Thus, in mid-1940, the British Empire stood alone against Nazi Germany and an increasingly hostile Europe. It seemed to be only a matter of time before Britain went the way of France and Hitler's "New Order" held sway over all. It was Churchill who turned this certain defeat into stalemate after the "Battle of Britain". It was Hitler who broke the stalemate and ensured his own ultimate defeat with his attack on Russia in June 1941. In the intervening 12 months Churchill bullied and badgered Britain into withstanding the German onslaught.

Bulldoggishly, Churchill clung to his policy of defeating Germany during a period when a British defeat seemed the more likely outcome. Offering little more than faith, Churchill's powerful oratory raised Britain to her feet and set her in a stance of determined resistance to Hitler. The defeat of Germany became virtually the sole national policy of Britain and all impediments to this end were liable to be swept away. As it became obvious that the British Empire alone could not bring Hitler down or ensure the security of Britain, Churchill looked to the United States for assistance. If the price of this assistance were to be the Empire itself, then so be it.

Menzies' initial reaction had also been to turn toward America to ensure Britain's immediate survival. In this there was little reason for argument with Churchill. However, their paths began to diverge as it became clear that Churchill was prepared to sacrifice the security of the Empire to ensure total victory. Moreover, it seemed to Menzies, his wildly aggressive policies threatened to destroy not only the Empire but Britain itself. This, then, was to be the basis of Menzies' modern crusade—to rescue the Imperial fortress from the infidel, Churchill, and, if need be, to come to terms with the enemy at the gates. Firstly, though, Britain would have to be made secure from the imminent threat of invasion.

Menzies and Bruce were of the view that the invasion threat had to be tackled in two ways—by pressing for a negotiated peace and by calling for America to decisively support Britain and so end the conflict. On 27 May Bruce met with the former Prime Minister, Chamberlain, and pressed the case for a negotiated peace. To forestall a British defeat, Bruce urged Britain to enlist the good offices of Roosevelt and Mussolini as mediators between the belligerents. This was almost a month before France finally collapsed and Chamberlain was sufficiently alarmed by the conversation to report the matter to the War Cabinet. There, the new Prime Minister, Churchill, called on his Ministers to exude confidence and proclaimed that "the bulk of the people of this country would refuse to accept the possibility of defeat."[1]

Churchill's biographer, Martin Gilbert, claimed to recognise a contrast in the attitudes of Bruce and Menzies at this time.[2] However, Menzies and Bruce were actually in close accord in their view of Britain's prospects. Both agreed that Britain faced a grave danger of defeat and that a negotiated peace might soon have to be concluded with Germany. At Bruce's suggestion, Menzies despatched an urgent message to President Roosevelt on 27 May imploring immediate American assistance for Britain. This message was predicated on their shared belief that a British defeat was imminent.[3]

On 30 May, in the middle of the Dunkirk evacuation, Churchill received a seven-page note from Bruce which proposed an international conference to arrange a peace settlement. Concluding, Bruce called for the struggle to cease and argued that "the further shedding of blood and the continuance of hideous suffering is unnecessary." Not surprisingly, Churchill was most scathing in his comments on the note.[4]

The Australian public reacted to the military disasters in Europe with renewed calls for a national government and a greater war effort. Menzies responded to the pressure by announcing an "all-in" war effort but stopped short at the introduction of conscription for overseas service. Such a move would only have triggered an acrimonious and divisive debate that would have weakened rather than strengthened the war effort. Still, Menzies' failure to introduce conscription gave a renewed impression that he was strong on rhetoric and weak on action.[5] As for a national government, Menzies made a renewed offer to accept a united administration but on condition that "the great union movement of Australia backed the Labor leaders and so reinforced the Cabinet that it would be able to express completely the desires of the Australian people".[6]

In practical assistance to Britain, Menzies released 49 Hudson aircraft on order from the United States and dispatched RAAF units to Singapore to allow RAF units to be used elsewhere. At the same time, more than a third of Australia's reserve of small arms ammunition was despatched to Britain. These were real sacrifices on behalf of the "Mother Country", that materially weakened Australia's own defence position.

Publicly Menzies kept up a brave front on the military defeats in France. On 27 May he cabled to Churchill with the pledge that Australians would devote "the whole of their resources to victory".[7] Nine days later, after the fall of Dunkirk, Menzies publicly described its evacuation as a "triumph" and a "symbol of what Britain would achieve in the future—an achievement which would lead to ultimate victory''. Even as the German tanks rumbled towards Paris, he challenged any ''defeatist ideas that France would capitulate . . .''[8]

On 22 June, the French government of Marshal Pétain accepted the German terms for an armistice. That day, Menzies wrote to Australia's Chief Justice, Sir John Latham, in terms that reveal his private view of Britain's chances. Latham had raised with Menzies the problem of Imperial allegiance should Britain be ruled by a puppet government and had suggested that the Empire attach itself to the United States until British independence was restored. Menzies described this view as ''undoubtedly a realistic one'' and assured Latham that he had ''certainly not excluded'' this possibility from his consideration. Further, he agreed on the importance of ''associating the Governor-General and the Chief Justice'' in any possible switch of Australian allegiance.[9] Thus, despite Menzies' resolute public stance, he was obviously beset with private fears of the defeat of Britain and the sundering of the Empire.

The fall of France, the hostility of Italy and the threat to Britain all increased Australia's concern with the situation in the Pacific. It was now apparent that Britain could not readily spring to Australia's assistance in the event of a Japanese attack. So Menzies and Bruce once again pushed vigorously for a general settlement in the Pacific that would remove the threat of war with Japan. Failing such a settlement, Japan was to be kept embroiled in her war with China. Either way, China was the loser.[10]

With Britain now so obviously occupied in Europe, Japan became bolder and increased pressure on Britain to stop war supplies to China through Hong Kong and Burma. Though this threatened to cripple the Chinese war effort, Britain was in no position to talk tough in the Far East, with the crucial battle for Britain about to begin.[11] For her part, Australia was anxious that the Burma Road not be closed. Closure could mean a Japanese victory in China, thus disengaging Japanese forces for adventures elsewhere in the Pacific. Closure would also be seen as a sign of weakness and might well encourage the Japanese to take liberties with other British interests closer to Australia, or even with Australia herself.

In London, Bruce sought to stiffen the British attitude on the Burma Road and, rather than retreat piecemeal before the Japanese, formulate a policy that would produce a general understanding in the Far East and assuage Japan's aggressive motivations. The plan was now familiar—a series of economic concessions allowing Japanese consumer goods into China and the British colonies; a guarantee of raw material supply for Japan's industries; and territorial adjustments in the Far East which would permit an agreed amount of Japanese expansion. Australia lost little, if at all, by this arrangement and had much to gain.[12]

On 9 July 1940, Menzies endorsed Bruce's efforts to achieve a resolution in the Far East. He indicated a certain exasperation with Britain which, he felt, did not appreciate the extent of the Japanese threat to Australia. As for China's lifeline, the Burma Road, Menzies could not "understand why some trifle of this kind should be allowed to stand in the way of a Japanese settlement". Instead, Japan must be allowed to "establish her commercial position in East Asia and get some assistance in what must be her real economic difficulties". Menzies urged that Britain should be "generous and understanding, without being abject". He told Bruce to impress Churchill that the nub of the problem was Britain's inability to send the long-promised fleet to Singapore. This had caused anxiety among the Cabinet which would be exacerbated by "any approach to Japan which stops short of being realistic and comprehensive".[13]

At least on the Far East, Menzies and Churchill were in some agreement that war with Japan must be avoided. To Churchill, such a war would be disastrous because of its effect on the British position in Europe; to Menzies, war with Japan would be disastrous because of its effect on Australia, which was in no position to defend itself. So, for reasons that were really diametrically opposed, Britain succumbed to Japanese pressure on the Burma Road. War supplies to China were suspended. As Halifax explained the situation to Hoare:

> I wanted to call the Jap bluff and tell them to go to the devil, but the Chiefs of the Staff were greatly alarmed and Winston was not prepared to take the risk. The United States, as usual, said they would do nothing and Menzies was very much disturbed, especially as we told him we could no longer promise a fleet for Singapore . . . [14]

Here, then, is where Australia and Britain diverged on the Far East. Britain was concerned to retain whatever she could in the area, to make limited concessions to Japan under duress and to hope that this gradual, delayed retreat would postpone the start of hostilities until Britain had regained sufficient strength to deal with them. Australia wanted a stop to the series of isolated concessions and instead favoured a comprehensive settlement of the whole Far East position that would blunt the Japanese will to expand territorially into South East Asia. Britain, though, realised that American opposition would prevent any agreement concluded at China's expense and the alternative of a unilateral Anglo-Japanese settlement would threaten the continuation of American co-operation with Britain in its fight against Germany. Britain's Empire in the Far East was therefore edged into a position of increasing peril because of Britain's overriding concern with the war against Germany.

As Menzies and Bruce sought to secure Australia's safety in the Pacific, Britain was beginning a fight in her own skies that would determine her immediate fate. The "Battle of Britain" lasted from July to November 1940 and represented the determined effort of Germany to destroy the Royal Air Force, as a necessary pre-condition for an invasion of Britain. Wave after wave of German bombers dropped their deadly loads on Britain's cities, factories and airfields. Meanwhile, across the English Channel, the Germans hastily assembled an invasion fleet to follow up any victory by their air force in the skies over Britain. Throughout that northern summer and autumn, the spectre of a British defeat loomed large, as the devastation wrought by the German bombing spread across the country.

In the midst of this titanic struggle, Lloyd George quietly contemplated his "inner confidential views about the War and its prospects". In a draft 27-page memorandum he set out these views for his close circle of friends and supporters. This pessimistic, albeit realistic, document is probably the most comprehensive outline of his views on the war. Victory, Lloyd George claimed, would only occur if Hitler was stupid enough to attack Russia or if Russia joined the Allies. Neither he rated as likely and his conclusion was that terms must therefore be sought in order to avoid a wasting war in which neither side could force victory.[15]

Such terms would not be on the lines of those agreed to by France, which had allowed a German occupation, nor could they involve any interference with the British Navy. Instead, Lloyd George envisaged that Britain could sue for peace after she had "fought what will be universally acclaimed as a valiant and triumphant fight for the defence of our shores...". It was all predicated on a view of Hitler as a rational statesman who wanted peace in order to allow "his programme of building a greater Germany up into one of the most prosperous and well organised communities in the world".[16] Lloyd George urged the creation of a fresh Cabinet prepared to deliberate on peace proposals and he also suggested the formation of an Imperial War

Cabinet including Dominion representatives, along the lines of that of the First World War.

Though Lloyd George had clarified his own mind on the war, he still considered it inopportune to make any political moves on his own account. He felt that a compromise peace could only be proposed once the fear of invasion had abated and the prospect of a "protracted war of devastation and starvation" stared Britain and Europe in the face. Only then would Britain be ready to reconsider "this war into which we have blundered without consideration or wisdom".[17]

At the beginning of October, Nancy Astor, continuing her own campaign to have Lloyd George in the War Cabinet "in order to 'hold Winston'", approached Hugh Dalton, Labour's Minister for Economic Warfare. Her appeal fell on barren ground. Dalton dismissed Lloyd George as being "senile" and a "Welsh Pétain" who "wrote articles in the Sunday press as though he were a neutral in the war".[18]

Even had Nancy Astor succeeded, Lloyd George was still not ready to join the Government. Although Britain had successfully resisted the German air assault in August and September, Lloyd George rightly calculated that the British people were far from ready to discard their existing leadership and sue for peace.[19] He therefore continued his patient waiting game. In the interim though, he and his advisers kept up their contacts with potential political allies.

The most important of these was Lord Beaverbrook, now Churchill's energetic Minister for Aircraft Production. Churchill and Beaverbrook had a relationship stretching back to the First World War. During that war, Beaverbrook had been influential in securing the British Prime Ministership for Lloyd George. Although Churchill and Beaverbrook had been close associates during those years, they had since drifted apart and had been diametrically opposed in the late 1930s on the potential threat from Germany. Churchill's choice was therefore not a case of finding a post for an old crony. His intention seems to have been to harness Beaverbrook's energy to the war effort and to divert him from any inclination to repeat his political power-broking activities of the previous war. In this latter aim, he was to be only partly successful.[20]

As Churchill's Minister for Aircraft Production, Beaverbrook was making almost manic efforts to produce fighter planes but was increasingly concerned at the numbers of these planes that were being assigned to other theatres, mainly the Middle East. This concern put him more and more at odds with Churchill, who was equally determined to see the Middle East sustained.[21] Hugh Dalton observed that

Lord Beaverbrook, Churchill's Minister for Aircraft Production in
1940–41
(NEWS LIMITED)

Beaverbrook had a blinkered obsession with the defence of Britain, but that he was also inclined to be ''very defeatist''.[22]

In early October, Liddell Hart claimed to recognise a shift in Beaverbrook's paper, the *Daily Express*, that indicated a softer attitude to the notion of a compromise peace. Accordingly, he forwarded a copy of a memorandum to Beaverbrook setting out his thoughts on the war. He triumphantly informed Lloyd George that he had received in return ''a pleasant note from Beaverbrook about my memorandum— naturally non-committal, yet implying that it carried some weight''.[23] Beaverbrook's reaction was, in fact, a far cry from that of nine months before, when he described himself as one of Liddell Hart's ''disciples'' and ''in complete agreement'' with Liddell Hart's work.[24] Still, Beaverbrook was now a Government minister and had to be more circumspect in the expression of his views.

It was about this time that Beaverbrook sent an envoy to establish contact with Lloyd George. The envoy gave Lloyd George a most depressing picture of the war and suggested that he should contact Beaverbrook with ''some plan for saving this country from the doom into which it is heading with its accustomed blind fury''. On the telephone, Beaverbrook urged Lloyd George to meet him in London, but was told by Lloyd George that there was no point in his joining the present Government as his views would not be heeded.[25] Still, Beaverbrook urged that they meet privately in London.

In the event, A. J. P. Taylor claims, by the time the two men met on 5 November the war situation had changed for the better and so removed any impetus for joint action. The German invasion of Britain was now postponed indefinitely. To Lloyd George, though, the outlook was little altered. British military successes were for him the necessary preconditions for an early and honourable peace. He admitted that such successes as the damage done to the Italian navy at Taranto on 11 November would ''encourage the war fever'' in Britain but he also claimed that it would ''make it easier for us to entertain thoughts as to a reasonable conclusion of the War''.[26]

While Lloyd George patiently waited for Churchill to stumble, Menzies' preoccupation with Churchill's fitness for office continued to grow. The bungled Dakar operation in late September reconfirmed his feelings about Churchill's impetuosity. A combined British–Free French force failed in its attempt to capture Dakar and secure French West Africa for the British cause. The involvement of an Australian cruiser in the operation had placed Menzies in an embarrassing position, since he had been told of it only after the news had been released to the press in Britain. Bruce urged that Menzies make a strong protest over the affair, particularly at the lack of information given to Australia during the course of the operation.[27]

Menzies angrily informed Churchill that it was "absolutely wrong" for Australia not to be adequately informed and that the "absence of real official information from Great Britain has frequently proved humiliating". As if this was not criticism enough, Menzies attacked the whole conception of the operation which he described as "a half-hearted attack" that had caused a "damaging loss of prestige". He concluded his message with a note of concern over the position in the Middle East, where the Italians had moved on Egypt, but had held back from engaging the numerically inferior British forces. Menzies pointedly expressed the hope that, unlike Dakar, the "difficulties have not been underestimated in Middle East where clear-cut victory is essential".[28]

Churchill was considerably taken aback by Menzies' trenchant criticism and the questioning of his strategic good sense. This was no doubt a very sore point with Churchill, who would have been mindful of past failures for which he was held responsible, ranging from the Dardanelles campaign of the First World War to the Norwegian fiasco of just some six months previously. In typical Churchill manner, he replied in kind, implying that Menzies was timorous for demanding an overwhelming chance of success prior to an operation and claiming that the Australian Government was more fully informed about Dakar than was the British Parliament. Lastly, he stoutly defended British efforts in the Middle East though rightly refusing to guarantee "clear-cut victory". The war would not be a smooth road to victory and Churchill pointedly informed Menzies that he would make no promises of victory in the Middle East and that "the only certainty is that we have very bad times indeed to go through before we emerge from the mortal perils by which we are surrounded."[29]

In London, Churchill also took Bruce to task over Menzies' cable[30] and Bruce later warned Menzies that Churchill had regarded it as a personal attack.[31] In order to clear the air, Menzies cabled Churchill assuring him of Australia's full support and putting a different and milder construction on his earlier criticism. At the same time, he refused to allow Churchill to get away with any implied criticism of Australia's war effort and pointed to the large Australian contribution in the Middle East, a contribution that gave rise to and justified his anxieties. Lastly, Menzies assured him that "Australia knows courage when it sees it and will follow you to a finish, as to the best of my abilities I certainly shall".[32]

Churchill accepted Menzies' assurances and apologised for his own strident retort.[33] Calmness now apparently returned to their relations, but the incident had confirmed and heightened existing prejudices held by both men. Menzies was confirmed in his belief that the British leader was a menace who could commit Australian forces willy-nilly to bold and hazardous ventures. For his part, Churchill was further confirmed in his belief of Menzies as an anxious ally wary of accepting the risks of war and eager to intrude on Churchill's decision-making prerogatives.

The strength of Menzies' reaction to the Dakar failure may be partly explained by his own precarious political position. Though he had recently won a general election, his majority was razor thin and, as he informed Bruce, the political position in Australia was "very difficult and anything may happen". Despite the election, Menzies observed that there were political conspirators "at every street corner".[34] His feeling of being hemmed in by his political enemies was no mere paranoia. According to a conservative colleague, Sir Frederic Eggleston, Menzies was right to feel threatened although, Eggleston claimed, he had only himself to blame. Writing to a friend in London, Eggleston bemoaned the fact that Menzies had "so many enemies in politics and has so few real friends". He also claimed that most of Menzies' colleagues were "eager for his blood" and that Menzies would have to "vacate the Prime Ministership in order to have any Government at all in Australia and this at the most crucial period we have ever faced".[35]

Despite the antipathy towards Menzies, there was no alternative leader in the conservative parties who could match his obvious powers and intellect. So, on 15 October he was unanimously re-elected leader of his United Australia Party following his Federal election success. The party meeting guaranteed him its "loyalty and support in the new Parliament".[36] Menzies, presumably, had no illusions about this expression of support. Indeed he again actively canvassed the creation of some form of national government, a move that received widespread press support.[37] The Australian Labor Party, though, was implacably opposed to any form of national government. Though Menzies enjoyed a good working relationship with the Labor leader, John Curtin, the party as a whole was mindful of previous national governments that had drawn off Labor members into essentially conservative administrations whose main purpose had been to frustrate the formation of Labor governments. With Labor's strength in the House of Representatives, there was a strong possibility that they might soon be able to form a government in their own right. Menzies' plan therefore came to naught.

On 17 October, the British press magnate Lord Kemsley cabled Menzies regarding a newspaper campaign he was mounting in his London *Daily Sketch* to achieve an Imperial War Cabinet. He asked Menzies for his opinion of the campaign as he felt it "necessary to urge this policy on our Government".[38] Menzies properly replied that he could make no public comment as it was a matter for discussion between governments.[39] However, during an after-dinner conversation with Britain's High Commissioner, Menzies opposed the creation of any Imperial War Cabinet requiring the constant attendance of Dominion Prime Ministers, though he urged that there should be a conference of Dominion Prime Ministers. In reporting Menzies' views to London, the High Commissioner pointed out that Menzies was "sure that the suggestion for such a conference ought to come from the United Kingdom and not from the Dominions".[40] Menzies had now made the first move in a campaign he intended should take him to the very pinnacle of power in London.

When Menzies' suggestion came before the British War Cabinet on 4 November, it was decided that a conference was too difficult to organise, but that Menzies be invited to come alone.[41] In April 1940, plans for just such a conference had met with discouraging replies from Smuts and Mackenzie King, neither of whom was keen to leave his divided society for discussions in London. In contrast, Menzies expected that such high-level discussions could only reflect creditably on him at home and such credit was what he desperately needed. Also, of course, the greater involvement of the Dominions would fulfil Menzies' conception of proper Imperial decision-making, and help to moderate Churchill's dictatorial leanings.

As if further to emphasise the precarious nature of his position in Australia, Menzies was savagely attacked by the Sydney *Sun* following a complaint he made regarding Australian apathy towards the war. Aiming straight for the head, the *Sun* riposted that it was "not apathy that is the trouble, but the lack of confidence in leaders who fail to lead".[42]

Menzies was now set on going to London. Though his motives were mixed, it was necessary to keep alive his local options, and the importance of recapturing the political initiative in Australia loomed large in his mind. This he could do by both playing the statesman's role in London and, hopefully, by achieving something concrete, of practical value to Australia. Two possibilities here were expediting the delivery of fighter planes and attracting British capital for the country's burgeoning secondary industries.

But while protecting his political position doubtless played its part in speeding Menzies towards London, undoubtedly the issue of deepest significance was the signals from London making it increasingly clear that the British Empire was imperilled under Churchill's leadership. Churchill had a marked disinclination to involve the Dominions in the decision-making of the war; his truculent refusal to countenance a negotiated peace and his attachment to total victory in the face of over-whelming odds presaged a debilitating struggle that would sap the Empire's strength to the point of exhaustion; and, Churchill's disdain for the established principles of Imperial defence had left the Empire in the Far East extremely vulnerable to encroachment by Japan. By his personal representations in London, Menzies apparently hoped to be able to restore the security of the Empire generally as a British priority of the first order. Little did he realise how far the Empire had slipped in this regard and the consequent scale of the task he had set himself in the Imperial capital.

On 25 November, Menzies approached his Advisory War Council, containing representatives of all the political parties, with a proposal to visit London. He referred to ''the alarming position in regard to the defence of Singapore'' and claimed that this and ''other matters which he had in mind'' necessitated his visit to London for talks with Churchill. This was approved by the Council.[43]

Before Menzies could move he was faced with another bout of political turmoil when the Labor Party proposed amendments to his Budget. Menzies took this as a challenge to his government and for a week the parties were in uproar with a widespread expectation that he would be defeated. He was relying for his survival on the vote of an Independent MP from Victoria and there was every chance that the vote would not be forthcoming. However, on 4 December, the Labor Party suddenly ended the crisis by accepting a compromise and dropping its amendments.

The backdown by the Labor Party occurred despite the opposition of the newly-elected Labor member, Dr H. V. Evatt, who was keen, above all, for Labor to take power. Evatt continued his pressure on Menzies by calling for a National Government under a Prime Minister other than Menzies. In this he was supported by the UAP member

Bill McCall, a long-time critic of the Prime Minister.[44] The call for a national government was backed as well by influential sections of the press, especially in Sydney.[45] Menzies, however, ignored the calls and pressed on with his planning for the visit, which had received backing from wide sections of the press.[46] There was a further impediment to be overcome in the form of a by-election on 21 December that could have given Labor a majority in the House of Representatives. In the event Menzies held on to his slender majority.

The timing of his trip now became important as Churchill began to come under increasing criticism. The waiting "Welsh wizard", Lloyd George, sensed impending military defeats that could well open the way for his own intervention. In late November he informed his future wife, Frances Stevenson, that he would go to London as soon as there was an opportunity for effective intervention in Parliament.[47] This, he thought, was imminent as it was "clear that Hitler is working up to something dramatic... The pot is boiling up. It will be hot and strong when it is ready."[48] The military pot was certainly beginning to boil, as the struggle for the control of the Mediterranean intensified, but Lloyd George's dire anticipations were premature. Britain was to experience dramatic military successes before again tasting the bitterness of defeats sufficient to threaten the political existence of Churchill.

Perhaps Churchill also sensed impending trouble at this time for, in December 1940, he tried to shunt Lloyd George off the political tracks and appoint him as British Ambassador to the United States following the death of the previous incumbent, Lord Lothian. Ironically, Menzies made strenuous efforts to stop Churchill offering the position to Lloyd George. Menzies was acting at the behest of the American President, F. D. Roosevelt, who feared that Lloyd George would strengthen the hand of the isolationists in America.[49] The Australian Minister in Washington, Richard Casey, urged Menzies to add his voice to appeals from the other Dominions calling for the appointment not to be made. This Menzies immediately did, informing Churchill that he would "prefer somebody whose views (were) calculated to stiffen American opinion", and suggesting the Foreign Secretary, Lord Halifax, for the post.[50]

The fact that Halifax subsequently became the British Ambassador has led some writers to conclude that Menzies and Casey played a crucial role in preventing the appointment of Lloyd George.[51] This was not the case since a firm offer of the Ambassadorship was nonetheless made to Lloyd George by Beaverbrook acting as a go-between for Churchill. Lloyd George declined the offer, supposedly on the advice of his doctor. But in reality, as A. J. P. Taylor indicated, Lloyd George had "hopes of a negotiated peace and of himself making it . . . ''[52]

It is interesting to speculate at this point as to Menzies' view of the war at the end of 1940. His opposition to Lloyd George's Washington appointment suggests that he had moved some distance away from his earlier support for a compromise peace. In fact, Menzies addressed himself to this very issue on 19 December during a luncheon speech in Western Australia. He sternly warned the assembled guests that those who "indulge in a hope that some temporary compromise may be arrived at are merely being guilty of treason to the cause for which we stand''.[53]

These sentiments, albeit rephrased, could just as easily have come from Churchill. However, this did not mean that Menzies was preparing to leave for London feeling an identification with Churchill's pursuit of total victory. As with many politicians, Menzies' public utterances cannot necessarily be taken as an accurate guide to his private feelings. He had already informed Bruce that he had to be very circumspect in expressing his beliefs as the press and his Cabinet colleagues stood ready to attack any hint of appeasement. Menzies' major preoccupation at this time was his political survival but it is likely that he still retained a tendency to support, whenever politically possible, a peace that would avoid the looming, total, world conflict and preserve the coherence of the Empire.

Over Christmas and New Year, Menzies spent a quiet time with his family at his Macedon house in the mountains outside Melbourne. Macedon was a traditional summer retreat for the Melbourne upper class and it preserved an air of England in the harsh Australian bush. With the Western Australian by-election confirming him in office, Menzies had plenty of time to ponder his future in discussions with family and friends. Here he was, at the summit of Australian politics, having just turned 46 years of age. It had been a fast climb by any standards and now he was finding the view not to his liking.

Menzies had already been tempted to leave politics in 1938[54] and his predicament in 1940 must have stimulated similar thoughts. The option of starting afresh in Britain in either politics or the legal profession was a real one. Menzies had already been to London three times, had formed a strong attachment to the country and had made friends in London's business and political circles. His view of the Empire and of his own "Britishness" meant that there was no psychological barrier to such a shift. From the evidence available at the present time, it is impossible to determine whether thoughts of such a shift had previously crossed Menzies' mind. However, his later alacrity to consider it suggests that the idea may not have been new to him.

When Menzies did come down from the mountains, he was struck by last-minute doubts about the wisdom of going to London. On 3 January 1941, he cabled Bruce that he was concerned about the political situation in Australia but still felt that ''much mutual benefit might result from visit provided I could be sure of prompt and sufficient opportunity for consultation [with] Churchill and chief Ministers''. Menzies asked Bruce to ''quite frankly'' give his views on the visit and assured him that ''as always I will be much influenced by your own opinion''.[55] When questioned by the press, Menzies refused to comment, saying only that ''When I know that I am going I will announce the fact.''[56]

In response to Menzies' cable, Bruce was certainly frank about the difficulties to be faced in London. Though he assured Menzies that discussions with British Ministers would be valuable, he also provided powerful arguments against the visit. He pointed out that at that time there was ''no definite line we would want to press on the United Kingdom Government in the field of major policy''. He also warned Menzies of Churchill's almost dictatorial control over major war policy and that any attempt by Menzies to ''pin him down to definite discussions of fundamental questions'' would be liable to strain their relations seriously.[57]

Bruce's cable should have given Menzies cause to ponder but, if it did, it was not for long. On 8 January, Menzies again approached his Advisory War Council with the proposal that he go to London. Again, he was given their support and assured that, when he spoke in London, he would be ''expressing the united opinion of the Australian people''.[58]

Rather than giving Menzies second thoughts, Bruce's warnings seem to have spurred him on. Perhaps it was because his portrayal of a dictatorial Churchill had confirmed Menzies' private fears and emboldened him to try and cut Churchill's power. At this stage, the outcome of the ''Battle of Britain'' had provided Britain with a breathing space, but nothing more. There was still no clear road to victory and any strategic blunder by Churchill might still result in rapid defeat. In this situation of relative hiatus, Menzies might well have considered that it was worth risking a dispute with Churchill in order to place the Imperial war effort on a sure footing. In addition, whatever the warnings from Bruce, Menzies' own precarious political position warranted the taking of considerable risks.

"Artie" Fadden, Australia's Acting Prime Minister during Menzies' 1941
visit to England
(NEWS LIMITED)

On 13 January 1941, Menzies announced he would soon be going to London for a brief visit to "discuss with the Prime Minister and other British Ministers matters of great moment related to Empire policy and co-operation between Great Britain and Australia in the conduct of the war". "Artie" Fadden, the Australian Treasurer and leader of the Country Party, was appointed as Acting Prime Minister. Lastly, Menzies assured Australians that his absence would be "as brief as possible" and that "Parliament shall meet early in March, as originally intended."[59] In the event, his visit was far from brief, lasting four months.

The prospect of Menzies' visit was well received in London. The *Times* noted that he was "already well known in this country, and his previous visits impressed everyone who met him with his ability, his clearness of mind, and his tenacity of purpose".[60] In its comment, the *Daily Telegraph* linked Menzies' visit with the possibility of holding an Imperial conference or forming an Imperial War Cabinet. However, as a portent of the conflicts to come, the paper judged that neither of these options was possible.[61]

The troubles that Bruce forecast for Menzies in his relations with Churchill partly arose, as said, from the latter's view of the Empire and of the Dominions' place within it. One of Menzies' major criticisms was the lack of consultation with, and information from, Britain. Churchill was determined that he be allowed to win the war in his own way and with the minimum of interference from his own War Cabinet, let alone from the Dominions. In a Christmas Day minute to the new Dominions Secretary, Lord Cranborne, Churchill urged him to restrict the flow of secret information to the Dominions since, he claimed, the "Prime Ministers of every Dominion are bound to inform their colleagues, who again no doubt inform their wives and private secretaries". Though Churchill said there should be "no change in principle", he ordered that "there should be considerable soft-pedalling in practice."[62]

Another issue that was to dog Menzies' steps in London was that of aircraft reinforcements for Australia and the British base at Singapore. In early January 1941 the British Chiefs of Staff had reduced the projected plane levels at Singapore from the recommended target of 582 to just 336 which they claimed "should give very fair degree of security..." Even this target was to be subject to the "general situation and supply of aircraft".[63] On learning of this, Churchill, however, denied his approval to what, he termed "these very large diversions of Force". He claimed that the "political

situation in the Far East does not seem to require, and the strength of
our Air Force by no means warrants, the maintenance of such large
forces in the Far East at this time".[64] So this major item on Menzies'
London agenda was effectively denied to him even before he left
Australia.[65]

The other matter of significance bearing on the success of
Menzies' trip concerned the military situation in Greece. The
possibility of German intervention was becoming increasingly certain
as the Italian attack on Greece continued to falter. The problem facing
Churchill, and Menzies, was the British obligation to reinforce Greek
resistance in the face of the expected German attack. These
reinforcements, which inevitably would have to include a substantial
Australian contingent, could hope neither to stop nor stem the
onslaught, and could only be dispatched at the expense of the British
position in Libya. Yet even before Menzies' visit was announced,
Churchill had all but determined on sending reinforcements despite
strong warnings that they would be lost.[66]

The stage in London was therefore set in such a way as to bring
Menzies into head-on conflict with Churchill if any of his major aims
were to be achieved. Neither of them could count on the unquestioned
loyalty of his political colleagues and each was very aware of being
surrounded by people eager to see him fall. On the military side, the
stunning British victories in Libya in January 1941 would soon give
way to disastrous defeats. This would exacerbate the turmoil surrounding Menzies in Australia, and at the same time seriously throw
into question the war leadership of Churchill. With Menzies in London
and military disaster in the Mediterranean, the issue of compromise
peace in Europe and appeasement in Asia was to take on a new life in
the spring of 1941. Menzies and Churchill were set on a collision
course, the outcome of which would determine the future of the very
Empire.

Notes

1. M. GILBERT, pp. 410–11
2. IBID., p. 410
3. DAFP, iii, Docs 260, 261, 280, Cable No. 344, Bruce to Menzies, 22 May
   1940; Cable, Menzies to Churchill, 22 May 1940; Cable, Menzies to Casey,
   26 May 1940
4. M. GILBERT, pp. 435–6; the note formed the basis of a cable to Menzies,
   DAFP, iii, Docs 308 and 309
5. See P. HASLUCK, i, ch. 5 for details of the Australian reaction to the crisis in

Europe. At least one major newspaper was unimpressed by Menzies' response to the crisis and demanded that he go to the United States to purchase aircraft and other war supplies. The paper further demanded that Menzies admit that Australia was "as unprepared, muddled, and confused as Britain was 18 months ago". *Daily Telegraph*, Sydney, 7 June 1940

6. *ADVERTISER*, Adelaide, 6 June 1940; *Courier Mail*, Brisbane, 4 and 8 June 1940
7. M. GILBERT, p. 410
8. *ADVERTISER*, Adelaide, 6 June 1940
9. LETTERS, Latham to Menzies, 20 June 1940; Menzies to Latham, 22 June 1940, MS 1009/1/5459–61, Latham Papers: NLA
10. *DAFP*, iii, Doc. 452, Cable, Menzies to Caldecote, 27 June 1940
11. LETTER, Halifax to Hoare, 8 July 1940, XIII:20, Templewood Papers: CUL
12. NOTE by Bruce for meeting with Sir Horace Seymour and Ashley Clarke of the Foreign Office, 5 July 1940, CRS M100, July 1940: AA; *DAFP*, iv, Doc. 14, Cable No. 520, Bruce to Menzies, 6 July 1940
13. *DAFP*, iv, Doc. 20, Cable, Menzies to Bruce, 9 July 1940
14. LETTER, Halifax to Hoare, 17 July 1940, XIII:20, Templewood Papers: CUL
15. LETTER, Lloyd George to Liddell Hart, 11 September 1940 with enclosed memorandum "The Situation", dated 11 September 1940, 1/450, Liddell Hart Papers: KC
16. *IBID.*
17. LETTER, Lloyd George to Duke of Bedford, 14 September 1940, G/3/4/7, Lloyd George Papers: HLRO
18. DALTON DIARY, 3 October 1940, Dalton Papers: LSE
19. A. J. P. TAYLOR (ED.), *My Darling Pussy*, London, 1975, p. 239
20. For Churchill's pre-war relationship with Beaverbrook, see K. YOUNG, *Churchill and Beaverbrook*, London, 1966; A. J. P. Taylor, *Beaverbrook*, London, 1972; Lord Beaverbrook, *Men and Power 1917–1918*, London, 1956
21. See PREM 3/33: PRO
22. DALTON DIARY, 27 September 1940, Dalton Papers: LSE
23. LETTERS, Liddell Hart to Lloyd George, 11 October 1940, 8 November 1940, 1/450 Liddell Hart Papers: KC
24. LETTER, Beaverbrook to Liddell Hart, 13 February 1940, 1/52/8, Liddell Hart Papers: KC
25. LETTER, Lloyd George to Frances Stevenson, 22 October 1940, A. J. P. Taylor (ed.), *My Darling Pussy*, pp. 243–5
26. LETTER, Lloyd George to Liddell Hart, 19 November 1940, 1/450, Liddell Hart Papers: KC
27. *DAFP*, iv, Doc. 141, Cable No. 843, Bruce to Menzies, 26 September 1940
28. *DAFP*, iv, Doc. 144, Cable, Menzies to Churchill, 29 September 1940
29. *DAFP*, iv, Doc. 152, Cable, Churchill to Menzies, 2 October 1940
30. *DAFP*, iv, Doc. 153, Note by Bruce of talk with Churchill, 2 October 1940
31. *DAFP*, iv, Doc. 154, Cable No. 873, Bruce to Menzies, 2 October 1940
32. *DAFP*, iv, Doc. 158, Cable, Menzies to Churchill, 4 October 1940
33. *DAFP*, iv, Doc. 160, Cable, Churchill to Menzies, 6 October 1940
34. CABLE, Menzies to Bruce, 4 October 1940, CRS M100, "October 1940": AA
35. LETTER, Eggleston to R. Mackay, 8 October 1940, MS 423/1/143, Eggleston Papers: NLA

36. COURIER MAIL, Brisbane, 16 October 1940
37. See SUN, Herald Melbourne, Courier-Mail, Telegraph, Brisbane, 15 October 1940; Sun, Sydney Morning Herald, Sydney, Advertiser, Adelaide, 14 October 1940
38. CABLE, Lord Kemsley to Menzies, 17 October 1940, A1608, M 33/1/1: AA
39. CABLE, Menzies to Lord Kemsley, 22 October 1940, A1608, M 33/1/1: AA
40. CABLE NO. 377, UK High Commissioner in Australia to Dominions Office, 23 October 1940, PREM 4/43 A/13: PRO
41. WAR CABINET CONCLUSIONS, 4 November 1940, Cab 65/10, W.M.282(40): PRO
42. SUN, Sydney, 12 November 1940
43. ADVISORY WAR COUNCIL MINUTES, 25 November 1940, CRS A2682, Vol. 1, Minute 39: AA
44. ARGUS, Melbourne, 7 December 1940
45. DAILY TELEGRAPH, SYDNEY MORNING HERALD, Sydney, 9 December 1940
46. SUN, Sydney, 12 December 1940, Age, Melbourne, 13 December 1940, Daily Telegraph, Sydney, 16 December 1940, Herald, Melbourne, 16 December 1940
47. In order to avoid German bombing, Lloyd George rarely stayed in London and spent most of the war at one or other of his country houses
48. LETTER, Lloyd George to Frances Stevenson, 21 November 1940, A. J. P. Taylor (ed.), My Darling Pussy, p. 247
49. CABLE, Casey to Menzies, 16 December 1940, CRS A1608, K 33/1/5: AA
50. CABLE NO. 1694, Menzies to Churchill, 16 December 1940, A1608, K 33/1/5: AA
51. A. WATT, Australian Diplomat, Sydney, 1972, p. 38
52. A. J. P. TAYLOR, Beaverbrook, p. 457
53. SUN, Melbourne, 19 December 1940
54. K. PERKINS, Menzies, London, 1968, p. 67
55. CABLE, Menzies to Bruce, 3 January 1941, CP 290/9, Bundle 1, Folder 5: AA
56. AGE, Melbourne, 4 January 1941
57. DAFP, iv, Doc. 246, Cable No. 14, Bruce to Menzies, 5 January 1941
58. ADVISORY WAR COUNCIL MINUTES, 8 January 1941, CRS A2682, Vol. 1, Minute 79: AA
59. AGE, Melbourne, 14 January 1941
60. TIMES, London, 15 January 1941
61. DAILY TELEGRAPH, London, 15 January 1941
62. MINUTE, Churchill to Cranborne, 25 December 1940, PREM 4/43B/1: PRO
63. CABLE NO. 39, CoS to Commander in Chief Far East, 10 January 1941, PREM 3/156/3: PRO
64. MINUTE D15/1, Churchill to General Ismay for CoS Committee, 13 January 1941, PREM 3/156/3: PRO
65. R. G. MENZIES, The Measure of the Years, London, 1970, p. 45. Menzies recalled that ''the whole reason for this wartime visit'' was ''to discuss what my Government believed to be a serious menace from Japan . . . and to urge the strengthening of the defences of Singapore''
66. R. SHERWOOD, The White House Papers of Harry L. Hopkins, i, London, 1948, p. 240

3

En Route to London

On 24 January 1941, Robert Menzies clambered into a Qantas Empire Airways flying boat in Sydney Harbour for the first stage of his trip to London. Taking leave of Australia was a quiet affair as news of his departure was embargoed for security reasons. For Menzies, it was a time of some foreboding. In the diary that he began for this trip, he wrote that, "for once in my life I am off upon a chancy undertaking."[1]

The other members of Menzies' party were F. G. Shedden, Secretary of the Defence Department, J. Storey, a member of the Aircraft Production Commission, and a private secretary each for Menzies and Shedden. The composition of the party reflected a primary concern with political rather than military matters. The glaring omission from the party was a senior serving officer to provide Menzies with a source of independent military advice. This was left instead to Shedden, who was well versed but not expert in military affairs. Storey's inclusion was designed to fulfil one of Menzies' main aims—to get British capital to expand aircraft production in Australia with an eye to increasing the pace of Australian industrialisation and securing for Britain the post-war Australian automobile industry. This would help strengthen the economic integration of the Empire and lessen the inroads American capital was making into Australia. Success in this enterprise would amount to a substantial political gain and to Menzies the prospect outweighed the political risks involved in a prolonged absence from Australia.

Menzies could easily have chosen to fly to England by way of America, but he had reasons for taking the much more dangerous route via Singapore and the Middle East. This section of the trip was to be in the nature of a personal fact-finding mission that would allow him to check on defence preparations in the Far East and on the military situation in the Middle East where three Australian army divisions were stationed. More important, however, was the political value in visiting the troops. It might not only help restore his prestige among them, but also among their friends and relations in Australia.

This must have been of major concern to Menzies. After all, the Australian Army Minister, Percy Spender, had only just returned from a visit to Singapore and the Middle East and could presumably have provided him with the facts he required. What Spender could not provide, though, was the elevation of Menzies' place in the hearts and minds of the Australian people. So the first stage of the trip was very much an attempt to build on the inconclusive election result of the previous October.

Although Menzies' primary purpose may not have been to gather facts, he could not help seeing the parlous defence position in the Far East. In Singapore, his first major stop on the way to London, Menzies seems to have been genuinely shocked by what he discovered. In this reputedly impregnable British naval base, Menzies found a state of mind among its defenders that he perceptively predicted pointed straight to defeat.

On 29 January, he had a conference with Singapore's commanders presided over by the Commander in Chief Far East, Air Chief Marshal Sir Robert Brooke-Popham. Privately, Menzies was most scathing in his comments on the calibre of the commanders. Brooke-Popham left Menzies with "a vague feeling that his instincts favour some heroic but futile" defence rather than "clear-cut planning..." Menzies blamed this firmly on Churchill, whose farewell exhortation to Brooke-Popham was to "Hold out to the last, my boy, God bless you. If your grandfather had not broken his neck playing polo at Poona, he would be proud of you this day!"[2]

Though the army commander General Bond was described by Menzies as tall and well groomed, he also acidly noted that Bond spoke with "that form of mental hiccups which reduces conversation to a series of unrelated ejaculations". Menzies concluded that, if Malaya were attacked, General Bond would die fighting, but too many of his troops would die with him.[3]

Not only was Menzies disappointed at the calibre of the commanders, he was also shocked to see at first hand the relative defencelessness of Malaya and Singapore. There were no major naval units to make Singapore a functioning base, the air force was woefully ill-equipped and the army lacked essential items of equipment. The situation at Singapore had long been a cause for concern in Australia and Menzies now felt it was imperative to strengthen its defences as well as seek to reduce the potential threat from Japan. He was determined that the Far Eastern defence issue be taken seriously in London. To bolster his case there, he ordered further staff talks in Singapore so that the results could arrive in time for his talks with British Ministers.[4]

So Menzies' fleeting Singapore stopover had produced a modification in the purpose of his visit to London. This steamy Imperial outpost seemed suspended in time and almost blissfully unaware of the spreading conflagration that would soon consume it. Each week, the Qantas flying boat still lumbered into Singapore with 400 dozen oysters from Sydney and took back fresh Singapore orchids for the weddings of Sydney "high society". Australia had long placed its trust in the idea of the naval base at Singapore providing the springboard for the British fleet in the event of war in the Pacific. It was supposed to be the heavily fortified citadel that would block the approach of an enemy towards Australia's practically defenceless shores. Menzies was horrified to find that the place was as defenceless as Australia itself.

Churchill's neglect of Singapore had deep implications. Menzies was slowly beginning to realise that the system of Imperial defence that once sustained the Empire was no longer operative. The Empire no longer mustered its resources to meet threats on different fronts. Instead, its strength was being drawn inward to protect its heart, Britain. A tourniquet had been applied to such distant limbs of Empire as Malaya, as if they were being left to wither or be cut away.

It would seem that Menzies still found it difficult to comprehend that Churchill would consciously expose part of the Empire to possible annihilation. In his diary, he questioned why no fighter planes could be diverted from North Africa to Malaya and why Churchill refused to give a definite commitment on the despatch of a British fleet to Singapore in the case of war with Japan. He complained bitterly that "misty generalizations will please and sustain the Japanese, and nobody else."[5]

With Singapore so obviously devoid of defences, Menzies became more convinced of the urgency of reaching a settlement with Japan before the Japanese called the British bluff and picked off the Imperial plums in the Far East. Though he claimed to disavow appeasement and wanted to tell Japan "where she gets off", Menzies' ideas were still aimed at allowing Japanese military expansion at the expense of third parties, as long as it stopped short of the Imperial boundaries. "The peg," he wrote, "must be driven in somewhere."[6]

As Menzies' flying boat droned onwards from Singapore, Churchill was even then consciously combating the forces in Britain that continued to favour a compromise peace. In response to newspaper comment critical of various of his Cabinet Ministers, Churchill mounted a vigorous counter attack. In a letter to the newspaperman Cecil King, Churchill likened the criticism in the *Daily Mirror* and the *Sunday Pictorial* to a fifth column. Such a fifth column, he claimed, would use a "perfervid zeal for intensification of the war effort. . .as a cloak behind which to insult and discredit one Minister after another". Churchill claimed that this campaign could ultimately be "switched over into naked defeatism, and a demand for a negotiated peace".[7]

Churchill, then, was certainly concerned about the possibility of a popular movement welling up to force such a compromise. Later, in a private talk with King, he also revealed his anxiety over the extent of his own political insecurity. When he had assumed the Prime Minister-ship in May 1940, Churchill had retained many of Chamberlain's former Ministers who had been heavily tainted by their involvement in the pre-war appeasement of Germany. Even Chamberlain was kept on as a senior Minister in Churchill's War Cabinet. Churchill was widely criticised for not making a clean sweep of these so-called "men of Munich" but their support was vital for his own survival. As Chur-chill now confided to King, "the MP's who had supported Chamberlain still formed a majority of 150 in the House, and he was not going to fight them as they were too numerous."[8]

This frank admission reveals a Churchill far removed from the popular post-war myth. At this stage of the war he was not an un-assailed colossus but, rather, a Prime Minister in office on sufferance from opponents otherwise eager for his political skin. Only Churchill's public popularity stayed their collective hands against him.

It was at this time that the Australian High Commissioner in London, Bruce, was promoting the idea of having "someone in the War Cabinet strong enough to stand up to the Prime Minister".[9] This idea was based on a perception of Churchill that accorded well with reality—that he was a brilliant but erratic leader who simply required a strong, critical opponent in Cabinet to neutralise his more impetuous ideas. This criticism existed before the war, and gained further currency after the Norwegian disaster in 1940. In the coming months of 1941 this criticism was to become epidemic among leading British politicians, soldiers and businessmen. It infected their view of Churchill and permitted Menzies to be touted as the strong cure-all for Britain's ills.

While those like Bruce agitated for a counter-balance to Churchill, Lloyd George continued to push for a compromise peace. He still could not envisage a British victory and predicted that, without a negotiated peace within 12 months "the war will be spread everywhere in the world, causing suffering and destruction beyond imagination and it will not be a whit nearer solution". To Lloyd George and his friends, Churchill was the stumbling block to any negotiation with Germany.[10]

Menzies, the man who would try to break the political deadlock in Britain, crush Churchill's power and end the war, was even then being built up in the minds of the British public. Some three weeks before he actually arrived in London, Menzies was being lauded in several organs of the British press as the "Empire's Youngest Premier...the Man with a Will". He was introduced to Britain as one of the outstanding personalities of the British Commonwealth who could "obliterate a sunset with a phrase". Ironically, he was described as being "averse to any kind of compromise" and one who would "rather lose a battle any day than agree to a patched-up settlement".[11]

He was further heralded as being a "staunch" but critical supporter of Britain, a "fearless thinker, a man of great intellect, and of strong character" and "one of the most charming of personalities, and one of the most distinguished individuals". Physically, Menzies was likened almost to a Greek god. Though he was already a rather paunchy politician, two papers described him as being "over six feet in height, broad and muscular in proportion". One of them also claimed that, at school, Menzies was a brilliant sportsman and had maintained his physical fitness by regular gymnasium exercise. Concluding, the paper claimed that Menzies "has captured the hearts of the whole of Australia, doubtless he will make as great an impression in Britain...".[12]

It was almost as if the press was composing an ideal *curriculum vitae* for the person needed to stand up to Churchill in the War Cabinet and, if necessary, succeed him as Britain's leader. By means of this repetitious, overblown account of Menzies and his abilities, the British press, sometimes consciously and sometimes not, created a vision of a physical and intellectual superman capable of leading an Empire. From contemporary photos it is difficult to square the obviously florid, overweight politician with the athletic, god-like figure of press description.

While the British public apparently read with rapt attention of this larger-than-life figure rushing to London to lend his support, Menzies must have been more than encouraged by these descriptions of himself. Never would such unalloyed and unabashed praise of a political leader be published in Australia. In fact, the Australian press had, and still has, a deserved reputation for carrying political criticism to great lengths. Menzies had suffered much at their hands and had left Australia with the cacophony of their criticism ringing in his ears. What a contrast, then, to read the heady articles published in Britain to herald his arrival. As his visit progressed, the praise would intensify and be such as to overwhelm even the humblest of men, and that Menzies was not.

While the British press was beginning to turn its attention towards his imminent arrival in London, he was still on the second stage of his journey from Australia. This part of his trip took him to Palestine and Egypt, where he was able to visit many of the Australian troops stationed in the Middle East.

With Germany now in control of most of Europe, the Middle East was the only area in which British land forces could tackle their opponents, in this case the Italians. In the Mediterranean, the British Navy continued to assert its dominance. Using her bases astride the Mediterranean gateways, Britain had contained the Italian Navy and was gradually destroying it. However, the cost was considerable and it was becoming clear that it effectively prevented the dispatch of any substantial British fleet to the Far East in the event of war with Japan. It was on the dispatch of such a fleet that Australia's defence plans hinged. As yet Australia was not fully aware that it and the rest of the British Empire in the Far East could no longer rely on their protective naval armour—that Britain could not sustain a major war on two fronts.

Menzies' arrival in the Middle East coincided with the closing stages of a dramatic military assault by the Imperial forces stationed in Egypt. For some months they had stood toe to toe with their Italian adversaries some 100 miles inside Egypt itself. Though numerically outnumbered, the British forces used their weight in armour repeatedly to outflank and defeat the Italians and force them into headlong retreat back into Libya. There, a succession of fortresses was overrun by the triumphant British forces. The 6th Australian Division played a prominent part in some of these engagements, capturing Tobruk on 22 January and taking 30,000 Italian prisoners. By the time Menzies arrived in the Middle East on 3 February, the Italian Army in North Africa had been decisively defeated and within days was cleared from the Libyan province of Cyrenaica. The victorious British now faced their vanquished Italian opponents some 500 miles from the Egyptian border.

Distance in the desert was a deceptive military asset as the German General Rommel would soon show. Ordered by Hitler to halt the collapse of the Italians, on 12 February he flew into Tripoli with audacious plans for turning defeat into victory. This he would achieve with consummate ease within a few months. His daring victories would be made possible by Churchill who, on the day of Rommel's arrival in Libya, ordered that the British advance be halted and that preparations be made to transfer much of the British forces (including Australians) across the Mediterranean to Greece, where a German attack was expected.

Menzies was blissfully unaware of these disasters in the making, disasters in which Australian troops were to be caught up. Instead, he exulted in the victories at hand and seemed not to notice the storm clouds on the horizon. The reception given him by the Australian soldiers did much to cloud his vision. The battle-hardened troops responded to him in a fashion to which he was quite unused. Menzies described a day reviewing the troops in Palestine as "A great day's programme, driving around the camps—troops drawn up in many places—salutes—great precision—with only the old and bold cooks calling out 'How are you Bob?' ".[13] He was obviously impressed by his being received as the national leader rather than the disputed head of a single, sectional party.

In a cable to Fadden in Australia, Shedden described Menzies' tour of the troops in Palestine as a magnificent success, with Menzies in "his very best form". Shedden claimed that the troops "looked forward to his visit with a keenness bordering on excitement" and they were anxious that Menzies should "gain a good impression of them as head of the Government and in order to be able to tell their folks at home how well they are doing".[14]

Menzies not only toured the troops in the relatively peaceful backwaters of Palestine and Egypt but also flew over hundreds of miles of desert to see the men in the front line of the headlong push against the Italians. On 9 February, two days after British and Australian troops stormed into Benghazi, Menzies took off on a 1000-mile round trip from Cairo to visit the scene of their battle. However, a sudden storm flooded the aerodrome at Benghazi and his plane was forced back to Cairo. Resolutely he confided to his diary that he "must not miss seeing these men". He was now riding high on the wave of popularity he had created among the troops and he was out to exploit it to the limit. Ecstatically, Menzies wrote in his diary that his journey so far had been "of great value and quite successful—beyond my expectations".[15] Two days later Menzies finally succeeded in landing at Benghazi where again the troops responded positively.[16]

Menzies and General Blamey (saluting) review Australian troops
in the Middle East, February 1941

So, though there was no Australian election immediately in prospect, the tenor of Menzies' inspection was very much that of an election campaign tour. While he certainly spent time in discussion with political and military leaders in the Middle East, the bulk of the visit was devoted to public relations. Menzies even had a movie camera with which he assiduously photographed people and events for showing in Australia. Often welcoming dignitaries or a group of assembled troops would be disconcerted to find themselves the target for Menzies' roving camera while patiently waiting to greet him.

It was not only Australian troops who were impressed. A visiting Conservative MP, "Chips" Channon, attended a reception for Menzies in Cairo and found him "jolly, rubicund, witty, only 46, with a rapier-like intelligence and gifts as a raconteur...".[17] He made a similarly good impression on the British naval Commander-in-Chief, Admiral Sir A. B. Cunningham,[18] although he found it curious that the Australian was "still obsessed with the idea that we should send 3 or 4 battleships to Singapore".[19] Menzies had still not fully realised that Britain's Mediterranean situation had made virtually impossible an Imperial naval commitment to the Far East.

On 13 February, he returned to Cairo from his tour of the forward battle areas. That night he attended a reception at the Turf Club where he addressed members of the British community on Australia's war effort. He received another rapturous reception and later reflected in his diary that "A prophet is never without honour save in his own country and among his own people."[20] This quotation was to be repeated later in Menzies' diary and undoubtedly sums up his intense feelings of frustration and anger at the way he was regarded in Australia.

Whereas in Australia Menzies was constantly criticised, even by his supposed supporters, he was to continue to meet with wide acclaim on his overseas trip. Unable to judge his deeds, the audiences outside of Australia had to make do with his words, and his oratorical gifts were such that his words were usually more than sufficient. The contrast in attitude inevitably encouraged thoughts of starting afresh in Britain and leaving his ungrateful Australian public to their own devices.

While Menzies was getting much-needed personal encouragement, the Middle East also gave him his first experience of war. During an early morning shave in Benghazi, he had a taste of his first enemy air raid. In the recently captured towns he was also able to view the inevitable destruction and wanton waste of resources that war brings in its train. He visited cemeteries and hospitals and though he was

Menzies inspects war damage in Tobruk, February 1941

impressed by the sight of massed troops marching in review, he was also perceptive enough to describe them as "mere boys, in the flower of their youth, many of whom will never see Australia again. War is the abomination of desolation . . . ".[21]

Looking at the vast expanse of desert over which thousands of men had fought and died, Menzies reflected that the "sweating tax-payers of Italy probably thought Libya was worth it, because it looked fine and large when painted the Italian colour on the map!". After wandering Tobruk's streets and talking with groups of Australian soldiers, he sadly wrote that they were "friendly boys wise now in terrible things".[22]

Despite the overwhelming British victories in the Middle East, Menzies does not appear to have been exactly invigorated by them. He seems, indeed, to have been more than a little dismayed at the costs in men and property already incurred in what was always just a secondary theatre of war. Perhaps, in his mind's eye, Menzies was even then transferring the death and destruction of war to Europe and counting the cost of Churchill's policy of total victory. If the sands of North

Africa could absorb so much blood and treasure, how much more would be lost if the war was pushed back into Europe? These thoughts may well have begun to occur to Menzies during his 10 days in the Middle East. They certainly did occur to him later in England under the impact of the Blitz.

If Menzies' Middle East experience caused him to muse on the futility of war, it also produced renewed apprehensions about Churchill's fitness for leadership. On 9 February, Menzies attended a dinner in Cairo where the guests listened to a radio broadcast by Churchill in which he spoke of the great victories achieved in the Middle East. Menzies felt the broadcast was directed at the "lowest common denominator among men—a hymn of hate...". His bitterness was exacerbated by the news that Churchill had replaced another of Chamberlain's former Ministers—Menzies' friend Malcolm MacDonald. MacDonald had been removed as Minister of Health and dispatched to Canada as British High Commissioner. In his diary, Menzies wrote sourly of Churchill's preference for "Yes-men" and commented cynically that "we shall have Brendan Bracken as a Minister next!"[23] Bracken was Churchill's loyal and long-time friend and confidant. As Menzies predicted, he was soon to be appointed to the Cabinet.

His time on the battlefield also gave rise to serious doubts about the qualities of Britain's military leadership. Though Menzies was full of admiration for Admiral Cunningham, he was not so sure about the Army Commander-in-Chief, General Wavell, or some of his subordinates. Though he claimed to like Wavell, Menzies also noted that he was "an almost sinister figure" and that the successes in Libya were not Wavell's but were "entirely directed by General O'Connor, with brilliance and success".[24]

On 12 February, Menzies flew to Barce in Libya where he met General "Jumbo" Wilson. Wilson did not help matters by criticising the conduct of Australian soldiers and Menzies was severe in his assessment of the general:

> *Not impressed. All complaints about the "irregular" conduct of Australians on camp and guard duty, and nothing about their great fighting. Only man of whole bunch who intelligently understands is O'Connor. Wilson seems tall, fat and cunning.*[25]

Unfortunately, O'Connor was soon to be captured in Rommel's counter-attack while Wilson was to be appointed to command the ill-fated expedition to Greece.

Menzies' view of British generalship was intensified by his dis-

Frederick Shedden, Menzies and General Blamey
over drinks in the Middle East, February 1941
(AUSTRALIAN WAR MEMORIAL)

cussions with General Blamey, Commander of the Australian Imperial Force (AIF). Blamey was concerned to congregate all the scattered Australian units in the Middle East into one cohesive Corps. "Australian forces," he told Menzies, "must be regarded as national, under national command" and all use of the units must be subject to his (Blamey's) consent. Blamey argued that Australia must stick rigidly to this principle and warned Menzies that "If you give these English generals an inch, they'll take an ell." [26]

In the Middle East Menzies received further indications that there could soon be an expedition to Greece in order to forestall an expected German invasion. Though Australians were likely to make up a large component of any such expedition and Bruce had already informed Menzies of his doubts about the wisdom of such a diversion, Menzies does not seem to have gone to any great lengths to investigate the matter while in the Middle East. Here had been an opportunity for Menzies to perform a real role as Australia's leader. He was on the spot in the Middle East at a time when a major new commitment of forces was being contemplated, just as the situation in the Far East suddenly looked liable to boil over into war with Japan. [28] Given that state of affairs, any Greek adventure would tie up most of Australia's experienced troops at a time when they could have been needed for the defence of their homeland. Sadly, Menzies let the opportunity pass and failed to have any serious talks with either Wavell or Blamey to satisfy his own mind on the operation. He was to arrive in London relatively ill-prepared and to have the Greek proposal thrust upon him almost immediately. In the absence of any meaningful discussions on the subject in the Middle East, Menzies was too readily to give his blessing to the project.

But it was not only Menzies' fault that he arrived in London ill-informed on Greece. As the Australian military historian David Horner has pointed out, General Blamey should have been aware of the strong possibility of a Greek expedition. [29] He should have briefed Menzies on the possibility of Australian troops being used and he ought to have assessed the prospects of such an expedition meeting with success. Apparently no such discussions occurred. For their part, Churchill and Wavell were also culpable for keeping Menzies in the dark during the build-up to the expedition.

Churchill was particularly set on sending a force to Greece but was also aware that such a force had but a small chance of success. In mid-January he had tried without success to have the Greeks accept a British force in anticipation of a German attack. On 26 January

Churchill confided to Wavell that they "must expect a series of heavy, disastrous blows in the Balkans, and possibly a general submission there to German aims".[30] On 3 February he informed the War Cabinet that: "Last year's history in N. W. Europe is likely . . . to repeat itself this year in S. E. Europe."[31] Despite the gloomy prognosis, Churchill reacted positively to an eventual Greek request for military assistance. On 12 February, he cabled to Wavell with his order to halt the Libyan advance and prepare to send aid to Greece. He also informed Wavell that the Foreign Secretary, Anthony Eden, and the Chief of the Imperial General Staff (CIGS), General Dill, were going to Cairo to oversee the change of strategy.[32]

The same day that Churchill was foreshadowing a major change in British strategy that would heavily involve the Australian forces, Menzies was in Benghazi conferring with Blamey, apparently on everything but Greece. Even though he was perfectly placed for consultations on any strategic changes in that theatre, no attempt was made to so engage him. Australia's official war historian, Gavin Long, claimed that Menzies was consulted by Wavell prior to 12 February on "the general proposal to offer a force to Greece". However, Long merely cited a cable from Wavell noting discussions with Menzies about Australia giving Wavell "certain latitude as regards use of their troops".[33] This concerned the use of Australian divisions and parts thereof other than as a single corps; it did not at all involve Menzies' agreement to Australian participation in Greece.

On 13 February, Menzies was back from Benghazi and spent his last full day in Cairo. Accompanied by "Chips" Channon and the wife of the Egyptian Prime Minister, Menzies spent two hours touring Cairo's bustling bazaar in search of a present for his wife. Then, after another reception at the Turf Club, he had a final interview with Wavell at 8 pm on the evening prior to his departure for London. Despite having received cables from Churchill and the Chiefs of Staff, Wavell seems to have still held back from putting Menzies fully into the picture on Greece. In his diary, Menzies merely noted blandly that Wavell was "clearly contemplating the possibility of a Salonika expedition".[34]

One can argue that it was incumbent on Menzies, even at this late stage, to postpone his departure for London and examine the Greek proposal, in all its aspects, with Blamey. Instead, he stuck to his schedule and flew out of Cairo on 14 February, the same day that Eden and Dill were leaving England for Cairo. Eden was carrying instructions from Churchill to send "speedy succour to Greece". "It is our duty'', wrote Churchill, "to fight, and, if need be, suffer with Greece . . . ''[35] Menzies, whose forces were crucial to the operation's success, was left to spend a week flying to London apparently in blissful ignorance of the crisis beginning to well up around him.

In his diary, he summed up the Middle East part of his trip. "I have worked like a nigger for these ten days," he wrote, "but I think the results may be of great value.''[36] Obviously, the full implications of Wavell's intimation had yet to be borne home to Menzies. Before too long, the Greek crisis would be very much in his mind, further threatening his position in Australia but at the same time undermining Churchill in London. Even then Lloyd George was stepping up his private attacks on Churchill, claiming that he had "picked him out of the political gutter, but wished now he had left him there''.[37]

Menzies' Middle East visit had made him more amenable to approaches from the anti-Churchill forces. It had strengthened his view of Churchill as an erratic warmonger and had made him determined to stand up to the British Premier. Menzies confided to Channon, who travelled with him to London, that he would not be "blitzed by Winston''.[38] Viewing the death and destruction had reinforced his distaste for war and emphasised the cost in life and property that a policy of total victory would entail. On the other hand, seeing the battlefield at first hand had allowed Menzies to adopt the air of a man familiar with military matters, with definite ideas on what was needed to win through—armoured vehicles and mechanised transport. Lastly, he had had a taste of personal adulation to which he was quite unused, and had found it to his liking. When it increased apace in London, he was easily swayed towards political adventures, particularly when the adventures were directed at Imperial salvation and focussed on himself.

NOTES

1. 1941 TRIP DIARY (hereafter Menzies Diary), 24 January 1941, MS 4936/13/3, Menzies Papers: NLA
2. MENZIES DIARY, 29 January 1941
3. IBID.
4. IBID.
5. IBID.
6. IBID.
7. LETTER, Churchill to Cecil King, 25 January 1941, C. King, pp. 97–8
8. KING DIARY, 31 January 1941, C. King, pp. 101–3
9. TALK WITH HARRY HOPKINS, 28 January 1941, CRS M100, "January 1941": AA
10. K. MARTIN, p. 289

11. *LANCASHIRE DAILY POST*, 31 January 1941; *Sunday Mercury*, Birmingham, 2 February 1941
12. *IBID* ; in fact, Menzies' only interest in sport was as a spectator. At school he "neither played nor took any interest in sport . . .", Sir P. Joske, *Sir Robert Menzies, 1894–1978*, Sydney, 1978, p. 8
13. MENZIES DIARY, 4 February 1941
14. CABLE, Shedden to Fadden, 7 February 1941, CP 290/9, Bundle 1 (14) S.C.2: AA
15. MENZIES DIARY, 9 February 1941
16. MENZIES DIARY, 11 February 1941
17. CHANNON DIARY, 5 February 1941, R. R. James (ed.), p. 290
18. LETTER, Cunningham to "Doodles" (his aunts), 10 February 1941, ADD.MS.52558, Cunningham Papers: British Library (hereafter BL)
19. LETTER, Cunningham to First Sea Lord, Admiral Sir Dudley Pound, 10 February 1941, ADD.MS.52561, Cunningham Papers: BL
20. MENZIES DIARY, 13 February 1941
21. MENZIES DIARY, 4 February 1941
22. MENZIES DIARY, 8 February 1941
23. MENZIES DIARY, 9 February 1941
24. MENZIES DIARY, 7 February 1941
25. MENZIES DIARY, 12 February 1941
26. MENZIES DIARY, 11 February 1941
27. CABLE, Menzies to Fadden, 14 February 1941, CRS A5954/613/"Visit of Prime Minister to United Kingdom—Objects of Visit and Details of Movements": AA
28. See DALTON DIARY, 7 and 10 February 1941: LSE; Cable NO. 76, Sir John Latham to Department of External Affairs, Canberra, 11 February 1941, CRS CP 290/9/1/5: AA; Letter, Pound to Cunningham, 8 February 1941, ADD.MS.52561/56, Cunningham Papers: BL
29. D. HORNER, *High Command*, Sydney, 1982, p. 66
30. CABLE, Churchill to Wavell, 26 January 1941, "The Prime Minister's Personal Telegrams 1941" V1/1, Ismay Papers: KC
31. DALTON DIARY, 3 February 1941: LSE
32. DEFENCE COMMITTEE (OPERATIONS) MINUTES, 11 February 1941, Cab. 69/2, D.O.(41)8: PRO
33. G. LONG, *Greece, Crete and Syria*, Canberra, 1953, p. 8
34. MENZIES DIARY, 13 February 1941
35. NOTE, Churchill to Eden, 12 February 1941, PREM 3/294/2: PRO
36. MENZIES DIARY, 13 February 1941
37. KING DIARY, 19 February 1941, C. King, pp. 107–12
38. Channon noted drily: "but he will be." Channon Diary, 16 February 1941, R. R. James (ed.), p. 292

4

First Impressions

O n 20 February, six days after leaving Cairo, Menzies was finally flying over his beloved England. His fellow passenger, "Chips" Channon, wrote that the "excitement of Menzies' Australian entourage was touching to see as they approached England for the first time".[1] Though this was Menzies' fourth trip to England in six years, it was possibly the first time he had seen it from the air. Certainly he was just as excited by the aerial view and wrote in his diary: "Came in across N. Devon. Many fields white with snow. The dark woods, the myriad hedges. What a lovely place at any time."[2] On landing in Poole harbour, Menzies was met by Bruce and then driven to London where he was lodged in a first-floor suite at the Dorchester Hotel.

The following morning, he woke to a welcoming editorial in London's *News Chronicle*. As the first shot in a campaign that would become widespread during the course of his visit, the paper called for the eventual formation of a "full Imperial Cabinet, responsible for all long-distance policies". And, in an argument dear to Menzies, the paper maintained that the "British Empire is a true world order: we should make the most of it".[3] Later that day, he met the British and foreign press at a conference organised by the Ministry of Information. He made a tremendous impact on those present and was thereafter practically assured of a good press in London.

Menzies' message was simple and designed to evoke a ready response. Britain, he said, was not alone. The whole Empire was behind her and would go all out to win. The timing of his visit was crucial. He brought a tone of vibrancy and optimism at the end of a hard English winter of bombing and blackouts. Seized on as a hero figure, as he swept into London on the tide of recent Anzac successes in Libya, he was able to bring first-hand reports of the battlefield and inspire his listeners with the extent of the victories at a time when there seemed no end in sight to the war.

The conservative *Daily Telegraph* warmly greeted Menzies as the personification of that "staunch and stalwart spirit which our Australian kinsmen have so characteristically shown in the Empire's time of supreme peril". His speech was described by the paper as having a "tonic quality of high confidence and resolution which will find a ready echo here".[4]

The *Birmingham Post* continued this elevation of Menzies into a larger-than-life figure capable of anything. The paper described him as a "commanding personality" with "the zeal of a youthful statesman of forty-six years". Menzies' massive build was judged as impressive, while his "confident control over utterances couched in the liveliest phraseology, without any apparent assistance of notes, shows that he has within him the real stuff of a public man".[5] Though it was too early for the press to make a direct comparison with Churchill, their descriptions of Menzies compared favourably with the popular perception of Churchill. The more usual comparison was with the American politician Wendell Willkie, who had just visited England. Menzies was usually judged the better of the two.

On that first Friday, Menzies also attended a lunch hosted by Bruce at the Savoy, where he met seven British Cabinet Ministers. One of the seven, Labour's Hugh Dalton, later described him as "very hearty, amusing and intelligent".[6] For Menzies' part, the lunch was "very easy and informal, and if there was any ice to break I did not notice it". Among the subjects discussed was the difficult problem of Irish neutrality, about which Churchill had very firm views. His ministers, though, were less constrained and Menzies noted how they had a "very free talk" even if they were all "plainly anti-R.C.".[7]

The Irish question had important implications for Australia with its large Irish community, most of whom were Labor supporters. If Menzies could do something to solve this problem he could presumably help to secure his own position by winning over some of the Irish-Australian voters. Irish neutrality also carried awful implications for the Empire. The policy of neutrality denied Irish ports to the ships of the Royal Navy and raised the possibility of a back-door German attack on Britain by way of Ireland. To prevent this possibility, Churchill might well feel impelled to station British forces in the country forcibly. This raised the spectre of an intra-imperial war that would, among other things, create dangerous splits within Australian society, likely to threaten its war effort.

Menzies was pleased to hear the Minister of Labour, Ernest Bevin, argue that it was now the time for a "commission from the dominions, chaired by U.S.A., to offer to settle the matter!".[8] Here then was an ideal opening for a budding international statesman, one that carried the added likelihood of domestic political benefit. However, when Menzies tried to exploit the situation he was to find himself faced with the implacable opposition of Churchill.

On Saturday, 22 February, Menzies drove to Chequers for his first weekend with the British leader. His initial sight of Churchill was not calculated to endear him to the rather staid Menzies who was rarely seen without his pin-striped, double-breasted suit. Menzies was shocked when Churchill entered wearing "what is called a Siren Suit; a dull blue woollen overall, with a zip fastener up the front".[9] It was hardly the garb in which Menzies would deem it suitable for a British Prime Minister to receive his Australian counterpart.

It was not only Churchill's clothes that Menzies found difficult to accept. It was also his total demeanour and method of argument. Menzies described their after-dinner talk in striking terms that boded ill for their future relationship. Menzies obviously held to his view of Churchill as a "menace" since he now wrote of him as a "tempestuous creature" who spent the evening

pacing up and down the room, always as if about to dart out of it, and then suddenly returning. Oratorical even in conversation. The master of the mordant phrase and yet, I should think, almost without real humour.[10]

In further contrast to Menzies' own predilections, the Australian was disturbed to note that Churchill seemed to enjoy hatred and to receive "a good deal of simple pleasure" from describing the Irish Premier, De Valera, as "a murderer and perjurer". This portended problems for Menzies' attempts to seek a solution to the problem of Irish neutrality. This was confirmed when Churchill refused to discuss any of the solutions that Menzies proposed.[11]

Just as Churchill inspired the British people with faith in ultimate victory, so he tried to do with Menzies. However, the Australian Prime Minister was after a solid basis for such optimism rather than a simple variation of the typical Churchillian radio exhortation. Instead, Menzies noted, all he received was a recitation of the view that America would eventually intervene in the war. In his diary, Menzies wondered:

Is he right? I cannot say. If the P.M. were a better listener and less disposed to dispense with all expert or local opinion I might feel a little easier about it. But there's no doubt about it; he's a holy terror—I went to bed tired![12]

On Sunday, 23 February, Menzies awoke at Chequers to a welcoming column in the *Sunday Times*. It predicted "amazing success" for Menzies in London and hoped he would "stay many days with us, for such buoyancy is catching". The paper described his speeches as being "couched in precisely that bluff eighteenth-century sea-dog strain that the people of this country, and their Prime Minister, most appreciate".[13]

Menzies continued in this tenor with a weekend radio broadcast during which he brought a message of assurance from "all the Empire beyond the seas". He promised that all of Britain's Imperial resources were pledged to work and fight alongside Britain until victory was attained.[14] The *Times* lauded Menzies for his speech, while the press throughout Britain carried favourable reports of his message.[15]

With the heady praise from the press flowing freely, the Greek problem that was to bedevil Menzies in London began to assert itself. Nearly two weeks after Churchill had instituted moves to send an expedition to Greece, he now brought the matter to Menzies' attention in the context of an after-dinner discussion. This was apparently Menzies' first realisation of the import of the expedition and its implications for Australia and himself as Prime Minister. He wrote in his diary of a "momentous discussion" on the "defence of Greece, largely with Australian and New Zealand troops". Menzies, much more a worrier than a warrior, confided to his diary that such a decision "which may mean thousands of lives is not easy. Why does a peaceable man become a Prime Minister?".[16]

It obviously came as a considerable shock to Menzies to have the Greek proposal foisted upon him as he lounged back with brandy and cigars at Chequers, and his private repugnance at directly deciding the fate of others contrasts sharply with the ease and even relish with which Churchill was apparently able to make such decisions. It provides further indication of Menzies' receptivity to the possibility of a compromise peace that would remove this necessity for difficult and distasteful life and death decisions.

The reason why Churchill raised the Greek question was because the Greek Government had that very day accepted Britain's offer of reinforcements. From that moment Australian troops were virtually committed to Greece and the detail of Menzies' concurrence had therefore to be cleared up. Eden, who was then in Athens, had made the British offer and cabled its acceptance to Churchill.

On receipt of the cables, the Permanent Secretary at the Foreign Office, Sir Alexander Cadogan, noted gloomily that the decision to help

Greece was "certainly respectable but we must eventually be beaten there".[17] Churchill informed Eden that, even though the proposal had still to be brought before the British War Cabinet and Menzies for approval, "you should proceed on the assumption that full approval will be given."[18]

Menzies was back in London on 24 February, the day Eden's cables were due to come before the War Cabinet for endorsement. Before the meeting Menzies discussed what he called the "Greek adventure" with Shedden and Bruce. He noted that he and Shedden "both favour scheme with some misgiving—Bruce is more doubtful".[19] If the Australians were tending to favour the expedition, they did so in the expectation that it had a fair chance of success. It is unlikely that Menzies would have agreed to commit Australian troops to a forlorn hope. And yet, that was the view of the expedition held by British leaders from Churchill down.

The British view was epitomised by Cadogan who wrote in his diary that the expedition to Greece "*must*, in the end, be a failure".[20] Similarly, one of the naval planners later admitted that the Admiralty had always expected to have to undertake eventually a Dunkirk-type operation in Greece. He noted that they were "in no doubt that the military support we could give Greece would not prevent her being over-run by the Germans" and that they foresaw another major evacuation under possibly far worse conditions.[21] These fears were soon to be borne out.

For their part, the Chiefs of Staff fully recognised that "the expedition must be a gamble" but they were hamstrung by the advice received from Dill and Eden. This had held out the hope of being able to stem the German advance successfully and the Chiefs of Staff were loath to countermand this advice.[22] They would also have had in mind Churchill's own support for the operation.

Menzies described the scene in the War Cabinet when the Greek expedition came up for discussion. He wrote with some horror that this momentous decision was dispensed with in just three quarters of an hour and "would have finished in ten minutes but for some queries raised by me...." According to Menzies, Churchill opened the discussion thus:

"You have read your file, gentlemen... The arguments are clear on each side. I favour the project." And then around the table, nobody more than three or four sentences. Does this denote the great clarity and directness of mind in all *these ministers, or has Winston taken* charge *of them, as the one man whom the public*

regard as indispensable! There may be a good deal in this business
of building yourself up *with the public by base arts so that you can*
really control a Cabinet.[23]

In his description of the discussion, Menzies included all the
elements that would increasingly impel him to challenge Churchill's
pre-eminence. There was Churchill's predilection for strategic long-
shots, his fondness for "yes-men", and Menzies' self-image as the one
man able to stand up to Churchill. Menzies wrote that he came away
from the meeting feeling "like a new boy who, in the first week at
school, commits the solecism of speaking to the Captain of the
School".[24]

Despite Menzies' critical view of Churchill and his Cabinet, and
his doubts about Greece, he still went along with the decision. Possibly
he was daunted at the prospect of opposing the unanimous view of the
British War Cabinet; then again he may have been swayed by assurances from Churchill that the expedition was more than just a forlorn
hope and that, if necessary, they "ought to be able to evacuate safely
all but the wounded". Even though the Chief of the Air Staff estimated
almost a two-to-one German superiority in the air, Menzies seems to
have relied on the optimism of Churchill in giving his conditional
support to the operation.[25]

Before Menzies' full support was given, he sought the approval of
the Australian War Cabinet to its troops being committed to this new
theatre of war. By so doing, Menzies effectively absolved himself from
individual responsibility and so spread the political danger of a possible
catastrophe. After the meeting, Churchill cabled to Eden in Cairo that
the decision was

> *unanimous in the sense you desire, but, of course, Mr. Menzies*
> *must telegraph home. Presume, also, you have settled with New*
> *Zealand Government about their troops. No need anticipate*
> *difficulties in either quarter. Therefore, while being under no*
> *illusions, we all send you the order "Full Steam Ahead".*[26]

The problem was that Menzies did retain illusions about the chances of
success in Greece and when these illusions were destroyed Churchill
bore the brunt of his fury.

If Menzies felt somewhat steamrollered over Greece, he did at least
come away from his first War Cabinet meeting with one prize—
Churchill had invited him to attend further War Cabinet meetings
while he was in London. This was not quite the benefit that Menzies

Churchill and his War Cabinet, 1941.
(From left, standing) Arthur Greenwood, Ernest Bevin, Lord Beaverbrook,
Sir Kingsley Wood; (seated) Sir John Anderson, Winston Churchill,
Clement Attlee, Anthony Eden
(NEWS LIMITED)

may have imagined it to be. Decision-making on the war was increasingly concentrated in the smaller War Cabinet Defence Committee (Operations) over which Churchill held practically undisputed sway. The War Cabinet then tended to rubber-stamp decisions already reached in the Defence Committee.[27] Nevertheless, it was an important public relations exercise for Menzies at least to appear to be taking part in the supposedly supreme deliberative body of the Empire.

Menzies' first experience of the War Cabinet not only confirmed his view of Churchill as a virtual dictator, but left him as well with a mostly poor opinion of Churchill's colleagues. If Churchill's power was to be countered, Menzies was now aware that he could count on little help from within the War Cabinet. Interestingly, Menzies saw Beaverbrook as one of the few independent minds in the War Cabinet.[28] Before long, these two men would be drawn into a cabal of convenience against Churchill.

Following the War Cabinet, Menzies went on to dinner with King George and Queen Elizabeth at Windsor Castle, where he stayed the night. The following day, he lined up the Royal Family for photographs in the castle courtyard and collected their autographs for his daughter, Heather. On a more serious note, Menzies also found uneasiness about Churchill among the Royal Family. The Queen, Menzies noted, "has the shrewdest estimate of all the Cabinet, including Winston, whose weakness for Yes-men she regrets" while, later, the Duke of Kent told Menzies that Churchill " 'has 6 ideas a day; they can't all be right!' ".[29] For such an ardent Royalist as Menzies, this apparent Royal displeasure with Churchill must have weighed heavily.

Menzies' public message now began to show a perceptible shift in which he laid increasing stress on the rigours of war that had still to be faced. Following his visit to Windsor, Menzies told the press that the war would be a long one and that Britain had yet to engage fully the real enemy. While undoubtedly true, these were warnings hardly calculated to fire the public ardour for prolonged conflict. When much of Britain was already reeling from regular bombing it was not encouraging to be told that things were to get much worse. In the light of his other activities, it is possible that Menzies was deliberately attempting to cool the war fever while ostensibly echoing the war cries of Churchill.[30]

On the evening of his return from Windsor, Menzies had dinner with the prominent Conservative MP Victor Cazalet. Cazalet was a director of the Dorchester Hotel and their dinner was probably suggested by him as a gesture of hospitality to a distinguished guest. Fresh from his discussions with the Royal Family, Menzies took the opportunity to unburden himself to Cazalet about Churchill's method of government and his gradual expulsion of the Chamberlain supporters from positions of power.[31] It is likely that Menzies was already beginning to test the political temperature in London to determine the extent of Churchill's support in Conservative Party ranks.

Cazalet immediately warmed to Menzies whom he judged as being very able and "just too clever for most Australians....". Though he seemed not to anticipate the depth of Menzies' bitterness towards Churchill, they were soon freely describing Churchill "as a dictator" as well as having long discussions on the appointment of Dominion statesmen to Governorships. According to Cazalet, Menzies suggested that he would like to become Governor-General of Canada after the war. Thus, just five days after landing in England, Menzies had let it be known that he could be counted among Churchill's critics, that he had his own ideas on the running of the war and that he was even then considering a future outside Australia.[32] Before long, Churchill's critics would begin to respond to Menzies' apparent feelers.

Meanwhile, the British press continued to build Menzies' image in the public mind. Beaverbrook's *Daily Express* mis-named him as "Big (6 ft. 2 ins.) 'Bill' Menzies" and described him lighting up one of Churchill's cigars and complaining of cigar prices in Britain.[33] Kemsley's *Daily Sketch* welcomed Menzies' inclusion in the War Cabinet while reiterating its call for "permanent members from all the Dominions, not merely a temporary member from one".[34] The *Times* likewise applauded the decision and termed his visit an "event of outstanding importance".[35] But while all this newspaper talk did create a dynamic image of Menzies in the mind of the British public and boosted his own self-image, it exaggerated his sense of the support he could count on in Britain. The alacrity with which the press latched on to Menzies and attributed to him outstanding leadership qualities was to an extent a reflection of an underlying anxiety over Britain's existing leadership.

As has been said, although the public at large still gave their allegiance to Churchill, men and women of wealth and substance were not as committed. Those with more to lose from a German victory or a long, drawn-out war were more precise in their calculations of British chances. Churchillian "blind faith" was not an adequate basis for safe investment and there were apparently many in the City loath to bank on a British victory.[36]

It was this growing disquiet in the drawing rooms of Britain that Lloyd George was sensing. On 24 February, he wrote to Beaverbrook, urgently requesting a meeting. "The time is coming," he said, "when I think it will be urgent that I should have another talk with you." Beaverbrook replied cautiously, agreeing to a meeting as, he noted, "I would like so much to hear your views on the immense issues which now impend".[37] Knowing the views of Lloyd George, the question of a compromise peace was no doubt high on the agenda of his talks with Beaverbrook. As for Beaverbrook, it would seem that while he had his main money on Churchill, he was not averse to laying side-bets on Lloyd George. As a potential Prime Minister, his views could not be ignored by a politicised press baron such as Beaverbrook.

The possibility of a compromise peace was also exercising other minds less sympathetic to the prospect. On 2 March, the Conservative MP Harold Nicolson wrote in his diary that he had "an uneasy feeling that when things get very bad there may be a movement...to replace Churchill by . . .some appeaser''. Nicolson maintained that the British people would endure any ordeal so long as there was some prospect of victory. But he privately lamented that there was as yet little light at the end of the tunnel ''beyond the light of faith''. Though Nicolson possessed this faith, he acknowledged the difficulty of propagating it among the public at large.[38]

By that time in February 1941, Britain had been largely withdrawn into her island fortress for more than eight months and there was no prospect in sight of her being able to sally forth in strength to tackle the German Army. Like an animal at bay, the British bulldog held off the German hounds while waiting for a miracle to rescue her. Churchill's solution was to savage the Italian lap-dog, harry the German hounds and hope that others would join in on Britain's side.

In this anxious atmosphere, Menzies was putting further emphasis on the enormity of the task that confronted Britain in winning the war. In his first public speech, at a Dorchester luncheon of the National Defence Public Interest Committee, Menzies told the guests that it would be ''folly for anybody to believe that we were [other than] at the commencement of the task facing us in winning the war''.[39] Though he wrote after the luncheon that his purpose was to ''encourage and lift up the people here'',[40] the tone of his remarks was as depressing to some as it may have been uplifting to others. This reflected Menzies' own ambivalence on the war—he wanted a British victory but shrank from paying the awful cost of achieving it.

This ambivalence was certainly not apparent to the British press, which extolled his luncheon remarks. At the lunch Menzies had been introduced as a twin to Churchill,[41] and the press clearly agreed. A *Daily Herald* columnist proclaimed that Menzies ''rose to the full stature of an Empire statesman yesterday'', the *Daily Mail* called the speech exhilarating, while the *Daily Telegraph* reported observers assessing it as the best speech they had heard at those lunches.[42] Speeches were one thing; changing the direction of British policy proved to be something completely different.

Following his successful speech at the Dorchester, Menzies went to the Foreign Office for a meeting on British policy in the Far East. In the absence of the Foreign Secretary, Anthony Eden, it was left to the Parliamentary Under Secretary, R. A. Butler, the Permanent Secretary, Sir Alexander Cadogan, and other officials to set out and defend the basis of the British policy. Menzies' suggestion was simple. Britain should decide on an acceptable limit for Japanese expansion, communicate that limit to the Japanese and declare war if it were transgressed. He also proposed a general settlement in the Far East that would satisfy the Japanese need for expansion short of threatening major British interests in South East Asia and, of course, Australia. The Foreign Office representatives tried to explain that any such settlement would be at China's expense which would upset America and thereby threaten United States support for Britain. Such support underpinned Britain's one hope for victory against Germany and was clearly not something that the Foreign Office was likely to put under threat.[43]

Though one Foreign Office official thought Menzies was "a first rate man",[44] Cadogan angrily described Menzies' proposal as "irresponsible rubbish".[45] However, Cadogan failed to convince Menzies of the Foreign Office viewpoint. Menzies left with a mounting sense of anger over a British policy that seemed to be sliding Britain into a Far Eastern war with which, Menzies now well knew, she was unable to cope.[46] In such a situation, Australia was liable to be seriously threatened.

With Menzies now seriously disturbed over British foreign policy in the Far East, the issue of Britain's defence capability against Japan took on an added sense of urgency. On 27 February, the day after his visit to the Foreign Office, Menzies tackled British Service Ministers and their Chiefs of Staff on how they would cope with hostilities breaking out in the Far East. The old assurance about sending a fleet was duly trotted out but, with three Australian divisions in the Middle East, Menzies was now equally concerned with the position in the Mediterranean. He was not prepared to sanction a Far East fleet formed at the expense of Britain's naval strength in the Mediterranean. After all, he argued, how could the naval forces be stripped from the Mediterranean "if you have land forces which cannot be deserted"? Two days of official talks had left Menzies clearly worried and he bitterly commented in his diary that: "Clear thinking is not predominant here. I can only hope that action and thought are not considered mutually exclusive."[47]

One reason for Menzies' mounting concern was provided by Shedden who, on 26 February, raised several serious questions about the commitment to Greece. It was he who suggested to Menzies that the Greek expedition would tie up British naval forces so that "the security of Singapore may hinge entirely on the question of American assistance". Shedden's doubts about Greece also seem to have deepened in discussion with Bruce and he now advised Menzies that any evacuation from Greece was liable to incur heavy casualties given that

British air strength in Greece was relatively small.[48] In the event, his prediction was to be proved correct.

Doubts about British war leadership also led to a suggestion by Shedden that Australia's General Blamey should lead the forces to Greece. Apart from the fact that most of the troops would be either Australian or other Dominion, Shedden argued that the appointment of Blamey would assure the Australian Government that "the Commander is directly responsible to it . . . for insuring that the minimum conditions essential in his opinion for the probable success of the operations are fulfilled". This line would have been partly prompted by the British appointment of General Wilson, an officer much disliked by Menzies, to head the Greek force, but there was also an underlying assumption in Shedden's argument that, under British control, Australian troops were liable to be committed to action with inadequate equipment or otherwise needlessly sacrificed.[49]

Lastly, Shedden raised again the suggestion, made at their discussion with Bruce on the previous day, that the comments of Blamey should be obtained on the proposed operation. Unfortunately, Shedden informed Menzies, a draft cable to Blamey along these lines was prepared but he had been unable to contact Menzies for his approval.[50] The cable thus lapsed and Blamey was not consulted. It was in fact the case that Blamey had serious doubts about the viability of the operation. Had his opinion been sought, it may well have tipped the scales, convincing Menzies to oppose the Greek expedition. Without Australian troops the operation could never have gone ahead, and some 16,000 casualties, 3000 of them Australian, would have been avoided.

Shedden's second thoughts had come too late to prevent Menzies cabling to Australia with a recommendation favouring the Greek expedition. With his clear recommendation before them, the Australian War Cabinet gave its sanction to the operation, albeit with some misgivings.[51] On 27 February, Menzies attended the British War Cabinet and, despite Shedden's doubts, passed on Australia's approval to commit two of her divisions to Greece. However, he did pass on the Australian concern that her troops be adequately equipped; that, if possible, their numbers be augmented; and that plans be completed beforehand for a successful evacuation if it should become necessary.[52] The fulfilment of these conditions was to become a matter of serious dispute between Menzies and Churchill when the Greek expedition came to its inevitable end.

While Menzies was becoming more aware of the pitfalls that faced him in London, his stocks continued to rise in the British press. On

28 February, he was pictured emerging from a War Cabinet meeting with Churchill beside him. It needed no caption to realise the obvious physical contrast between the two men—Menzies tall, straight and beaming towered over the hunched, aged and impassive Churchill.[53] On the 29th the *Star* described him as possessing "all the dash, humour and resource of what Australians are now entitled to call the Benghazi spirit" while the *Daily Mail* welcomed him as "the representative of our magnificent kinsmen who have done, and are doing, and will do all that lies in their power to beat our enemies".[54]

On 2 March came the first public mention of a possible political future for Menzies in Britain. It was in Beaverbrook's *Sunday Express* that a columnist suggested that Australia should export Menzies and added that "a few men like Menzies would transmogrify Westminster." The columnist described Menzies as a "red, rough, tough barrel of a fellow" who was "plainly far more concerned with the future of the world than with his own future as a politician".[55] Again there was the implicit contrast between Menzies' youthful dynamism and Churchill's aged doggedness. The contrast for Menzies, though, was between his ecstatic reception in London and the continual sniping in Australia. This contrast was to become even more marked.

It was at Chequers that Menzies rose to read of his political future in Britain as outlined in the *Sunday Express*. This was his second weekend with Churchill and the close contact had forced some grudging admiration from Menzies. The Australian could not help admiring Churchill's astonishing grasp of military detail and even his determined pursuit of victory. It was certainly with some admiration that Menzies wrote in his diary that "Churchill's course is set. There is no defeat in his heart."[56]

It would seem that in the close atmosphere of Chequers, Menzies might have been partially infected by Churchill's resolution. However, he still felt that the "real tyrant" of Churchill was the "glittering phrase—so attractive to his mind that awkward facts may have to give way".[57] And, while Menzies could admire Churchill's resolution, it did not mean that he fell in with it. "In every conversation," Menzies wrote, "he ultimately reaches a point when he positively enjoys the war."[58] This Menzies could never do.

Hugh Dalton also spent part of that weekend at Chequers. His diary suggested that Churchill partook in some banter at Menzies' expense and that Menzies sat through lunch "rather silent, a little over-awed . . .".[59] Despite Churchill's apparent dominance of the situation at Chequers, Menzies told interested journalists that he could outlast Churchill in their late-night talks and that more than once he "grabbed half the conversation".[60]

On the occasion of such high-level discussions with Churchill and other ministers, Menzies would often be accompanied by Shedden and sometimes Bruce. Shedden, though, was also pursuing activities of his own. Of particular interest was the resumption of his relationship with the British Cabinet Minister, Lord Hankey. Shedden had worked under Hankey in the 1930s when the latter was Secretary to the Committee on Imperial Defence, as well as being Secretary to the British Cabinet. Now Shedden occupied the equivalent position in Australia. Hankey had been brought into the Government by Chamberlain and while Churchill had retained him, he was steadily reducing the power and influence of this loyal Chamberlainite. Hankey retained serious misgivings about Churchill's fitness for leadership—he had earlier referred to him as a "rogue elephant"[61]—and he was now frustrated at being partly prevented by Churchill from bringing his considerable experience to bear on the problems of the war.

During Shedden's stay in London, he and Hankey were to lunch together seven times at the United Services Club while Shedden also visited Hankey at his country home in Surrey.[62] What transpired at this series of meetings is not recorded save for Shedden's note that they discussed "Machinery for Higher Direction. War Policy Generally".[63] This suggests that Churchill's running of the war dominated their talks and Shedden presumably acted as a conduit, passing Hankey's criticisms on to Menzies.

Much criticism of Churchill was to arise out of his handling of the expedition to Greece and the subsequent defeat on Crete. To a certain extent he became the prisoner of his own rhetoric in the Greece affair. Eden and Dill had gone to the Middle East convinced that Churchill was set on such an expedition and that their task was merely to facilitate its occurrence. Thus, when even Churchill himself began to have doubts about its continued wisdom, his loyal lieutenant in Athens, Eden, helped to lock him into the decision by repeatedly according the operation a fair chance of success. Now, on 1 March, Churchill informed Eden that, while he was "absolutely ready to go in on a serious hazard if there is reasonable chance of success", Eden should ensure an escape clause for Britain in the case of the expedition facing certain defeat.[64]

At the War Cabinet meeting on 3 March, Menzies expressed his own anxiety about Greece. Though he "fully agreed in principle" with the War Cabinet decisions, Menzies said he was now worried about the timing of the enterprise and sought an assurance that it had been taken into account by the Chiefs of Staff. It looked increasingly as if the British force would arrive too late to be able to halt the Germans. The Chiefs of Staff promised to present their view on this aspect of the matter.[65] Unfortunately for Menzies, Churchill was absent from this meeting with a heavy cold and no diversion from previous policy was possible without him. Menzies sarcastically described the meeting as "very like cold soup" and wrote that he "must discover the secret of having my cabinet unwilling to decide any important question in my absence".[66]

The following day Churchill was able to attend the War Cabinet where he now admitted that the "prospects in the Balkans were not promising". Though he offered the opportunity for the Cabinet to "take a final view of the whole position in the light of the information to be received in the next few days", Churchill still maintained that he was "most disinclined" to oppose the view of his men on the spot in Athens—Eden and Dill.[67] Churchill was now trying to have it both ways—to have the operation continue but to slip out from under the heavy cloak of responsibility in case it failed.

In the Mediterranean, Churchill's naval Commander-in-Chief, Admiral Cunningham, felt constrained to give a final warning to the First Sea Lord, Admiral Pound, of the risks the expedition would face. Though he expressed support for the policy, Cunningham advised Pound that his resources were "taxed to the limit and that by normal security standards my commitments exceed available resources".[68]

Though Menzies had much the same opinion as Cunningham on the necessity for the Greek operation, he was not as aware of the enormous risks that his troops would be facing. He assumed that the military opinions emanating from the Middle East were based on a sober assessment of military factors. However, for a time, the military commanders forgot the precepts of their profession and used political rather than military criteria to justify their views.

Not only were the troops committed to Greece in dire peril, but their fellow soldiers in Libya were now coming under threat. Rommel had arrived in Tripoli on 12 February and a steady stream of German troops built up under his command. The *papier mâché* Italian Empire now had a solid centre that would soon allow it to roll British Imperial forces far back into Egypt. If Churchill had stuck to his task, he probably could have cleared the Italians from North Africa. Instead, he split his forces between Greece and the Middle East and brought disaster on both fronts. Before long, it would be the British who stood in danger of being thrown bodily from the whole Mediterranean area.

Menzies remained in a state of optimism over the visit as a whole.

On 3 March, an Australian official in London noted that, though Menzies had had a "tremendously strenuous time", he was "looking very fit and brown" and "has had a grand tonic effect" on Britain.[69] Socially, Menzies was a roaring success. The Conservative MP "Chips" Channon described a dinner party he gave for Menzies on 3 March as "one of the gayest and most riotous festivals" he had ever held, with Menzies telling "lengthy stories with great gusto. . . ".[70]

On 4 March, the *Daily Telegraph* published a photograph of Menzies that had been touched up by a reader to portray him as John Bull, the personification of the English nation.[71] In less than two weeks Menzies had said much to move the British people. Now another important speech brought further praise.

This time Menzies addressed a luncheon gathering of the Foreign Press Association on the preservation of the peace in the Pacific. He warned strongly against drifting into an atmosphere where war with Japan was considered inevitable rather than just possible. He argued that "the Pacific Ocean could be made pacific if all its people were frank, sensible and tolerant in understanding one another".[72] It was very much in the tenor of the talks he had with the British Foreign Office and Menzies later claimed that it was to the Foreign Office that his speech was directed. Still, the Japanese journalists at the lunch thought there was a message in it for Japan and pronounced themselves "very pleased".[73]

The British press was similarly pleased. Kemsley's *Daily Sketch* judged it as "great political wisdom and the foundation for a sane and prosperous policy in the Pacific"; moreover, it was "good sense of the sort likely to be understood all over the world".[74] The *Daily Telegraph* went even further and described Menzies as "rapidly becoming Dominion orator No. 1" with a remarkable speech that was "characterised by the frankness and realism we have come to associate with the John Bullish presence and the deep voice of the Australian Prime Minister".[75] It was left to a *Daily Herald* columnist to raise the obvious and portentous possibility that some people "may call this an appeasement speech" though, for himself, the columnist merely judged it as frank.[76]

With just on two weeks of his visit completed, Menzies cabled Fadden with a review of his results to date. Significantly, Menzies' own assessment was that the main value of his visit was its effect on the general opinion and the spirit of the people in Britain. He reported a good response to his speeches and a very real enthusiasm about what Australia was doing.[77] Menzies was therefore very aware of the personal impact he had made to date.

As for Churchill, Menzies informed Fadden that his experience as British Prime Minister had "obviously ripened his judgment and he combines in a unique way most remarkable fighting and driving qualities with an astonishing mastery of the details of both plans and equipment". He went on, however, to inform Fadden that he was disturbed by the refusal of Churchill's Cabinet to entertain an independent view and the fact that there was therefore a shortage of criticism. Moreover, he revealed that he was unimpressed with the Foreign Office whose Far East policy "seems to be one of drift".[78]

As for Greece, Menzies told Fadden that he had no faith in Yugoslavia or Turkey providing aid. As this creation of a "Balkan front" was one of Churchill's major justifications for the Greek expedition, Menzies again put himself at variance with Churchill's strategy. He also expressed concern with the "abortive" and "mismanaged" attack on Castelorizzo[79] and the arrival of German mechanised units at Tripoli. In view of these factors he reported that he had requested that the Greek operation be re-examined by the Chiefs of Staff.[80] In the main, though, this report of his visit so far was predominantly optimistic. Both Menzies and Churchill were still riding high on the wave of British victories in the Middle East. It was a wave that was about to collapse abruptly.

NOTES

1. CHANNON DIARY, 20 February 1941, R. R. James (ed.), p. 293
2. MENZIES DIARY, 20 February 1941
3. *NEWS CHRONICLE*, London, 21 February 1941
4. *DAILY TELEGRAPH*, London, 22 February 1941. See also *Star* and *Daily Express*, London, 22 February 1941
5. *BIRMINGHAM POST*, 22 February 1941
6. DALTON DIARY, 21 February 1941, Dalton Papers: LSE
7. MENZIES DIARY, 21 February 1941
8. *IBID*.
9. MENZIES DIARY, 22 February 1941
10. *IBID*.
11. *IBID*.
12. *IBID*.
13. *SUNDAY TIMES*, London, 23 February 1941
14. *DAILY MIRROR*, London, 24 February 1941
15. *TIMES*, London, 24 February 1941. See also *Morning Advertiser, Daily Herald, Daily Mail, Daily Mirror, Evening News, Daily Telegraph, Daily Express*, all of London, *Manchester Guardian, Glasgow Bulletin, Glasgow Herald, Scotsman, Newcastle Journal, Yorkshire Post, Yorkshire Observer*, 24 February 1941
16. MENZIES DIARY, 23 February 1941

17. CADOGAN DIARY, 23 February 1941, D. Dilks (ed.), p. 358
18. CABLE, Churchill to Eden, 23 February 1941, "The Prime Minister's Personal Telegrams 1941", VI/I, Ismay Papers: KC
19. MENZIES DIARY, 24 February 1941
20. CADOGAN DIARY, 24 February 1941, D. Dilks, p. 358. See also Dalton Diary, 19 February 1941, Dalton Papers: LSE
21. "MY LIFE", autobiography of Admiral Sir William Davis, p. 233, WDVS 1/3, Davis Papers: CC
22. "POLICY IN THE MIDDLE EAST AND EASTERN MEDITERRANEAN", Report by Chiefs of Staff Committee, 24 February 1941, Cab. 66/15, W.P.(41)39 (Revise): PRO
23. MENZIES DIARY, 24 February 1941
24. *IBID.*
25. WAR CABINET CONCLUSIONS/CONFIDENTIAL ANNEX, 24 February 1941, Cab. 65/21, W.M.20(41): PRO
26. CABLE, Churchill to Eden, 24 February, 1941. "The Prime Minister's Personal Telegrams 1941", VI/I Ismay Papers: KC
27. On the day of Menzies' first War Cabinet meeting Hugh Dalton wrote in his diary that it was "meeting less and less . . . and nothing of great importance is discussed. One of its members says it is hardly worth belonging to any more." Dalton Diary, 24 February 1941, Dalton Papers: LSE
28. MENZIES DIARY, 24 February 1941. Even so, at a dinner with Dalton two days later, Menzies was noted by Dalton to be "abusing Beaverbrook very freely". Dalton Diary, 26 February 1941, Dalton Papers: LSE. For his part, though, Menzies noted that "Dalton & Co. hate and distrust Beaverbrook!!!!" which further established Beaverbrook in Menzies' mind as somewhat distanced from other members of Churchill's Government. Menzies Diary, 26 February 1941
29. MENZIES DIARY, 25 February 1941
30. *SCOTSMAN*, 26 February 1941
31. CAZALET DIARY, 25 February 1941, R. R. James (ed.): *Victor Cazalet*, London, 1976, p. 254
32. *IBID.*
33. *DAILY EXPRESS*, London, 26 February 1941
34. *DAILY SKETCH*, London, 26 February 1941
35. *TIMES*, London, 26 February 1941
36. DALTON DIARY, 25 February 1941, Dalton Papers: LSE
37. LETTER, Lloyd George to Beaverbrook, 24 February 1941; Letter, Beaverbrook to Lloyd George, 27 February 1941, G/3/6/46, Lloyd George Papers: HLRO
38. NICOLSON DIARY, 2 March 1941, Sir H. Nicolson, p. 149
39. *AGE*, Melbourne, 27 February 1941
40. MENZIES DIARY, 26 February 1941
41. *LIVERPOOL POST*, 27 February 1941
42. *DAILY HERALD, Daily Mail, Daily Telegraph*, London, 27 February 1941
43. "RECORD OF A MEETING in Mr. Butler's Room in the Foreign Office", 26 February 1941, CRS A5954, Box 629, "Prime Minister's Visit to U.K., 1941: Discussions on Brief: Part 1(1)—Political": AA
44. LETTER, Sir Horace Seymour to his wife, 27 February 1941, SEYR 2/4, Seymour Papers: CC
45. CADOGAN DIARY, 26 February 1941, D. Dilks (ed.), p. 359
46. MENZIES DIARY, 26 February 1941. See also Sir John Kennedy, *The Business*

of War, London, 1957, p. 190
47. MENZIES DIARY, 27 February 1941
48. "FUTURE EMPLOYMENT OF THE A.I.F.", Note, Shedden to Menzies, 26 February 1941. CRS A5954, Box 587, "Middle East Position": AA
49. *IBID.*
50. *IBID.*
51. WAR CABINET MINUTES, 26 February 1941, CRS A2673/5/838: AA
52. WAR CABINET CONCLUSIONS/CONFIDENTIAL ANNEX, 27 February 1941, Cab. 65/21, W.M.21(41): PRO
53. *MANCHESTER GUARDIAN, Evening Standard*, London, 28 February 1941
54. *STAR, Daily Mail*, London, 1 March 1941. See also *The People*, London, 2 March 1941
55. *SUNDAY EXPRESS*, London, 2 March 1941
56. MENZIES DIARY, 2 March 1941
57. *IBID.*
58. MENZIES DIARY, 1 March 1941
59. DALTON DIARY, 2 March 1941, Dalton Papers: LSE
60. *DAILY HERALD*, London, 3 March 1941
61. LETTER, Hankey to Hoare, 12 May 1940, HNKY 4/32, Hankey Papers: CC. Hankey doubted "whether the wise old elephants (Chamberlain & Halifax) will ever be able to hold the Rogue Elephant (Churchill)" and he further noted that he did not "feel any confidence in the new administration"
62. SHEDDEN ENGAGEMENT BOOK, CRS A5954, Box 612, "Engagements in London, 22-2-41−2-5-41": AA
63. "F. G. SHEDDEN−List of Interviews to April 1941", CRS A5954, Box 612, "Engagements in London 22/2/41−2/5/41": AA
64. CABLE, Churchill to Eden (in Athens), 1 March 1941, "The Prime Minister's Personal Telegrams 1941", VI/I, Ismay Papers: KC
65. WAR CABINET CONCLUSIONS/CONFIDENTIAL ANNEX, 3 March 1941, Cab. 65/22, W.M.22(41): PRO
66. MENZIES DIARY, 3 March 1941
67. WAR CABINET CONCLUSIONS/CONFIDENTIAL ANNEX, 4 March 1941, Cab. 65/22, W.M.23(41): PRO
68. CABLE NO. 1132, Cunningham to Pound, 4 March 1941, ADD.MS.52567, Cunningham Papers: BL
69. LETTER, Alfred Stirling to Peter Heydon (Australian Legation in Washington), 3 March 1941, CRS A3300/215: AA
70. CHANNON DIARY, 3 March 1941, R. R. James (ed.), p. 293
71. *DAILY TELEGRAPH*, London, 4 March 1941
72. *AGE*, Melbourne, 4 March 1941
73. *DAILY HERALD*, London, 4 March 1941
74. *DAILY SKETCH*, London, 4 March 1941
75. *DAILY TELEGRAPH*, London, 4 March 1941. See also *Scotsman*, 4 March 1941
76. *DAILY HERALD*, London, 4 March 1941
77. *DAFP*, iv, Doc. 330, Cable M.1, Menzies to Fadden, 4 March 1941
78. *IBID.*
79. For details of the Castelorizzo operation, see W. S. Churchill, *The Second World War*, iii, Sydney, 1950, p. 659; M. Gilbert, *Finest Hour*, London, 1983, pp. 1014−15.
80. *DAFP*, iv, Doc. 330, Cable M.1, Menzies to Fadden, 4 March 1941

5

The Problems Begin

On 4 March 1941, the first echelon of the British expeditionary force left Egypt by ship for Greece. In Berlin, Hitler had already ordered plans for the German occupation of Greece in order to protect the southern flank of his forthcoming attack on Russia. The British force was therefore steaming steadily into the jaws of its enemy. Menzies had some misgivings about the Greek expedition but he was still blissfully unaware of the fate which awaited it. After two weeks in London, he remained relatively optimistic about the chances of success for his troops in Greece and for himself in the Imperial capital.

Menzies' view of Churchill had moderated somewhat. He had spent two weekends at Chequers, and had not escaped the force of the British leader's charisma. Though he remained convinced that Churchill's almost dictatorial powers needed to be curbed, he was now somewhat more inclined to admire Churchill the man.[1] He had not, however, lost sight of the fact that he and Churchill were opposites by nature.

For Churchill's part, his view of Menzies also seems to have improved since the Dakar dispute of the previous October. Churchill's secretary, John Colville, claimed that Churchill placed Menzies in that category of men "with whom it is agreeable to dine".[2] And, of course, Menzies' fairly ready concurrence with the Greek expedition must have helped to allay any doubts Churchill entertained about Menzies' fighting spirit.

The first substantial disturbance during Menzies' visit came not from London, but from Canberra. Menzies' speech on 3 March calling for peace in the Pacific was viewed with suspicion by many in Australia. The Advisory War Council had recently caused alarm on the home front by alerting the population to the deteriorating situation in the Pacific. Menzies' declaration that war was not inevitable in the Pacific seemed to belie the statements of the War Council and even smack of appeasement towards Japan.

The Australian press generally praised Menzies' speech,[3] with the *Age* calling it a "masterly declaration of the true Australian mind, robust in tone yet conciliatory, firm but persuasive".[4] The Japanese Consul-General likewise found the speech to his liking. He described it as a statesmanlike utterance and called for it to be "embodied in some concrete form such as an agreement, declaration, or trade treaty . . . ".[5]

Labor members of the Australian Parliament were not so enamoured with Menzies' speech and moved quickly to raise the matter at the Advisory War Council. In London, Menzies received notice of the growing storm when he was closely questioned by the Australian press representatives on the implications of his speech. It was in sharp contrast to the acclaim with which the London papers had received his speech and Menzies was rather taken aback. He angrily wrote in his diary:

Some noodle thinks my speech about the Pacific was "appease-ment". What a perversion. What a tyranny over inferior minds words and phrases exercise. . . . Our true policy vis a vis Japan is firmness and friendliness! the two are not inconsistent.[6]

With this first hint of possible trouble, Menzies dispatched a cable to Fadden seeking to allay any concern. He informed Fadden that the speech was "primarily addressed to the Foreign Office which . . . seems to me to have adopted a fatalistic attitude towards our relations with Japan". Menzies specifically denied that he was suggesting a policy of appeasement but argued that "we must have a positive policy of thrashing out our differences and if necessary telling Japan just where the limits of tolerance are."[7] However, Fadden was already meeting with the Australian War Cabinet which was worried about the growing furore among some sections of the press and the Labor Party.[8] At its behest, Menzies issued a public statement disclaiming any support for "what is known as 'appeasement'" and denying any conflict with the Labor Party. "In brief," he said, "I have always understood and maintained that Australia's Pacific policy is one of peace unless it is necessary to go to war to resist an aggressor."[9]

Menzies' strenuous denials did nothing to change the fact of his implicit support for compromise in the Pacific. However, his subtle semantic shift apparently did help to calm the situation and Fadden now assured Menzies that there was no need for concern, that the issue would die a natural death.[10] Whatever the long-term political effect, the immediate Australian reaction confirmed for Menzies the danger of appearing to be an appeaser, even by implication. He was never again to be so caught out but rather kept his public mask in place and maintained a strident total victory tone in all his public utterances. He would now go all out to outdo Churchill in his militancy.

The furore over Menzies' speech threw into sharp relief the reception he was receiving in London. On 5 March, Beaverbrook's *Daily Express* increased the tempo of its praise. The paper described Menzies as a "forthright man with splendid vision" who had brought with him the "fresh air of the Pacific". More significantly, the paper claimed that Menzies was not only opposed to "people who talk 'New Order' flimflam" but was equally opposed to "people who talk fluff about Anglo-American friendship".[11] While the former was presumably a reference to Hitler, the latter was probably an oblique reference to Churchill who increasingly looked to America for Britain's present and long-term salvation. Thus Menzies was already being touted as the champion of Empire and opposed to Churchill's building of political bridges across the Atlantic. In this, Menzies' opinions and concerns were very much in accord with those of Beaverbrook.

Other newspaper publishers were able to assess Menzies when he dined that same day as the guest of the Newspaper Proprietors' Association. After Menzies gave them an account of his experiences in Libya, Lord Rothermere offered Menzies, apparently in jest, a post as Special Correspondent should he ever leave politics.[12] Not only were the "press barons" apparently impressed with Menzies, but he was also very much *persona grata* with their journalists.[13]

The press went much further than simply uncritically reporting his speeches. It seemed determined to create a superman out of Menzies. No doubt there was a psychological imperative operating to make Britain's allies appear all-powerful when Britain was under such grave threat, but it is also clear that there was a widespread desire to welcome a political figure who could stand up to and possibly replace Churchill. In the *Star*, Menzies was reported to convey an "extraordinary sense of a powerful personality with immense reserves of strength". He was, the paper claimed, the "embodiment of the young, virile nations of the British Commonwealth" while the war had given his oratory a "theme worthy of the latent powers of the man".[14] The *Daily Express* similarly commented that Menzies "speaks with such force...that many who have heard him liken his oratory to that of John Bright".[15]

Meanwhile, the *Manchester Guardian* noted the political impact flowing from Menzies' sudden success in London. The paper pointed out that his visit had "naturally revived suggestions that a regularly constituted Imperial War Council should now meet, as in 1917''.[16] It is impossible to determine whether Menzies was actively promoting these suggestions at this early stage of his visit. It is possible that he merely took them up later and amplified them when they provided an avenue of escape from his own political difficulties.

On a personal level, Menzies was also moving closer to Beaverbrook. But while Beaverbrook's papers were actively promoting him, Beaverbrook as the Minister for Aircraft Production was proving rather niggardly in despatching aircraft to the Far East. Menzies sought to get his agreement to such reinforcement and also to the transfer of greater aircraft production capacity to Australia. For their part, Beaverbrook and the British government were anxious to satisfy Menzies but, of course, at the minimum cost to themselves. After all, it was in Europe that the fighting was taking place.

On 5 March, Menzies lunched at the Savoy with the Secretary of State for Air, Sir Archibald Sinclair. He found the talk very useful and left convinced that he would get results and that Singapore would be heavily reinforced with fighters.[17] The following day, Menzies dined with Beaverbrook at Claridges and he came away further satisfied that he would achieve substantial results.

Moreover, Menzies was being drawn into Beaverbrook's circle of influence. At the Claridges dinner, Menzies gave an account of his Libyan visit to the 20 or so guests. He was delighted to receive a good response to his talk and he again reflected: "A prophet is never without honour save in his own country and among his own people." As for Beaverbrook, Menzies found him friendly and he was led to believe that Beaverbrook would accede to his plans for boosting aircraft production in Australia.[18]

Next morning, Menzies again met Beaverbrook for more concrete discussions about aircraft. Menzies was particularly keen to get a commitment of modern Hurricane fighter planes for Singapore. Australians were familiar with the achievements of the Hurricane during the Battle of Britain and such a commitment to Singapore would have carried important political benefits for Menzies as well as making a valuable contribution to the defence of Malaya. But sending modern fighters to Singapore would have contravened Britain's strategic conception of the war which was to concentrate British arms in the fight against Germany and Italy. Beaverbrook therefore laughably assured Menzies that the 170 Brewster fighters which had been allotted to Singapore were "as good as, if not better than, existing Hurricanes".[19] Menzies realised the planes really had to be Hurricanes for the commitment to be of any benefit and he therefore simply omitted to mention the Brewsters when he reported the discussion to Fadden.[20] Instead, he kept up his requests to Beaverbrook for Hurricanes.[21]

Menzies' repeated requests for Hurricanes suggest that he was not fully aware of Churchill's view of the war. According to this view, risks had to be run in the Far East in order to defeat Germany decisively. Even if Japan were to enter the war, Churchill did not envisage any large-scale diversion of resources other than those needed to stem the flow of Japanese expansion. Australia therefore suffered from serious shortages of vital military equipment and was in potential peril if Japan entered the war. It was incumbent on Australia's political leader to do everything he could to correct this situation during his two and a half months in London. This clear duty was set out by Colonel Wardell, Australia's Military Liaison Officer in London.

On 6 March, Wardell informed Shedden that he himself could do no more to get the military equipment Australia needed. Wardell argued that Australia was getting all

> *we can expect on the view of the strategical position held by the*
> *C.I.G.S. This is the crux of the situation and the only way that*
> *we can get better deliveries of important . . . items of equipment is*
> *for the Australian point of view of the strategical position to be*
> *put forward on the highest plane possible.*[22]

It is not clear whether Shedden passed on the gist of this minute to Menzies. But even if he did, Menzies was too hamstrung by competing loyalties and interests to act upon it.

Menzies saw Australia only as part of the larger British Empire. He could not envisage Australia without the Empire, and the defence of the Empire as a whole and particularly its heart, Great Britain, could not in Menzies' mind be completely separated from the defence of Australia. Though Menzies would push hard to obtain planes for Australia, he would not use his position to undermine basic British strategy if such a change would lay Britain open to greater risk. So British Ministers found that they could quickly abort Menzies' claims for equipment for Australia by graphically describing the position in the mother country.[23]

Moreover, of course, Menzies had before his very eyes a graphic illustration of Britain's plight. Living and travelling around central London, Menzies was continually exposed to the bombed-out ruins of the city he loved. This also helped to blunt the force of his appeals on behalf of Australia. After all, how far could he push for anti-aircraft equipment for Australia's peaceful cities when British cities were being bombed almost daily?

On 5 March, Menzies toured the devastated inner London areas of Gray's Inn Road and Lincoln's Inn Fields, areas of special import to him as a lawyer. Later, in his diary, Menzies wondered

*what tragedies of lost or ruined lives must lie behind these
scattered bricks. It is a bedlamite world, and the hardest thing in
it is to discuss and decide (as we do in War Cabinet) policies
which, even if successful, must bring the angel of death into many
homes. In public affairs at this time the successful leader is he
who ignores the individual and thinks and acts in broad terms.*[24]

To Menzies' credit, it would seem that he was finding it difficult to forget the effects on individuals of policies to which he felt forced to agree.

The policy uppermost in Menzies' mind at this time was the deteriorating position in Greece. German troops were moving into Bulgaria as preparation for an attack on Greece. In Athens, Eden still undertook to commit British forces though, in advising Churchill, he admitted that the "hard fact remains that our forces, including Dominions contingents, will be engaged in an operation more hazardous than it seemed a week ago".[25] The Secretary to the Defence Committee, General Ismay, later claimed that Churchill and his colleagues in London were "almost relieved" when they received this cable from Eden. According to Ismay, the cable "gave us the opportunity of withdrawing with honour from what now seemed to be a very risky military adventure...".[26] The problem was that Churchill's emissaries, Eden and Dill, seemed to have been so fired with Churchill's enthusiasm for a "Balkan front" that they remained committed to a Greek expedition whatever the setbacks.

After the War Cabinet meeting on 5 March, Menzies complained bitterly that things were going badly and questioned how Eden could "commit us on facts which he must know are most disturbing and which have an Empire significance?".[27] Even more disturbing for Menzies was a cable from Fadden urging Menzies to re-evaluate the commitment to Greece in the light of a possible thrust by Rommel against the depleted British forces in Libya.[28] This cable, which was sent prior to Australia learning of the latest setbacks, shifted the responsibility for Australia's participation back towards Menzies. It also revealed a new level of concern in Australia over the implications of the decision to assist Greece.

On 6 March, Menzies was shocked to find that Eden had subsequently signed a military agreement to help Greece notwithstanding the declining chances of success. In effect, Eden had committed Australian troops without referring the matter to the Australian Government. Menzies was furious and, at a further meeting of the War Cabinet, spoke strongly about consulting the Dominions before grave decisions were made affecting them.[29] Nevertheless, he accepted Churchill's argument that they now had no choice but to carry out the agreement reached at Athens, despite the fact that no reason was offered why the operation should succeed.[30]

What seemed to worry Menzies more than its chances of success was the manner in which the commitment was publicly presented to the Dominions. He made it clear that he would go along with the commitment only so long as Australia was kept in the dark on how it had arisen.[31] Menzies was well aware of the outcry that would occur in Australia if it were known that Australian troops had been sent to Greece as a result of an agreement reached in Athens by a British Cabinet Minister, especially when the Australian Prime Minister was in London supposedly overseeing Australian interests. Churchill took up Menzies' point and urged Eden to forward a precise military appreciation as Eden had so far given "few facts or reasons . . . justifying the operation on any grounds but *noblesse oblige*".[32]

By the time Menzies replied to Fadden on 8 March he could cite an impressive list of military and political leaders who favoured the expedition. Menzies argued that the proposal was not hopeless and that the "overwhelming importance to our position in relation to the world at large and particularly America of not abandoning the Greeks . . . should be the decisive consideration". He noted that British troops were even then on their way to Greece and he asked for Fadden's early concurrence to the commitment.

Despite the still-entertained hopes of success, Menzies implicitly acknowledged that the troops were possibly headed for disaster. He took solace in the fact that the "first Australian units will not go into position in Greece much before the end of the month by which time many things may have happened".[33]

If Menzies was now concerned about Greece itself, he was also beginning to realise that the whole affair would have serious repercussions in respect to the possible dispatch of a British fleet to the Far East in the event of a Japanese attack.

On 8 March, Menzies visited the Admiralty and impressed upon its First Lord, A. V. Alexander, that he preferred to return to Australia with a definite promise of naval assistance to meet a Japanese attack even if the assistance was "less than they had perhaps, in the past, been led to suppose".[34] Menzies therefore acknowledged that Australia could no longer expect to see the British fleet steaming towards them at the first sign of a Japanese attack. What he was after was some specific statement of the assistance Australia could expect if Japan attacked.

Throughout the century and a half of British settlement in Australia, the Royal Navy had provided the basic guarantee of Australia's defence. Till now no serious threat had eventuated and Australia had never had to test the worth of the guarantee.

The concept involved, of the Royal Navy maintaining a seven seas capability and patrolling extensively rather than actually basing units in colonial waters, had allowed successive generations of Australians to sleep more or less peacefully in their beds. Now when they anxiously scanned their ports and harbours for the smokestacks of British warships, they saw only troopships transporting the produce and men of Australia to the war in Europe. Though Menzies might personally discount the possibility of a Japanese attack against Australia, he was conscious that it was politically imperative for him to make preparations for such an eventuality.

In the probable absence of the British fleet, Menzies pointed out to Alexander the need for the "strong re-enforcement of our air forces at Singapore" which should "certainly include sufficient quantities of Hurricane fighters".[35] Again, Menzies came away from this meeting with no concrete assurance, other than on the supposed poor fighting ability of the Japanese, which seems to have partly allayed his fears.[36]

But the fear of the Japanese ran deep in the Australian psyche and it was a political necessity for Menzies to return with some noteworthy defence achievement. In the absence of ships, it really meant fighter planes, hence his concern to get a commitment of Hurricane fighters. As has been noted, such a commitment would have cut across Churchill's strategic priorities and the two men found themselves increasingly at odds over this issue. In the meantime, though, their personal relations continued to improve, with Menzies spending his third weekend with Churchill at Chequers.

Another guest at Chequers that weekend was the Commander-in-Chief of Britain's Home Forces, General Sir Alan Brooke (later Lord Alanbrooke). Brooke later recalled the jolly atmosphere that prevailed as "one of the first occasions on which I had seen Winston in one of his real light-hearted moods".[37] Churchill, although ill with bronchitis, also managed to captivate Menzies, who was forced to admit that it was

> *superb to hear him cross-examining and directing the experts. He is a marvellous master of all sorts of war-like detail, but, contrary to impression, does not dictate to the experts. But he insists on* action.[38]

On a more serious note, Menzies had a talk with another fellow guest, Colonel Donovan, head of America's Office of Strategic Services (the forerunner of the present Central Intelligence Agency). Menzies was impressed with Donovan and they had a long talk during which the American argued in favour of establishing communications between Churchill and Ireland's De Valera.[39]

This was just what Menzies wanted to hear as it could provide him with a mediatory role between the two parties and, if successful, could produce enormous political benefit in Australia. Anglo-Irish agreement would also help to reduce the chances of a German invasion of Britain and would cement the fragile ties of Empire, a matter of much importance to Menzies. So, Menzies now had it confirmed that it was a propitious moment to try and bridge the rift between Ireland and Britain. Though he knew of Churchill's intransigent attitude, Menzies apparently felt he could circumvent this by publicly approaching De Valera for an agreement. When Churchill maintained his intransigence and dashed Menzies' hopes, the bitterness of the Australian Prime Minister was to be great indeed.

Though Menzies only noted the Irish part of his talk with Donovan, the two men presumably also discussed the situation in Greece. Donovan had just returned from a visit that took him through the whole Mediterranean region. In a report for Roosevelt he had supported British efforts to form a "Balkan front" as being the only way for Britain to get to grips with Germany and beat her in the field.[40] Donovan's views were apparently important in convincing British leaders that deserting Greece would have serious repercussions in Washington. However, there is evidence that Donovan had private reservations and had told at least one British official that they should "on no account send more troops to back up the Greeks, and in the event would not even have to justify the apparent desertion".[41] Whatever Donovan now told Menzies, the latter did not see fit to record it and apparently stayed steady on his Greek setting.

That same day, General Blamey approached the Australian

government seeking to make his views known on the Greek expedition. This was the first intimation that Menzies would have of any possible misgivings by the Australian Commander. It now really was too late to reverse the decision to aid Greece and Blamey's cable was a serious embarrassment to Menzies. He had all along assured his Australian colleagues that Blamey backed the expedition. Menzies had, however, neither sought nor received Blamey's personal confirmation of such backing. As we have seen, he had, instead, relied on advice from the British Army Commander in the Middle East, General Wavell, that Blamey had been consulted and was in agreement with the decision. Menzies now found that the Greek expedition was causing him increasing political problems in Australia with Blamey stressing the extremely hazardous nature of the operation.[42]

On 11 March, Menzies wrote to Churchill to pass on the comments of his Australian colleagues who were becoming distinctly uneasy about Greece. In his letter, he asked Churchill to provide the "military basis of the opinion favouring the venture".[43] Menzies now seemed to be trying to form a solid front with Churchill to repel any political attacks from Australia.

On 14 March, Menzies tried to spread the political risks of any disaster in Greece. Until then he had not informed the Advisory War Council, with its Labor Party component, of the decision to send Australian troops to Greece. He now saw the folly of this omission and advised Fadden that he should discreetly inform the War Council, "not showing them the actual telegrams but giving the substance of the proposals".[44] If Menzies hoped for *post facto* Labor Party endorsement of the decision, he was to be disappointed. The Labor Party rightly refused to accept responsibility for a decision in which it had taken no part.[45]

Like Menzies, Churchill was also anxious to spread the political risk of the looming disaster. Eden was the obvious "fall guy" and, on 14 March, Churchill cabled him in Cairo urging that he stay on in the Middle East "until the opening phase of this crisis has matured". "No one but you," Churchill cabled, "can combine and concert the momentous policy which you have pressed upon us and which we have adopted."[46] This was a clear warning by Churchill that, if there was a political cost to pay over Greece, Eden would be the one to pay it.

Meanwhile, Menzies pressed on with his attempts to get British capital more heavily involved in Australia's war industries. On 10 March, in Churchill's absence, Menzies addressed the War Cabinet at great length on Australia's contribution to the Imperial war effort.

He called for a bold British policy to transform Australia into a mass producer of aircraft for the Empire east of Suez. Even heavy bombers, Menzies said, would not be beyond Australia's capability. Further, the production of planes was just the means to a long-term end. And the end Menzies had in mind, and with which he vainly tried to interest the War Cabinet, was to secure the Australian automobile industry for British capital. He stoutly maintained that there was "no reason why the United States car should be allowed to capture the Australian manufacturing possibilities".[47]

Two days after proposing this to the War Cabinet, Menzies addressed a dinner meeting at the Savoy chaired once again by Lord Nathan. Again, he spoke at length on Australia's manufacturing effort and, more importantly, its potential. Later he had a long talk with the economist J. M. Keynes on "the importance of blending war effort with an eye on post-war work—e.g. aeroplanes and motor cars in Australia".[48]

There was in this a further contrast between himself and Churchill. Whereas Churchill was forging the British national will to win the war and gave little thought to the post-war world, Menzies was using the war to fashion the shape of Australia in a peacetime he still hoped would not be too far distant.

Elsewhere, the British press was beginning to suggest the need to obtain Menzies' permanent presence in London. On 9 March the *Sunday Chronicle* claimed that he had "made such a markedly favourable impression on politicians here that the idea of an Imperial War Cabinet is being seriously mooted". The paper advised its readers to "Watch Mr. Menzies."[49] The British public, however, still had its eyes firmly fixed on Churchill. The press campaign doubtless made them aware of Menzies' presence in London but its main effect was to boost Menzies' self-image to unreal proportions and to foster a belief that his self-image was a projection of a more popular perception.

On 11 March, Menzies was further flattered to find personal confirmation of this press support, as well as to receive notice of a possible political future for him in Britain. At a luncheon engagement, he was approached by the press baron Lord Kemsley, who told him that "we must not let you leave this country!". Menzies wondered in his diary "what journalistic stunt he will be working", but there was no suggestion that Menzies tried to dissuade Kemsley from his task of retaining him in London. In fact, Menzies' diary provides a glimpse of what may have lain behind Kemsley's suggestion and what would have been certain to arouse the interest of the ambitious and anxious

Australian. Menzies confided that he had an "Interesting talk on future of the Conservative Party. After Winston, what?".[50]

Three days later, Menzies again met with Lord Kemsley, this time in more private surroundings over tea at the Ritz, and we can presume that Kemsley went further into his plans for Menzies' prolonged detention in London. This expression of powerful press support, together with the possibility of a political vacuum if Churchill fell from power, may well have provided the basis in Menzies' mind for the idea that it was not beyond him to make a bid for Downing Street.

Also on 11 March, Menzies was made aware that he could as well count on considerable political support if he chose to switch his attention to Westminster. He addressed a meeting of the Empire Parliamentary Association at which, Kemsley's *Daily Sketch* reported, he was given a remarkable ovation by more than 200 British MPs from all political parties. In fact, the enthusiasm of the audience was such that Menzies later confided to his diary that at least some of the British MPs "would not mind my defeat at Canberra if they could get me into the Commons. OMNIS *IGNOTUS* PRO MAGNIFICO".[51] Menzies' descent into Latin roughly translates as "any humble man (i.e. colonial) may become great" and is a wry reflection that he would not be exchanging the Prime Ministership of Australia for a mere backbench seat in the Commons.

As the signs increased that Menzies could fruitfully pursue a political career in London, Fadden enquired as to when Menzies would be leaving London. Menzies had earlier indicated that he planned to leave by the end of March and Fadden wanted to know whether he could confirm this to the Australian Parliament.[52] This put Menzies in a quandary. He had not yet achieved anything of substance in London, and there was the tantalising prospect to consider that he might yet be able to stay on permanently. Both these strands needed further time to develop and Menzies hung back from replying to Fadden's enquiry.

On 13 March, Menzies had a further opportunity to cement his relationship with Beaverbrook. He left his Dorchester suite for an afternoon with Beaverbrook inspecting aircraft. Though Menzies made no note of what transpired, there was presumably plenty of time for the sort of intimate discussions that would allow both men to see where they each stood. Whatever the nature of their discussions, Menzies was sufficiently delayed by them to miss the first part of a War Cabinet meeting, including a discussion of military policy in the Balkans and the Middle East.[53]

If Menzies and Beaverbrook were moving closer together, Beaver-

brook was still chary of supplying Menzies with the planes that he so
desperately needed. On 15 March, Sir Archibald Sinclair wrote to
Beaverbrook to co-ordinate the British offer of planes for Australia. He
informed Beaverbrook that Britain could not send Menzies away
empty-handed and then listed his proposed promise of planes. Delivery
was to be staggered over the next two years and there was little immediate succour for Australia's defence. As for the types of planes to
be provided, they were mainly the largely outdated Brewster Bermudas
for which Britain had little use. Sinclair assured Beaverbrook that he
would also make clear to Menzies that the delivery dates were not firm
and would depend on the circumstances at the time. All in all, Sinclair
argued, this proposal was "no more than a reasonable concession to
Australian wishes and needs".[54]

There was precious little in Sinclair's proposals for Menzies to get
excited about. Yet Beaverbrook prevailed on Sinclair to restrict his
promises still further, moaning about whether there would be "anything left for the poor wretches who pay taxes in Great Britain?".
Sinclair was well aware of Beaverbrook's anxieties and was quick to
assure him that he would not give Menzies any firm delivery promises
and agreed that Britain "must see that these Dominions do not strip us
of everything. . . ."[55] Menzies was as yet blissfully unaware that he was
set to return to Australia almost empty-handed so far as planes were
concerned.

In this, Beaverbrook proved himself the consummate politician,
appearing to be the ally of everyone while steadily furthering his own
particular interests. He would push Menzies' political prospects in
Britain and align with him on various issues against Churchill in the
War Cabinet, but he would not countenance Australia's defence being
secured at any considerable cost to Britain and ensured that Menzies
would not get satisfaction on the matter. At the same time he was
careful to conceal his moves from Menzies who seemed oblivious to
Beaverbrook's manoeuvring and convinced that they were becoming
firm allies.

Still, Menzies was getting satisfaction in different directions. A
Sunday Times columnist wrote on 16 March that the maximum use
should be made of his presence in London and urged that Britain and
Australia be "brought into the very closest mutual understanding". It
was further suggested that other Dominion and Indian leaders be
brought to London for talks with Churchill and Menzies to better co-
ordinate the war effort. Also, taking up one of Menzies' prime concerns, the columnist pointed to the largely latent potential in the

Dominions for production of ships, aircraft and munitions.[56]

Meanwhile, he was no closer to securing his political position in Australia. Indeed, his position there was becoming increasingly perilous. In Britain, on the other hand, Menzies was being seen as a leader with something to offer. From now on, he was to be increasingly torn between these two widely separated futures.

NOTES

1. MENZIES DIARY, 4 March 1941. After viewing some of Churchill's oil paintings, Menzies described him as a "versatile genius"
2. J. COLVILLE, *Footprints in Time*, London, 1976, p. 129
3. *TIMES*, London, 5 March 1941
4. *AGE*, Melbourne, 5 March 1941
5. *TIMES*, London, 5 March 1941
6. MENZIES DIARY, 5 March 1941
7. *DAFP*, iv, Doc. 336, Cable M.3, Menzies to Fadden, 5 March 1941
8. *DAFP*, iv, Doc. 334, War Cabinet Minutes, 5 March 1941
9. *DAFP*, iv, Doc. 338, Cable No. 17, Menzies to Fadden, 6 March 1941
10. *DAFP*, iv, Doc. 339, Cable No. 112, Fadden to Menzies, 7 March 1941
11. *DAILY EXPRESS*, London, 5 March 1941
12. MENZIES DIARY, 5 March 1941
13. *PRESS NEWS*, London, 6 March 1941
14. *STAR*, London, 8 March 1941
15. *DAILY EXPRESS*, London, 8 March 1941
16. *MANCHESTER GUARDIAN*, 8 March 1941
17. MENZIES DIARY, 5 March 1941
18. MENZIES DIARY, 6 March 1941
19. "NOTES on P.M.'s Discussion at Ministry of Aircraft Production 7 March 1941", CRS A5954, Box 617, "Review of United Kingdom Government's War Policy. Ministry of Aircraft Production": AA
20. CABLE NO. 21, Menzies to Fadden, 12 March 1941, *ibid.*
21. NOTE of a conversation between Menzies, Shedden and Bruce and First Lord of the Admiralty, A. V. Alexander, and Vice Chief of the Naval Staff, Admiral Sir Tom Phillips, 8 March 1941, AVAR 5/5/13, Alexander Papers: CC
22. MINUTE 427/17/2, Colonel Wardell to Shedden, 6 March 1941, CRS A5954, Box 628, Paper No. 21, Supplies from the United Kingdom: AA
23. CABLES M.20 & M.24, Menzies to Fadden, 12 March 1941, CP 290/9, Bundle 1(13)SC: AA
24. MENZIES DIARY, 5 March 1941
25. CABLE, Eden to Churchill, 5 March 1941, in W. S. Churchill, *The Second World War*, iii, p. 88
26. NOTES by Ismay for Churchill re his history of World War II, Greek Expedition, II/3/57/2, Ismay Papers: KC
27. MENZIES DIARY, 5 March 1941

28. CABLE NO. 102, Fadden to Menzies, 6 March 1941, MS4936/31/290/13, Menzies Papers: NLA
29. MENZIES DIARY, 6 March 1941
30. WAR CABINET CONCLUSIONS/CONFIDENTIAL ANNEX, 6 March 1941, Cab. 65/22, W.M.25(41): PRO
31. IBID.
32. CABLE, Churchill to Eden (Cairo), 7 March 1941, "The Prime Minister's Private Telegrams 1941", VI/I, Ismay Papers: KC
33. DAFP, iv, Doc. 344, Cable M.13, Menzies to Fadden, 8 March 1941
34. See fn. 21
35. IBID.
36. MENZIES DIARY, 8 March 1941
37. "NOTES ON MY LIFE", iv, p. 260, 3/A/IV, Alanbrooke Papers: KC
38. MENZIES DIARY, 9 March 1941
39. IBID.
40. REPORT BY DONOVAN, undated but sent by the British Ambassador in Spain, Sir Samuel Hoare, to Cadogan on 27 February 1941 and passed on to Churchill on 10 March 1941. PREM 4/25/5: PRO
41. LETTER, Desmond Morton to Lord Hankey, 6 March 1941, HNKY 11/14, Hankey Papers: CC
42. G. LONG, *Greece, Crete and Syria*, Canberra, 1953, p. 17
43. LETTER, Menzies to Churchill, 11 March 1941, PREM 3/206/3: PRO
44. CABLE M.27, Menzies to Fadden, 14 March 1941, AA CP 290/9, Bundle 1(13) SC: AA
45. ADVISORY WAR COUNCIL MINUTES, 18 March 1941, CRS A2682/2/228: AA
46. CABLE, Churchill to Eden (Cairo), 14 March 1941, "The Prime Minister's Personal Telegrams", VI/I, Ismay Papers: KC
47. "THE AUSTRALIAN WAR EFFORT", Statement by Menzies, 10 March 1941, Cab. 66/15, W.P.(41)55: PRO
48. MENZIES DIARY, 12 March 1941
49. SUNDAY CHRONICLE, London, 9 March 1941
50. MENZIES DIARY, 11 March 1941
51. IBID.
52. CABLE NO. 122, Fadden to Menzies, 10 March 1941, MS 4936/31/290/13, Menzies Papers: NLA
53. WAR CABINET CONCLUSIONS, 13 March 1941, Cab. 65/18, W.M.28(41): PRO
54. LETTER, Sinclair to Beaverbrook, 15 March 1941, BBK D/32, Beaverbrook Papers: HLRO
55. LETTERS, Beaverbrook to Sinclair and Sinclair to Beaverbrook, both 16 March 1941, BBK D/32, Beaverbrook Papers: HLRO
56. SUNDAY TIMES, London, 16 March 1941

6

Triumph
in the Provinces

*I*n mid-March 1941, the war had entered a new phase. Britain had scored dramatic victories over the Italians in the Middle East, but her sniping at the edges of Germany's new Europe had been without much effect. Churchill had now thrown down the gauntlet to Hitler by his dispatch of the British expedition to Greece. Within weeks, Hitler would accept his puny challenge and throw it back in his face. As a result of this badly conceived enterprise Churchill would not only lose his tentative toe-hold in Europe but have his grip on the entire Middle East seriously loosened.

As the thousands of Australian, New Zealand and British troops sailed across the Mediterranean to Greece, Menzies packed his bags in London and left for a week-long tour of Britain's industrial heartland. It effectively removed any influence he might have had on the developments in the war. In particular, the Australian military commitment to Greece now proceeded without the protective care that only Menzies could really provide. The subsequent allegations concerning ill-equipped troops might well have been avoided if Menzies had taken a constant and conspicuous interest in their welfare. It seems that, having committed Australian troops, Menzies was content to let events take their course.

The issue that led Menzies to leave London was the familiar one of Australia's industrial expansion. To date, Australia had merely assembled imported car components and Menzies had in mind the production from Australian materials of an all-Australian car, albeit controlled by British capital. This would be a major jump in Australia's transformation from a largely agricultural and pastoral society to one with a major industrial base.

Much of Menzies' hope for attracting British capital was centred on the Rootes Company, makers of the Humber car. It seems that the company had encouraged this hope and was assiduously cultivating

One of Menzies' factory visits.
With him (from left) J. A. Cole, Chairman of Humber Ltd; John Storey,
member of the Aircraft Production Commission of Australia; and William
Rootes, President of the Society of Motor Manufacturers

Menzies' allegiance. Rootes put three chauffeur-driven limousines,
complete with Australian flags, at Menzies' disposal during his provincial tour. Menzies reportedly told a journalist later that the only way
in which he could slow their race through the countryside was to ask to
use his movie camera. Then, Menzies recalled, ''the whole cavalcade,
police escort and all, pulled up with a flourish, much to the conster-
nation of some people in little villages, who thought that the invasion
had begun.''[1] Apart from the transportation, W. E. Rootes also accompanied him throughout the tour. By the completion of his London visit,
Menzies had apparently come to an understanding with Rootes that the
company would be given a secure position in the future Australian
automobile industry.

But any decision to transfer vital production facilities to Australia
rested with the British War Cabinet. As Minister for Aircraft Production, Beaverbrook was likely to exercise a major influence on any

question of this nature. So, whatever interest Menzies could arouse among British industrialists, it was in London that the ultimate sanction would be given. It appears that Menzies' earlier contacts with Beaverbrook had left him with the impression that government approval would be automatic. As he toured the factories of the Midlands, he was presumably acting on this assumption. It was only after arousing the interest of the industrialists that Menzies found his efforts had come to naught. Without War Cabinet approval nothing left Britain and it was not to be forthcoming.

While Menzies may have been more profitably occupied bringing his influence to bear in London, it is extremely doubtful whether he could have achieved any diversion of industrial resources whatever the focus of his attention. British production was fully committed to the war, especially while a German invasion remained a possibility; Australia was far from the spheres of conflict and the transfer of productive capacity from Britain could only disrupt the flow of supplies in the war zone. But the dashing of his hopes added to the frustration and anger he already felt towards Churchill's government.

Menzies' tour of the provinces may well have had a double purpose, since it allowed him to take the political temperature outside of London and to impress his presence on a wider public audience. Whether he had this in mind when planning his tour is unclear. But it is clear that he made the most of the opportunities provided by the tour to build on his public image. And, to achieve success with the British public, Menzies rightly judged that he had to be seen as being at one with Churchill. He told the press in Manchester, therefore, that Churchill was a "bobby dazzler" and a "real crackerjack" who thrived on combat and was "one of the great fighting leaders in all history".[2]

His tour had taken him to the front line in Britain's air war with Germany, the industrial heartland where German bombers had concentrated much of their terror. Here he found the people unbowed by their experience and stalwart in their support for Churchill and his handling of the war. On 19 March, Menzies' convoy of cars arrived in Sheffield. Despite bomb damage to a third of the city, Menzies found the public spirit unaffected by adversity. He noted in his diary that, despite the serious damage, industries were "going magnificently. Spirit superb. No surrender. *No compromise.*"[3] Menzies' emphasis on the fact that the public were not in a mood to brook compromise seems to have given him pause in considering his own position on the war. And yet, as an outsider with a penchant for rational thought, there was little to convince Menzies that the war was winnable for Britain.

In Coventry, Menzies publicly mused on this "strange mad war" in which civilians had to bear the brunt of the fight. He claimed that the Germans were aiming to "destroy British production and the morale of the people, in the hope of causing the latter to seek a compromise peace".[4] In fact, he argued, the bombing produced the opposite effect on the British public. In fact, it was more with puzzlement than admiration that Menzies noted the popular reaction to German bombing. However, it was a reaction that he had to take into account.

Just as Menzies had been greeted by cheering soldiers in the Middle East, he now received a similar reception from this industrial front line. He took every opportunity produced by his tour to address meetings of workers in the factories and cities he visited. In the Lucas works at Birmingham he was greeted by cheering crowds, while the Rootes factory in Coventry set up a vast meeting where Menzies addressed thousands of men and women. On 21 March, he addressed a massive meeting of 20,000 workers at a Bristol munitions factory.[5]

Newspaper reports told of tumultuous welcomes which affected even Menzies' "customary calm". When he waved his hat to the crowds the response was reported to be deafening. One paper described a worker in the audience yelling that Menzies was "a great man", a comment that produced wild applause from his fellow workers.[6] This popular adulation went further to build in Menzies' mind the idea that he might well have a constituency within Britain. In fact, he was so encouraged by the results of his tour that, on 20 March, he decided to remain in Britain for an extra two weeks to pursue what he described as "great possibilities", which apparently centred on his continuing hopes for the transfer of industrial resources to Australia.[7]

With Menzies now determined to prolong his stay in England, he had to somehow convince his Australian colleagues of the need for it. Accordingly, on 21 March, he cabled Fadden informing him of promising negotiations that he had to complete before he could usefully depart. Menzies confided that Rootes and Rolls-Royce had both expressed interest in extending their operations to Australia and that the aim would be not only to build aircraft during the war but to lay the foundation for building motor cars afterwards.[8]

It is extraordinary that, with German military might in the ascendant and Australian troops preparing to meet them in combat in Greece, Menzies' concern should be with Australia's peacetime industrial growth. While Australia anxiously watched Japan's military expansion, Menzies was eagerly noting the "real spirit of interest" among British manufacturers and their "genuine desire to actively assist with Australia's post-war development".[9] What Australia needed, and urgently, was modern fighter planes, not skeleton automobile factories.

Menzies' provincial tour had a heady effect on the ambitious Australian. It opened up a vision of a firmly British industrial future for Australia and the cementing of the economic bonds of Empire. Menzies enthusiastically reported to Fadden that he was "more optimistic of the good mutual results" than ever before. Obviously, the achievement of this vision would secure Menzies' political future in Australia. However, it was hardly a valid vision to pursue in the depths of a war that required every ounce of energy to secure a favourable outcome. Menzies' optimism was also fuelled by a phenomenon with purely British implications. This was what Menzies called the "amazing popular reception" he personally received during his tour. He would soon have to face the question of whether or not to cash in on his apparent popularity in Britain.[10]

The last major stop on Menzies' tour was at Plymouth where he was the guest of Lady Astor. He was suddenly thrust firmly into the firing line when Plymouth was subjected to intense German bombing throughout the night of 21 March. He was dining with Lady Astor, Rootes and the admiral of the local naval base when the air raid sent them hurrying to the basement. There, Menzies and Lady Astor engaged in a spirited political argument to divert their attention from the bombing. Menzies later recalled that Lady Astor then "took the stage with a magnificent performance of mimicry of certain well-known persons". Menzies was himself an accomplished mimic with a cruel streak that could make his subjects squirm. Menzies probably also demonstrated his talents in this sphere and, as the bombs rained down around them, Churchill would doubtless have featured in his repertoire.[11]

Some 400 citizens of Plymouth were killed or seriously injured that night. The scale of the attack also left its mark on Menzies. He described it as "the queerest experience, and no longer will I believe there is anyone who is not frightened by concentrated bombing". Later, while inspecting the damage, an exploding time bomb reportedly caused Menzies to throw himself on the roadway and cover his face with his tin hat.[12]

Meanwhile, in his diary Menzies noted his private reaction to the devastation. He deplored the wanton destruction of property but claimed that he was "in a grim sense glad to have seen it". Though he reaffirmed his support for peace, he now argued that it would be a "tragedy for humanity if it comes before these beasts have had their own cities ravaged". In his own "hymn of hate", Menzies responded to the bombing with a conviction that the "Hun must be made to learn through his hide..."[13] Unlike Churchill, though, Menzies did not preclude a peace short of total victory. On a positive note, Menzies' experience in Plymouth enhanced his reputation in Britain with widespread newspaper coverage of his heroism and the fact that he lent his car to transport women and children from their bombed homes. Even the American papers were beginning to take note of Menzies' impact with one describing his "biting speech" as "second only to Winston Churchill's".[14]

While Menzies was engaged on his provincial tour, Lloyd George continued to wait patiently. His military adviser, Liddell Hart, remained convinced of the folly of pursuing total victory. He wrote rather presciently that, even if Britain could decisively defeat Germany, it would be "likely to entail our subservience to the United States — if not the supremacy of Soviet Russia in Europe".[15] This was much the view of Menzies, who foresaw a widened and prolonged war sounding the death knell of the British Empire. Meanwhile, Lloyd George continued to spread a depressing view of Britain's chances and paint Churchill as a dangerous warmonger.[16]

At the end of his tour, Menzies once more set out for Chequers to dine with the British leader. Here, Menzies was given another example of Churchill's abrasiveness and dislike of criticism. Menzies informed him that during his visit to Plymouth he had noticed serious short-comings at the naval dockyards. In an interesting indication of the relationship between the two Prime Ministers, Churchill immediately took Menzies' comments as a personal attack. Years later, Menzies recalled that Churchill had responded to the criticism with a "Nel-sonian broadside".[17]

Menzies had now been in England for a month and absent from his office in Australia for two. As yet he had nothing of significance to show for his efforts. Part of his problem lay in the widespread expectation he had created in Australia that he would be able to arrange the transfer of industrial capacity.

Menzies was apparently so confident of success that he kept the accompanying Australian press representatives fully informed of his activities and they in turn reflected his optimism in their cabled reports.[18] Hence the need to prolong his stay in the hope of a favourable turn of events. This was readily acceded to by Fadden, who agreed that it would be foolish to prejudice his chances of success by returning too early and promised to do his "utmost at this end to keep affairs on an even keel".[19] In fact, Fadden was finding Menzies' office to his liking and he was widely regarded as performing well in his stead.

A further portent of potential trouble for Menzies in Australia came with the call by the Melbourne *Sun* for his return. The paper was one of those controlled by Keith Murdoch and Menzies had previously been able to count on him for support. Murdoch, however, had become increasingly critical of Menzies' inability to achieve political unity and he was apparently now also frustrated by Menzies' failure to provide dynamic war leadership. The *Sun* rather caustically commented that Menzies' provincial tour had become a "procession from one scene of carnage to another" and it called for his early return to Australia where "much important work in connection with our war effort remains to be done".[20] Even the Melbourne *Age*, which usually supported Menzies to the full, expressed concern at the continued absence of the nation's leader during wartime.[21]

With his future in Australia largely riding on the success of his efforts to attract British industrial capital, Menzies was naturally furious to learn of possible plans to manufacture American aircraft engines under licence in Australia. He mistakenly believed the proposal had been approved by the Australian Government in his absence and immediately cabled Fadden, taking the "strongest exception to this decision which renders quite futile all my discussions with aero-engine manufacturers here". Menzies ordered Fadden to suspend government approval if possible. If it were not possible, Menzies angrily announced that he would "at once terminate my conversations with British firms".[22]

Fadden seems to have been quite taken aback by the sharpness of Menzies' cable and was quick to assure him that the Government had not taken any such decision in his absence, although he admitted that they were exploring the possibility.[23] Menzies' reaction further suggests that he had no clear conception of just how serious his country's situation was, and how crucial the rapid expansion of its defence industries. It seemed to matter not a whit whether the American proposal would produce better engines in a shorter time—what concerned Menzies was that the plans for industrial expansion should be seen to emanate from his efforts, that they be under the control of British capital and that they further his vision of Imperial integration.

Though this furore turned out to be a storm in a teacup, there were other issues arising that would prove to be more intractable. Britain's serious shipping problems were forcing it to cut back on the transportation of primary products over such long routes as from Australia. This had devastating implications for Australia's primary industries and Menzies was given the task of easing the situation.[24] He was unable to resolve it fully before leaving London. In fact, Australia was really only rescued by the Japanese attack in December 1941 which created a tremendous demand for primary products from American forces based in the South West Pacific.

At the same time, Menzies' continuing concern with the problem of Irish neutrality was helping to establish him in a position of opposition to Churchill. Menzies had already informed Fadden that he intended to visit De Valera in Dublin and had requested that the Australian Cabinet supply him with a

> *most emphatic expression of opinion that this problem concerns the security of the whole British Empire and that Australia cannot and will not remain indifferent to the continuance of a policy which materially helps Germany and may vitally injure us.*[25]

Though Fadden immediately complied with his request, it took Menzies almost three weeks to raise this supposedly urgent matter at a meeting of the British War Cabinet on 24 March.

He told the Cabinet that he was trying to arrange an interview with De Valera and asked that he be permitted later to make "some public statement of his views on the Eire position". Though this was agreed to, the War Cabinet also felt impelled to stipulate that its present policy towards Eire would continue.[26] This should have indicated to Menzies that his chances of reconciling the two sides would be slim. Yet he persevered and, in doing so, further aligned himself with those elements critical of Churchill's leadership. On 28 March, he lunched with Geoffrey Dawson, editor of the *Times*, with whom he discussed Ireland. Both men were clearly worried about where Churchill's Irish policy was leading and Menzies later complained in his diary that Britain "must not just drift into an Irish War".[27]

Of more far-reaching concern for Menzies' political future was the increasingly dubious nature of the Greek expedition. Menzies' ill-considered support for the operation was becoming more of an embarrassment to him and threatened to negate any positive achievements he might bring away from his visit. The imminent failure of the Greek expedition also threatened to loosen Britain's hold on the Mediterranean and to put the Suez Canal within Germany's grasp. The Suez was a vital Imperial axis that carried much of the peacetime trade between Britain and her Empire in the east. The possible loss of Egypt and the Suez had awful implications, in Menzies' view, for the interdependent British Empire.

The Labor Party members of Australia's Advisory War Council had suggested that Menzies be urged to re-examine the Greek commitment in view of the probable defection of Yugoslavia and the added defence responsibilities facing Australia in the Far East. It put the onus on Menzies once more to provide a personal assurance as to the viability of the expedition.[28] Moreover, the Labor members pointed out that they felt no responsibility for the Greek expedition and that, if their policy had been pursued, Australian troops would not have been in the Middle East in the first place. They now suggested that some, if not all, of the Australian forces be returned to Australia to prepare for the possibility of a Japanese attack.

Though Fadden assured Menzies on 27 March that these views were repudiated by the Australian War Cabinet, which stuck by the Greek commitment, he nevertheless stressed that Menzies should keep in close touch with the British government and "acquaint us of any developments which you consider should be brought to our notice".[29] That Fadden felt it necessary to make this point betrayed an uneasiness that would not have escaped Menzies' attention.

In fact, that same day, Fadden dispatched a further cable to Menzies posing problems of a much more serious nature. The Australian Government had only then received dispatches from General Blamey outlining his misgivings regarding the Greek commitment. Blamey now claimed that the whole operation was "most hazardous" and denied that he had ever been consulted on its advisability by his British superiors. Fadden claimed that the failure to consult Blamey deeply affected the question of Empire relations and warned Menzies of the potential embarrassment if the lack of consultation was made public. Fadden had accepted Menzies' mistaken assurance that Blamey agreed to the Greek operation and had proclaimed this to the Advisory War Council and the Parliament. The whole business was beginning to appear rather tawdry, even sinister, and to pose problems for which Menzies had no easy solution.

In his cable to Menzies, Fadden also noted that Blamey had included in his dispatches a copy of a letter sent to Menzies on 5 March outlining his doubts on Greece. Fadden was clearly puzzled as to why Menzies had not informed his colleagues of this important communication and he asked Menzies for an explanation.[30]

Menzies could easily explain why he had not informed Fadden of Blamey's letter—he had not yet received it himself. In his reply to Fadden on 29 March, he rightly noted that it was "curious for Blamey to write and not cable on matters of such urgency". Further, Menzies reiterated that he was "certainly informed of Blamey's agreement" and he was puzzled why Blamey should now regard himself "merely as receiving instructions". Still, Menzies undertook to take the matter up with Churchill.[31]

As for the continuing viability of the Greek commitment, Menzies disposed of Blamey's doubts and assured Fadden that, while it was undoubtedly hazardous, it still had reasonable chances of success. Moreover, he claimed that these chances were improved following the anti-German coup in Yugoslavia and he expressed renewed faith in a "Balkan front" built around Yugoslavia, Greece and Turkey to resist German moves southward. He now argued that no chance to form such a front should be neglected and that the British expedition to Greece "may prove the decisive factor in stiffening resistance".[32]

Menzies' confident assertions were but a hollow echo of Churchill's rhetoric, the result of his own lack of independent military advice. He obviously now felt locked into the Greek commitment and placed all his hopes on the successful outcome repeatedly predicted by Churchill.

The core of Churchill's Balkan strategy was the Turkish army, ill-equipped but numerically strong. It was this force that Churchill wanted to stimulate into action against Germany. It was a simplistic head-counting exercise by Churchill that paid little account of fighting ability. Menzies too readily accepted Churchill's Mediterranean strategy; but then so did many of Britain's military leaders who should have known better.

To pursue his Mediterranean strategy, Churchill had sent Admiral Kelly to Turkey to stimulate Turkish interest in joining the British war effort. Ironically, at a time when Menzies was agreeing to place so much faith in the Turks, Kelly was complaining to a colleague that the "Turks have not the faintest intention of doing, under any conditions, anything in the nature of offensive action" and that they were "quite unmoved by any treaty obligations".[33]

It is significant that Kelly was writing on 28 March 1941, the day after a coup in Yugoslavia had restored the pro-British elements to power. Whereas Kelly knew that even this would leave Turkey unmoved, Churchill, and Menzies, took great solace, believing that it might well represent the beginning of the cherished Balkan front.[34]

The Yugoslavian coup came at just the right time to rescue

Menzies temporarily from his increasingly querulous colleagues. At the same time there were British military victories in Eritrea and Ethiopia and a great naval victory against the Italian fleet. Taking them all together, Churchill was enormously heartened and swung his weight behind Menzies in order to quieten Australian anxiety.

In a cable to Fadden on 30 March, Churchill admitted that the Greek commitment originally looked like a "rather bleak military adventure dictated by *noblesse oblige*". He now claimed that Britain's recent successes meant that they could "cherish renewed hopes of forming a Balkan front with Turkey comprising about 70 Allied divisions. . .". Churchill further informed Fadden that the expedition to Greece should be seen not as "an isolated military act, but as a prime mover in large design". Nevertheless, while claiming that the risks of the expedition had lessened, Churchill still cautioned Fadden that the results were "unknowable".[35] The respite this cable afforded Menzies was to be short-lived. Over the next month the news of British forces was to be almost universally bad, with one disaster closely following another.

While Menzies may have appreciated Churchill's assistance in his own political difficulties, he was being drawn ever further into the issues surrounding the possibility of transferring his talents to London. On 25 March he dined at the Ritz with a group of young Tories with whom he discussed "post-war reconstruction and the future of the Conservative Party".[36] Menzies may even then have been sounding out his prospects in British politics. Certainly, discussing the future of the Conservative Party was far removed from his brief as Australian Prime Minister.

As for his view of Churchill, Menzies seemed to seesaw according to the prevailing military situation. On 26 March, when things were still looking grim in Greece, Menzies was highly critical of Churchill and pessimistic about Britain's chances in the war. He described in his diary attending a conference at Downing Street, presided over by Churchill, on the "Battle of the Atlantic". The outcome of this extended conflict was crucial to Britain's survival. The enemy was the German submarine fleet which was desperately trying to sever Britain's lifeline to North America. Churchill had come under critic- ism for not according this battle sufficient priority and throwing British resources instead into less vital, largely symbolic bombing raids on Germany. Tending to support this view, it was, therefore, a rather critical Menzies who now faced Churchill across the Downing Street conference table and looked for reassurance about the epic battle in the

Atlantic. Instead of reassurance, Menzies found Churchill "pale, unpleasant and strained" and he came away from the conference with a spectre of defeat in view. Menzies confessed privately that the battle "looks lousy" and that he lacked "*real* faith in the navy".[37]

Not only was the outlook bleak, but the possibility of averting disaster seemed impossible under Churchill's iron rule. Menzies was again shocked to note Churchill's political and military subordinates at the conference acting like schoolboys in the presence of the head-master.[38] Not one of them seemed able to counter Churchill's commanding hold over their deliberations and there were few arguments thrown up to restrain his aggressive temperament. With little to brake Churchill's wilder inclinations, Menzies feared that the Imperial procession could easily plunge off the track. As such a disaster loomed closer in the weeks ahead, Menzies would make frantic efforts to extinguish Churchill as Britain's driving force.

But before Britain was plunged into its defeats of April–June 1941, Menzies experienced a new burst of optimism following a series of minor British victories during the last week of March. British forces overwhelmed the Italian army in Ethiopia and Eritrea and sank five Italian warships in the Mediterranean. With his temporary oscillation into optimism, Menzies also took a kinder view of Churchill and his handling of the war. On 31 March, Menzies admitted to himself:

> *Winston's attitude to war is much more realistic than mine.*
> *I constantly find myself looking at "minor losses" and saying*
> *"There are some darkened houses." But he is wiser. War is*
> *terrible and it cannot be won except by lost lives. That being so,*
> *don't think of them.*[39]

In the flush of victory, Menzies could be less critical of Churchill but he remained painfully aware of the deep gulf that separated their attitudes to the war. When the victories turned to defeats this gulf would again loom large and Menzies' criticisms of Churchill would reappear and grow in intensity.

While he was busily fending off attacks from home and anxiously watching the situation around the Mediterranean, the British press was steadily stressing his merits to the populace and suggesting he stay on in London. The *News Chronicle* claimed that "no Dominion states-man has created so marked or so favourable an impression in this country" and described him as a "big, handsome man, forceful, very much alive, keenly observant, well-informed, full of courage and re-solution and (incidentally) a speaker of the first order".[40] The *Observer* was similarly heavy-handed in its praise, claiming that Menzies had "found a place among the most heartening and pleasing public speakers of the moment". It then went much further with the suggestion that he would make an "admirable member of the War Cabinet, like General Smuts in the last struggle".[41]

It is possible that, by now, Menzies was himself inspiring these suggestions for it is certainly doubtful that they would be made without his connivance. The *Observer* editorial, in particular, was written by J. L. Garvin, a close confidant of Lady Astor, who had so recently been Menzies' hostess in Plymouth. The accompanying praise, though, would have been unsolicited and served to quicken the pace of Menzies' ambition. This was further developed at the end of March when a British publisher offered to produce a volume of his London speeches.[42]

During April 1941, Menzies' stocks would continue to rise among the British public, while military reverses would produce increasing questions about Churchill's fitness for leadership. Like two giant pincers, columns of German tanks would push east from Libya into Egypt and south from Bulgaria into Yugoslavia and Greece. Egypt, the cornerstone of British power in the Middle East, seemed set to be crushed in the middle. Not only the military outcome, but the political outcome in Australia and Britain, would begin to dominate the conversation in the corridors of power.

Notes

1. SMITH'S WEEKLY, Sydney, 26 April 1941
2. BIRMINGHAM POST, 18 March 1941
3. MENZIES DIARY, 19 March 1941
4. TIMES, London, 21 March 1941
5. MENZIES DIARY, 19, 20 and 21 March 1941
6. AGE, Melbourne, 20 March 1941. See also *Age*, 21 March 1941
7. MENZIES DIARY, 20 March 1941
8. CABLE NO. 30, Menzies to Fadden, 21 March 1941, CRS CP 290/9, (15) SC: AA
9. IBID.
10. IBID.
11. DAILY TELEGRAPH, Sydney, 24 March 1941
12. IBID.
13. MENZIES DIARY, 21 March 1941
14. DAILY MIRROR, New York, 24 March 1941
15. "REFLECTIONS", note by Liddell Hart, 17 March 1941, 11/1941/18, Liddell Hart Papers: KC

16. LOCKHART DIARY, 19 March 1941, K. Young (ed.), p. 93
17. "CHURCHILL AT SEVENTY-FIVE", article by Menzies in *New York Times Magazine*, 27 November 1949, reprinted in R. G. Menzies, *Speech is of Time*, London, 1958, p. 52
18. *AGE*, Melbourne, 20, 21 and 22 March, 1941
19. CABLE NO. 156, Fadden to Menzies, 24 March 1941, MS 4936/31/290/13, Menzies Papers: NLA
20. *SUN*, Melbourne, 25 March 1941
21. *AGE*, Melbourne, 19 March 1941
22. CABLE NO. 36, Menzies to Fadden, 25 March 1941, AA CP 290/9, (15) SC: AA
23. CABLES NO. 160 AND 163, Fadden to Menzies, 25 and 26 March 1941, MS 4936/31/290/13, Menzies Papers: NLA
24. CABLE NO. 161, Page to Menzies, 26 March 1941, AA CP 290/9, Bundle 1(11) SC: AA; Note of a meeting with Mr Arthur Greenwood, Lord Woolton and Sir Frederick Leith Ross, 26 March 1941, CRS M100, "March 1941": AA; Cable No. 45, Menzies to Fadden, 30 March 1941, AA CP 290/9, (15) SC: AA; War Cabinet Conclusions, 31 March 1941, Cab. 65/18, W.M.33(41): PRO
25. *DAFP*, iv, Doc. 331, Cable M.2, Menzies to Fadden, 4 March 1941
26. WAR CABINET CONCLUSIONS, 24 March 1941, Cab. 65/18, W.M.31(41): PRO
27. MENZIES DIARY, 28 March 1941
28. ADVISORY WAR COUNCIL MINUTES, 25 March 1941, CRS A2682/2/237: AA
29. CABLE NO. 173, Fadden to Menzies, 27 March 1941, AA CP 290/9, Bundle 1(11) SC: AA
30. *DAFP*, iv, Doc. 370, Cable No. 176, Fadden to Menzies, 27 March 1941
31. *DAFP*, iv, Doc. 373, Cable M.35, Menzies to Fadden, 29 March 1941
    See also PREM 3/206/3: PRO
32. *IBID.*
33. LETTER, Kelly to Admiral Cunningham, 28 March 1941, KEL 42, Admiral Kelly Papers: NMM
34. MENZIES DIARY, 29 March 1941
35. CABLE NO. 162, Churchill to Fadden, 30 March 1941, PREM 3/63/13: PRO
36. MENZIES DIARY, 25 March 1941
37. MENZIES DIARY, 26 March 1941
38. *IBID.*
39. MENZIES DIARY, 31 March 1941
40. *NEWS CHRONICLE*, London, 30 March 1941
41. *OBSERVER*, London, 30 March 1941
42. MENZIES DIARY, 31 March 1941

7

Defeat After Defeat

*T*he final week of March 1941 saw the highwater mark of British fortunes for the year. From the first week of April an alarming series of military defeats threw Britain's war machine off balance and almost extinguished hopes for an eventual victory against Germany. Rommel was to launch a daring onslaught on the depleted British forces in Libya and rapidly overrun the scenes of Britain's recent victories. In the Balkans, German tanks were being assembled for a sudden thrust against Yugoslavia and Greece that would quickly rout the much smaller and ill-equipped British, Australian and New Zealand forces.

Menzies had then been in England for nearly six weeks and was as yet unable to point to one solid achievement that could justify his now prolonged absence from Australia. Now, during the first week of April, nearly everything began to go wrong for him in his role as Australian Prime Minister.

On the personal side, he was stricken by a bout of homesickness and depression that could not be relieved by life in London.[1] Part of his depression was probably caused by the uncertainty and indecision that beset him.

The call for Dominion representation in the War Cabinet was steadily gaining ground. This was no doubt partly inspired by Menzies in talks with accompanying journalists. But it also arose from the very real admiration that Menzies generated in London. Still, the very idea of Dominion representation betrayed an underlying uneasiness with the war's direction and the competence of the present War Cabinet members.

The argument for Dominion representation went in two directions. Some advocates claimed to recognise great qualities in Menzies and urged that he be included in the War Cabinet as a representative of Dominion interests generally. Others hearkened back to the Imperial

War Cabinet of the First World War and pressed for the return of this system, based on representatives from each of the Dominions. Menzies firmly favoured the first alternative, with accompanying changes in War Cabinet personnel.

There were arguments against Dominion representation. One journal acknowledged the pressure for an Imperial War Cabinet arising from Menzies' visit but argued that such a Cabinet was both unnecessary and inappropriate for the circumstances.[2] The Australian press, which had been calling for Menzies' return, now received reports of calls for his continued retention in London.

On 1 April, the Melbourne *Herald* reported that Menzies had been

> *sounded on the possibility of his remaining in Britain indefinitely*
> *. . . They are saying on all sides. ''Here's a man with an*
> *intellect that matches Winston's. Why can't we keep him here for*
> *a while to continue in Cabinet?''* [3]

Though the *Herald* report admitted the obstacles facing Menzies' elevation to the British War Cabinet, it nevertheless supposedly established an overwhelming call for Menzies to remain in London. Menzies' close association with the Australian press corps in London suggests that he at least partly inspired this report. It certainly served his purpose of emphasising his success in London while at the same time testing the Australian reaction to the possibility of his staying on.

If Menzies was hoping that Australia would readily allow him to remain in Westminster, he was to be disappointed. The Melbourne *Age* reacted to the reports by suggesting that they were inspired by Menzies' political enemies in Australia who sought to be rid of him. It assured its readers that the reports were bound to cause him embarrassment and that it could be ''taken for granted that Mr. Menzies will brush aside all such blandishments''. It pointedly argued that, during wartime, the ''one thing that Australia cannot dispense with for any indefinite length of time is the leadership of the elected Prime Minister'', and that Menzies doubtless would be ''sensitive to his responsibility in this respect''.[4]

Two days later, the *Age* again editorialised against his remaining in London. This time it took as its theme the idea of formalising Dominion representation in British decision making. Responding to such a call in the House of Lords, the *Age* firmly opposed any formalised procedure and proposed instead the institution of periodical visits by senior Ministers.[5] The *Age* had been a stalwart supporter of

Menzies and its stand would have made Menzies aware of the opposition he could expect to face if he formally proposed staying on in
London.

Nevertheless, Menzies was beset by other worries at this time that
increasingly impelled him to ignore this opposition and turn towards
Westminster. Australia had become aware of the implications that the
Greek expedition had for Britain's Far East strategy in the event of war
with Japan. The Dominion down under could no longer be assured of a
powerful British naval reaction to a Japanese attack. Fadden now
pressed Menzies to establish the scale of naval reinforcement Australia
could confidently count on. The conservative political parties had
always opposed the Labor strategy of local defence and placed their
reliance on British naval power. There were serious political implications if it were widely realised that Australia now lay practically
defenceless, at the mercy of Japanese military intentions.

On 1 April, Menzies responded to Fadden's anxieties by assuring
him that he had the matter well in hand. He informed him that he had
''already asked the Admiralty to prepare a scheme of naval re-inforce-
ment East of Suez and this is being done as rapidly as possible'' and
that ''you may assume that before I leave I will have all material
answers''.[6] However, Menzies' confident assurances were shattered
when the Admiralty refused to give any such definite scheme.

Additionally, the proposal to increase aircraft production in
Australia became increasingly vexed. Menzies' visit to the provinces
had elicited interest from industrialists but his plans now foundered on
the rocks of political opposition from, of all people, Beaverbrook.
Menzies had written to Churchill following his return from the provinces with an outline of his proposals for boosting aircraft production
in Australia. On 1 April, Beaverbrook gave his opinion of the project
to Churchill. Seemingly giving his support, Beaverbrook promised to
do ''everything we can to encourage the scheme which Mr. Menzies
outlines to you''. He claimed that it was ''our desire that aircraft
capacity should be built up in every Dominion''. However, Beaverbrook's real attitude was revealed when he noted that he only supported the scheme in principle and that Menzies should ''recognise the
difficulties that exist''.[7]

In point of fact, Beaverbrook was the principal difficulty in
Menzies' quest for fighters, as he amply demonstrated the following
day when responding to a New Zealand request for aircraft. Though
the request had the support of Sinclair as the Secretary of State for Air,
Beaverbrook stonewalled the proposal. He instructed his staff to file it

away and bluntly announced that he would "not take any notice of it at all".[8] Ironically, he was even then informing Churchill of a two-fold increase in aircraft production over the previous 12 months and a three-fold increase in fighter production.[9] However, Beaverbrook's fears of a German invasion put him in determined opposition to any dispersal of this increased strength to the defenceless Dominions. Despite the encouraging noises he made to Menzies, the Australian was destined to be disappointed in his quest for aircraft.

Apart from his hopes for boosting aircraft production, Menzies was also seeking to transfer part of Britain's ship-building capacity to Australia where it would be free from air attack. A thriving ship-building industry was an important base for an infant industrial economy and the Labor Party had likewise placed much stress on this possibility in its talks with Menzies prior to his departure from Australia. Menzies was now forced to report to Fadden that British ship-building interests were determined to "keep our activities confined to naval craft so as not to build up competitive yards for other vessels in the post-war period". Menzies urged that Australia press on regardless with mechant ship construction. "In view," he wrote, "of the prospect of meagre shipping space for exports, merchant ship construction would appear to be an essential corollary both from the practical and political angles."[10] However, the problem for Menzies was that the chances of his being able to announce any shift in ship-building to Australia had considerably diminished.

An associated problem pressing on Menzies was, as we have seen, the cutback in British import programs. The Australian Cabinet was now seriously alarmed about the implications of this for Australia. In a cable to Menzies, Fadden forecast that it would "spell the death-knell of our primary industries if war were prolonged". The Cabinet was most bitter about the British Government using the opportunities provided by the Lend-Lease Bill to buy American rather than Australian foodstuffs. And behind it all was an implicit criticism of Menzies for being in London when the cutbacks were made and not putting forward the Australian view with sufficient force. Menzies was now urged to "press in strongest manner possible the views of Cabinet and endeavour to secure some modification of the proposed restrictions".[11]

The following day, Australia's Minister of Commerce, Earle Page, cabled an additional appeal to Menzies. He told him that Australia (in effect, Menzies) "must fight hard against the damage to our economy which the proposed restrictions would cause". Page argued that it was not the shortage of shipping but the easier conditions in the American market that were causing the cutbacks. He pressed Menzies to get some firm understanding of Britain's willingness to buy Australian surpluses. This, Page said, would be a great achievement and, as an added incentive, he held out the prospect of Australia concluding a trade agreement with the United States if Menzies could not reach agreement with Britain.[12] Menzies was loath to countenance such a prospect, which would threaten the economic foundations of Australia's ties with the Empire. He was now faced with more problems than when he had arrived in London and they had become more intractable.

There now occurred a sudden turnaround of British fortunes in the war that had additional and serious implications for Menzies' political future in Australia. The elated expectations of North African victory following the initial British successes in Libya collapsed as Rommel counter-attacked. Wavell was forced into a hasty withdrawal, and Benghazi, the Libyan town so recently visited by Menzies, was evacuated. The 7th Australian Division, about to embark for Greece, was ordered to the western desert to try to stem Rommel's advance. Thus, the half-completed transfer of forces to Greece was now suspended and the forces already landed doomed to defeat.

Ironically, Menzies now received from Fadden a fresh military appreciation by Blamey of the situation in Greece. Fadden pronounced himself more confident of the outcome as a result of Blamey's analysis. But he also raised the question of the air strength allotted for Greece which, he informed Menzies, seriously disturbed the Australian Cabinet. Menzies had earlier given Fadden ample assurances regarding the air strength in Greece and Fadden now flung in his face the fact that Blamey had reported the air strength to be less than half that claimed by the British Government and backed by Menzies.[13]

With this discrepancy in mind, Menzies' colleagues in Canberra emphasised as strongly as they could that the greatest possible effort had to be made to provide immediately the air strength envisaged when they first approved the Greek expedition. They also passed on Blamey's urgent plans for the army in Greece to be reinforced "to the limit of the capacity of Greece to contain and lines of communication from Egypt to Greece to maintain them".[14] This cable was redundant even before it was sent. The German attack in Libya made major reinforcement impossible and sealed the fate of the forces in Greece. Furthermore, Menzies was no longer in London to receive Fadden's appeals. He had left for Ireland to pursue his quest for an Anglo–Irish rapprochement.

Menzies and Stanley Bruce, Australian High Commissioner to Britain
1933–45
(AUSTRALIAN WAR MEMORIAL)

It was an unfortunate time for Menzies to be absent from London. With the latest string of cables from Australia, there was certainly enough to be done there without concerning himself with the vexed question of Irish neutrality. However, he had set himself on a course to Dublin from the time of his arrival in London.

On his way to Dublin, Menzies addressed Belfast's Reform Club, giving a view that he was often to repeat. He told his audience that the war would "leave its mark on their descendants for generations". But, Menzies asked, "What does it matter if we are bankrupt, as long as we are free?".[15] It was hardly a position calculated to encourage and inspire.

In Dublin, Menzies conferred with the Irish Prime Minister, De Valera, and his Ministers but there was little he could achieve. He had gone without any message or support from Churchill and could only make proposals on a personal basis. Despite a late-night session with ample quantities of Irish whiskey, he was unable to move the Irish

Government from its understandable position of being unwilling to join in the war against Germany. Nevertheless, Menzies decided to put his political observations into a memorandum for Churchill.[16] Ireland was an issue on which Churchill was vulnerable to criticism since his unbending attitude appeared to be leading Britain towards hostilities with a member of its own Empire. Menzies' attempts at peace-making could therefore serve to embarrass Churchill as well as help his image among Irish-Australians.

On his arrival back in London, Menzies was given notice by the High Commissioner, Bruce, that his political survival in Australia depended on wringing substantial concessions from Churchill. On 7 April, Bruce submitted a draft letter to Menzies, urging him, apparently, to present it to Churchill. The letter was a blunt ultimatum setting out conditions for Australia's continued participation in Britain's war effort.

Bruce held out the prospect of the Menzies government falling and Australia's overseas forces being recalled when the Australian people realised their country had been put at risk by the Imperial military commitment. Australia, he wrote, could no longer rely on British naval protection and, if Japan attacked, ''a position it is not pleasant to contemplate would face us''. If Australia was to continue to allow her forces to serve overseas, two conditions must be met. Menzies had to be ''satisfied as to the adequacy of the Air reinforcements it is proposed to send to the Far East'' and had to be given ''reasonable assurances as to obtaining the planes required for the re-equipping and expansion of the Royal Australian Air Force''.[17]

There is no indication that Menzies accepted the tenor of this letter or that he even submitted it to Churchill. He was loath to press Britain too hard on the supply of aircraft since he felt her need was the greater. He was also loath to admit that Imperial defence arrangements were designed to draw off the strength of the Empire for the protection of Britain while leaving the outlying Dominions covered by copious paper treaties and little else. Ultimately, he did make demands on Churchill but it was to establish his own position in London rather than to ensure Australia's security from invasion by Japan.

On 6 April, following his trip to Dublin, Menzies travelled to Beaverbrook's country house at Leatherhead in Surrey. In his diary, Menzies described Beaverbrook as ''clear headed and forceful'' and noted his ''love of scandal and direct language''.[18] Their relationship was obviously now much closer though Menzies did not record details of their discussion. Fortunately, another of Beaverbrook's guests kept a

more complete record of events and noted how Beaverbrook ''came in
with Menzies. . . A big, powerful man who has plenty of self-confidence
and common sense. . . ''. Menzies freely criticised Churchill's handling
of Ireland and attacked the Conservative Party for being out of touch
with the people. On the looming defeats in Greece and Libya, Menzies
expressed concern about the effect on his political position in Australia.
There was also much debunking by Beaverbrook and Menzies of
Churchill's vision of a Balkan front now that it was obviously a
chimera. Moreover, this observer confided to his diary that Menzies
seemed very much under the influence of Beaverbrook.[19]

The criticism of the war's direction by Menzies and Beaverbrook
is even more significant when it is realised that the full scope of the
Libyan disaster was as yet unknown and the debacles in Greece and
Crete were yet to occur. As the full panorama of disaster unfolded,
their criticisms became more trenchant and a firm alliance of convenience developed between the two men in opposition to Churchill.

On 6 April, as Menzies enjoyed the convivial company of Beaverbrook, Hitler launched operation ''Retribution'' against Yugoslavia
while the German Air Force struck a decisive blow against the Greek
port of Piraeus, effectively isolating the British forces in Greece from
further large-scale assistance. The grand plan for a Balkan front was
now in tatters and Greece, 1941, was looking very much like Norway,
1940. Just as Norway had extinguished Chamberlain's power, so now
Greece seemed to presage Churchill's end.

Menzies' initial reaction to the German attack on Yugoslavia was
one of optimism—or rather, that was the stance he took publicly. He
predicted that Yugoslavia would mount a strong and effective resistance which would provide Britain with a Balkan front. He further
suggested that, with Turkey's co-operation, ''such resistance can be
built up across the whole of the Balkans as will provide a serious
military embarrassment to Germany''.[20] As we have seen his private
view was a good deal less confident.

At the War Cabinet on 7 April, the Permanent Secretary at the
Foreign Office, Cadogan, noted that the meeting was very gloomy and
that Menzies was ''evidently worried and rather critical''.[21] Menzies
informed the meeting of a cable from his Australian colleagues expressing anxiety about the situation and recalling that he had assured
them of military advice that discounted the chances of a German attack
in Libya. Menzies now stated the obvious conclusion—that the attack
in Libya would prevent any further reinforcement of Greece—to which
Churchill agreed.[22] The shock to Menzies must have been considerable.

The columns of Australian troops he had so recently reviewed in the Middle East were now marching blindly over a military precipice.

Menzies was aware that his political future in Australia was severely threatened. Even if he did not retain a long-term ambition to keep his Australian post, it was necessary in the short-term as a springboard into British politics. After the War Cabinet meeting, he noted grimly:

> *Things have gone wrong in Libya. Wavell's estimates of possible attack from Tripoli grossly falsified, and we are in danger of. . . retreat and grave loss. Wish my people in Australia would hang to central idea of helping Greece, and would not assume that I am not raising obvious points about equipment etc.*[23]

Menzies may have been raising obvious points but if so he had not been pressing them very far. In fact, for nearly half the previous three weeks, he had been absent from London and unable adequately to represent Australian interests in regard to the Greek force. As events worsened in Greece and Libya, Menzies did push much harder, but it was now too late and he was faced with implacable opposition from Churchill.

While Menzies was writing grimly of the British defeats, Churchill was steeling Wavell to blunt the German thrust in Libya. British forces, including the Australian 9th Division, were retreating towards Tobruk and Churchill cabled Wavell that the town should be "held to the death without thought of retirement".[24] Menzies had visited Tobruk during his tour of the Middle East and had seen the ease with which it had been captured by British forces despite its extensive fortifications. It was therefore with considerable foreboding that Menzies learnt of Churchill's latest instruction and he readily foresaw a massive defeat for the Australian troops and consequent embarrassment for himself.

With Britain seemingly set for disaster in Greece and Libya, the movement for a compromise peace gathered strength. After a meeting of 23 British Members of Parliament on 2 April, Lloyd George's military adviser, Liddell Hart, was approached by their spokesman, the Labour member R. R. Stokes. He requested that Liddell Hart address a larger meeting of MPs on the "war situation and strategy connected therewith", with the intention of creating a "really well-supported alternative to the 'bitter-end' policy so many of the present Government are pursuing".[25]

Though 23 members was not a mass movement, there had been 63 invited to the 2 April meeting. The members who did not attend were presumably known to be sympathetic to a compromise peace but un-willing to commit themselves publicly. The prospect that would soon face Britain—of being thrown ignominiously from the whole Mediter-ranean—would cause the pace of protest to quicken. Defeat, or at least a ruinous stalemate, appeared to stare Britain in the face.

Liddell Hart's political mentor, Lloyd George, was also preparing to move out of the political wilderness in the belief that his time was coming. Frances Stevenson informed Liddell Hart that "Lloyd George had a great time in the House last week...and his success has given him renewed confidence and he seems to be ever so much better".[26] The coalescing of the anti-Churchill forces had begun and Menzies and Lloyd George would soon be at their head.

On 8 April, the British War Cabinet met in an even more gloomy atmosphere. The news from the Balkans was bad, and in Libya, two British generals had been captured by the Germans. Menzies' criti-cisms of British war leadership, so far largely latent, now made them-selves manifest. He complained at length in his diary that British generals were "behind the times" and that he was

> *horrified to hear Churchill saying,* à propos *of Tobruk to which we are retreating and where we hope to make a stand,* "If stout hearted men with rifles and machine guns cannot hold these people until the guns come up, I must revise my ideas of war." *Well, he should revise them quickly.*[27]

Menzies was also apparently letting his criticisms be known to a wider audience. Lord Cadbury reported to the Minister for Economic Welfare, Hugh Dalton, that there were "great complaints by the Australians that their troops have been put in a bad place".[28] Menzies' depression was now deep and he wrote portentously that the "clouds were dark and there is a lurid patch in the sky—I hope not sunset".[29] The future of the Empire seemed to hang in the balance and it was Churchill who had put it at such grave risk.

The following day, Churchill went to the House of Commons to move a motion of congratulations for the armed forces on their recent victories. These victories had now either evaporated or been over-shadowed by the alarming situation in Greece and Libya. As Hugh Dalton anxiously noted, Churchill would "have a job to-day when he moves a motion, now a bit time-soiled, of congratulations to our Forces for recent victories...".[30] Though Churchill could announce a further British victory in distant Eritrea, he also had to acknowledge another setback in Greece where German troops had now taken control of the strategically important northern city of Salonika. One member noted that this news brought a "silent wince of pain throughout the House".[31]

One of those wincing was Menzies, who had gone to the Commons to hear Churchill expound on Libya, Greece, and the Battle of the Atlantic. The reaction of the House allowed Menzies to assess the political temperature at Westminster. Interestingly, he thought Churchill's speech was poor and that the British Premier was "earth bound and hesitating and failed to electrify the House".[32] The conditions were approaching when political change would appear imperative. Already, Dalton was predicting that conditions were ripe for a political upset.[33]

Later that day, Menzies met with Beaverbrook and had what he considered as a "good talk regarding aircraft production". Menzies later wrote that Beaverbrook was "active, concise and knowledgeable, hates red tape, and grows on me". They both agreed on the urgent need for the mechanisation of the army and complained that Britain's generals had "let us down—the Germans are too clever for them".[34]

Menzies and Beaverbrook were now in virtual alliance, each motivated by a conviction that the war was being mishandled. Each had a lifelong attachment to the Empire and was concerned that it was now in peril. Beaverbrook was an inveterate power-broker and Menzies could well be the "coming man" or, at least, part of the motive force that would bring political change. This explained Beaverbrook's ready attachment to Menzies.

Menzies' attachment to Beaverbrook can be similarly explained. Menzies saw him as the one man of power who could stand up to Churchill. If the direction of the war was to be changed, it was likely that Beaverbrook would have to throw his weight behind the change for it to be successful. Beaverbrook's personality no doubt also played a part in confirming Menzies as a firm admirer. A. J. P. Taylor later wrote that Beaverbrook "well knew how to steal the hearts of men" and that he had "a gift for making you feel when you were with him that you were the most important person in the world".[35] Menzies was just the sort to be susceptible to the kind of blandishments Beaverbrook was adept in delivering. In the fateful weeks ahead, their interests and their impulses would be as one.

Menzies was now set on a path that would take him even further from Churchill. Not only was Churchill blocking his attempts to secure the defence of Britain's Far East Empire, but his military moves had placed the entire Empire in peril. As the military situation in the Mediterranean deteriorated, the political implications would steadily press Menzies into an alliance of convenience with those seeking Churchill's fall.

NOTES

1. MENZIES DIARY, 1 April 1941
2. *IMPERIAL REVIEW*, April 1941
3. *HERALD*, Melbourne, 1 April 1941
4. *AGE*, Melbourne, 2 April 1941
5. *AGE*, Melbourne, 4 April 1941
6. CABLE M.37, Menzies to Fadden, 1 April 1941, AA CP 290/9, Bundle 1(13) SC: AA
7. MINUTE, Beaverbrook to Churchill, 1 April 1941, BBK D/416, Beaverbrook Papers: HLRO
8. LETTER (copy), Sinclair to Churchill, 2 April 1941, with note by Beaverbrook, BBK D/32, Beaverbrook Papers: HLRO
9. MINUTE, Beaverbrook to Churchill, 5 April 1941, BBK D/416, Beaverbrook Papers: HLRO
10. CABLE M.40, Menzies to Fadden, 2 April 1941, AA CP 290/9, Bundle 1(13) SC: AA
11. *DAFP*, iv, Doc. 377, Cable No. 185, Fadden to Menzies, 2 April 1941
12. CABLE NO. 195, Page to Menzies, 3 April 1941, AA CP 290/9, Bundle 1(1): AA
13. *DAFP*, iv, Doc. 382, Cable No. 197, Fadden to Menzies, 3 April 1941
14. *IBID.*
15. *AGE*, Melbourne, 5 April 1941
16. MENZIES DIARY, 3–5 April 1941
17. LETTER, apparently drafted by Bruce for submission by Menzies to Churchill, 7 April 1941, CRS M103, "1941": AA
18. MENZIES DIARY, 6 April 1941
19. LOCKHART DIARY, 6 April 1941, K. Young (ed.), pp. 94–5
20. *AGE*, Melbourne, 7 April 1941
21. CADOGAN DIARY, 7 April 1941, D. Dilks (ed.), p. 370
22. WAR CABINET CONCLUSIONS/CONFIDENTIAL ANNEX, 7 April 1941, Cab. 65/22, W.M.36(41): PRO
23. MENZIES DIARY, 7 April 1941
24. CABLE T.54, Churchill to Wavell, 8 April 1941, M. Gilbert, p. 1055
25. LETTER, Stokes to Liddell Hart, 7 April 1941, 1/450, Liddell Hart Papers: KC
26. LETTER, Frances Stevenson to Liddell Hart, 8 April 1941, 1/450, Liddell Hart Papers: KC
27. MENZIES DIARY, 8 April 1941
28. DALTON DIARY, 8 April 1941, Dalton Papers: LSE
29. MENZIES DIARY, 8 April 1941
30. DALTON DIARY, 9 April 1941, Dalton Papers: LSE
31. NICOLSON DIARY, 9 April 1941, Sir H. Nicolson (ed.), p. 161

32. MENZIES DIARY, 9 April 1941
33. DALTON DIARY, 9 April 1941, Dalton Papers: LSE
34. MENZIES DIARY, 9 April 1941
35. A. J. P. TAYLOR, *A Personal History*, London, 1983, p. 221

8

The Battle Lines
Are Drawn

*T*he gloom pervading London continued through the second week of April 1941. Thousands of British troops were captured in Libya; German forces steadily overcame resistance in the Balkans; the war at sea worsened with the loss of much merchant shipping to U-boat attack; German bomber raids on Coventry inflicted serious damage to aircraft factories. While Menzies was concerned with the turn of events, his intention was still to leave London on 18 April for the journey home. He now concentrated, for a time, on completing outstanding matters and bringing his extended visit to a close.

One matter outstanding was the question of the British reaction if Japan entered the war. The Far Eastern fleet that had been so often promised in such an eventuality was no longer feasible without a virtual evacuation of the Middle East. Churchill had previously promised that Britain would not allow her interests in the Mediterranean to impede the dispatch of a fleet to the Far East. However, it was now plain that the Far East would not be allowed to outweigh the Middle East. In the worst eventuality, Britain's possessions and dominions in the Far East would be relinquished in the hope of later recovery. Nothing could be allowed to impede the fight against the main enemy —Germany.

Menzies had acknowledged that Britain's commitments around the Mediterranean would detract from any Far Eastern fleet. He made no attempt to dispute that, but rather requested that Churchill give him some definite undertaking regarding British reinforcement of the Far East to replace the traditional undertaking about a fleet. Menzies particularly wanted to be able to tell his Australian colleagues that Britain would boost the air forces in the Far East. Included in any increase should be Hurricane fighters.

On 9 April, the British Chiefs of Staff submitted to the Defence Committee (Operations) their draft reply to Menzies' request. There was little of political sustenance for Menzies. They rejected any use of Hurricanes in the Far East, as they could only be provided at the expense of the Middle East. Instead, they claimed that the Brewster Buffalo would be "eminently satisfactory and would probably prove more than a match for any Japanese aircraft".[1] Putting aside the point that it later proved hopelessly inferior to the Japanese Zero, the Buffalo could not match the public recognition factor of the Battle of Britain Hurricane. They would therefore be of little solace to Menzies.

As for the question of a Far East fleet, Menzies acknowledged that it could not be provided immediately in response to a Japanese attack, given Britain's commitments in the Mediterranean. However, he did seek an undertaking from Churchill to dispatch eventually a fleet according to some definite timetable, albeit an extended one. In their reply, the Chiefs of Staff refused to consider withdrawing from the Mediterranean or to give any definite undertaking on the transfer of a fleet to the Far East. All they would be committed to was the dispatch of a battle cruiser and a carrier to the Indian Ocean and their ability to do more would be judged entirely on the situation at the time.[2] Since Menzies had already promised his Australian colleagues to return with a definite naval commitment from Britain, the reply of the Chiefs of Staff held out the prospect of considerable political embarrassment.

When the Defence Committee (Operations) met to approve the reply to Menzies, it was clear that he would get little joy from the British Ministers. Despite Menzies' proclaimed success in London, the British Government was not very concerned to ease his political difficulties. Partly, of course, Britain's military setbacks increased the pressure to concentrate their forces in the northern hemisphere. Churchill was particularly prominent in playing down the risks in the Far East and adamantly proclaimed that it would be foolish to further reinforce Malaya and that the completion of its defences must be subordinated to more pressing needs elsewhere.[3]

Not only did Churchill not approve Menzies' request for Hurricanes, but he also supported the Chiefs of Staff in their refusal to set down a timetable for the naval reinforcement of the Far East. He termed such a timetable the "height of folly" and urged that they merely repeat to Menzies the general promise already given. This now outdated promise was for Britain to abandon everything in order to resist a major attack on Australia. But, as Churchill indicated, Britain's "great interests" in the Middle East prevented any premature rush to Australia's side in the case of "a few raids by Japanese cruisers".[4] In the event, British help was not forthcoming even when the Japanese threat was overwhelming. There had been an implicit re-ordering of British priorities that had set the Middle East above Britain's Empire in the Far East.

The Dominions Secretary, Lord Cranborne, tried to explain the basis of Menzies' problem. The Australian Prime Minister, Cranborne claimed, needed a specific assurance on naval reinforcements in order to satisfy the Labor Opposition which was "composed of men who were entirely isolationist in their view and thought of nothing but the protection of Australia". If this explanation was intended to elicit sympathy for Menzies' political plight, it failed miserably. The Labour Party Leader, Clem Attlee, argued that it would be "wrong to give Mr. Menzies a worthless promise with which to delude his people" and that it was up to Menzies to educate them. Churchill agreed, maintaining that it would be "wrong to give up sound strategical ideas in order to satisfy the ignorance of the Australian Opposition".[5]

Menzies' failure to gain significant concessions from the British War Cabinet was further demonstrated when the Defence Committee moved on to discuss Menzies' request for aircraft for Australia. The Secretary of State for Air, Sir Archibald Sinclair, informed the Committee that he proposed offering 12 Beaufighters for delivery in December 1941. If pressed, he might increase this to 20 aircraft. However, Sinclair assured his colleagues, Australia would only get her Beaufighters after 22 Home squadrons had first been supplied and when production of the planes would be running at 150 per month. He also proposed delivery by mid-1942 of 243 Brewster Bermudas, a "type of aircraft in which the Royal Air Force was not particularly interested . . .", as well as 94 Hudsons by December 1941. The Hudsons were, in fact, aircraft that Australia had on order from the United States but had allowed Britain to take over in mid-1940. Despite the poverty of Sinclair's proposal, there was still considerable discussion before it was approved and only after Churchill had enjoined him "not to promise more than was absolutely necessary".[6] So there was little to comfort Menzies when the Defence Committee finally approved the report by the Chiefs of Staff. Menzies, though, was not destined to learn of the failure of all his efforts until just prior to his departure from London.

Following the Defence Committee meeting, Sinclair and Beaverbrook met with Menzies on the morning of 10 April. The proposed deliveries of aircraft that Menzies accepted at this meeting were even less than those Sinclair had indicated to the Defence Committee. Menzies tended to fall in with the minimum British suggestions whenever possible and failed to press hard on Australia's behalf. As he later argued to Fadden, Britain was "sincerely desirous of helping us to the greatest extent possible" and "cannot be pressed unduly, particularly in view of the pressure I have recently been exercising for the provision of adequate air strength in the Middle East and on which they are taking almost heroic steps".[7]

Menzies' ready acceptance of the arguments of Beaverbrook and Sinclair was done in the face of advice and pressure from his own advisers, Bruce and Shedden. It was left to Bruce to indicate to the meeting that it would be a "little difficult to convince the Government and people of Australia that the whole of the requirements of the United Kingdom must be satisfied before any of the Australian aircraft were released". Though he admitted that Britain was in the battle zone, Bruce argued that "Australia might find herself there at any moment."[8]

In his diary, Menzies noted that Shedden had also argued that the risks in Australia were as great as those in Britain. But Menzies wrote, "I do not agree."[9] Perhaps it was the new-found alliance of interest between Beaverbrook and Menzies that caused the latter to mute his calls for ensuring Australia's security. Then again, the safety of Britain as the Imperial heart always loomed large for the Australian Prime Minister.

Apart from aircraft for Australia, Menzies also informed Fadden that he had secured a categorical assurance that should war occur in the Far East there would be an immediate review of air resources to meet the dangers on all fronts.[10] This categorical assurance was the most that Menzies was able to extract from Britain. Yet, it went without saying that war in the Far East would cause a review of air resources. What had to be established was the order of priorities in such a situation. If the Far East remained the lowest priority, then such a review meant nothing to Australia's security. Menzies made no attempt to establish the priorities for the Far East in such an eventuality. His professed concern for the defence of the Far East following his visit to Singapore now seemed to have evaporated under the pressure of events in London.

As Menzies' hopes for his London visit continued to crumble, he made frantic attempts to patch up some semblance of success or at least to project a picture of fighting for Australia's interests. The Greek expedition was a particular worry to Menzies. After a visit to the War Office on 10 April, he dispatched a relatively reassuring cable to Fadden which tried to put the worsening situation in Greece into a good light. But he also informed Fadden that he now had no doubt that British military authorities had ''grossly underestimated the speed of German movement and the German power of organisation''. Moreover, he pronounced himself to be much disturbed by the general failure in London to realise the full implications of mechanisation and he promised that there would be ''some plain speaking in the War Cabinet on the whole matter during the next few hours''.[11]

That same day, Menzies' report on his visit to Eire came before the War Cabinet for discussion. Menzies proposed that the Dominions Secretary should now go to Dublin in an attempt to arrange a meeting between Churchill and De Valera. While Menzies met with a considerable measure of support, mainly from Beaverbrook, he was effectively vetoed by Churchill who argued that ''only the closer approach of the United States to the war would lift the Irish problem into a new setting.''[12]

Given the attitudes of himself and De Valera, Churchill's analysis was no doubt correct. Menzies, though, was furious at this brusque dismissal. He complained bitterly in his diary that Churchill had patronisingly described his Irish memorandum as very readable, but had then exhibited the ''blank wall of conservatism''. Menzies railed against Churchill being ''*not* a receptive or reasoning animal'' and predicted that the British Government would eventually have to fall in with his proposal.[13] So, on Ireland too, Menzies and Beaverbrook found themselves again aligned against Churchill. Menzies' concern with Churchill's leadership deepened.

With his Irish proposals thus rejected, Menzies was free to concentrate his attention on the fate of Australian troops in Greece and Libya. It seemed that in both places there could soon be massive defeats for the Australians. Eden and Dill had now returned to London and Menzies questioned them closely when they presented their reports to the War Cabinet on 11 April. At Tobruk, where Australian troops were surrounded by Rommel's tanks, Menzies raised the spectre of an ignominious surrender and questioned whether it was the ''right place to make a stand?''.[14] Dill assured Menzies that Tobruk could be defended and that Britain was concentrating her energies on forming armoured rather than infantry divisions.[15]

On another level, the appearance of Eden at the War Cabinet gave Menzies his first chance to assess the performance of the man often tipped as a possible successor to Churchill. While Menzies described Eden's account of his negotiations in the Middle East as being "coherent and indeed lucid", the Australian Prime Minister seemed more concerned to see how Eden would measure up as a future Prime Minister of Britain. Since Menzies now had the prospect of Downing Street firmly in his own mind, it was presumably with some relief when he confided to his diary that he did not judge Eden "as of sufficient tonnage to be P.M."".[16]

On 12 April, Menzies and Churchill tried to put the war behind them for a day when they travelled, albeit separately, to Bristol where Churchill was to confer another honorary degree on Menzies. However, Bristol had been the scene of a German bombing raid on the night of 11 April and it was amid smouldering ruins that the ceremony went ahead.[17] It was a very emotional time and Churchill rose to the occasion with a speech that Menzies judged as the best he had heard him make. Though Churchill received an enthusiastic reception from the people of Bristol, so too did Menzies. His prolonged stay and succession of speeches had now sufficiently impressed Menzies' presence on the people that he was able to note in his diary that "I am now recognised wherever I go, and autograph books are produced."[18] He soon had a chance to turn this popularity to good account as disillusionment with Churchill's leadership spread through the ranks of the British elite.

Lloyd George was now confidently predicting major political changes once the full scope of the unfolding disaster in Greece became apparent. He also took heart from the fact that the *Daily Mail* was now printing articles by Liddell Hart which were critical of the strategic direction of the British war effort. Lloyd George claimed that this revealed a "certain change in attitude of the press and therefore of their readers". [19] The Conservative MP Harold Nicolson also noted a shift in the public mood. The public, he wrote, are "bored by talks about the righteousness of our cause and our eventual triumph" and want "facts indicating how we are to beat the Germans".[20]

On Sunday, 13 April, following his visit to Bristol, Menzies went to Coppins where he met the Duke and Duchess of Kent, Nancy Astor and others. He noted that the Duchess was "sorely tried by the events in the Balkans", a feeling that Menzies no doubt shared. He then went on to Cliveden, Nancy Astor's residence, where Menzies talked with Lord Astor and the editor of his *Observer* newspaper, J. L. Garvin, on "mechanization and Ireland". He was considerably boosted by Garvin's praise for his Irish memorandum which Garvin described as "the most penetrating account of the Irish position he had ever read''.[21] Through their control of the *Observer* and the *Times*, Lord Astor and his brother John provided important pillars of support for Menzies.

Churchill, meanwhile, was frantically trying to reverse the trend of military disasters. He professed himself to be optimistic about the situation in Libya when he cabled to Roosevelt on 13 April.[22] However, his real view was more adequately portrayed at the Sunday morning meeting of the Defence Committee. He held out the prospect of Britain being driven out of Egypt and commanded that a supreme effort be made to avert such a disaster.[23] Churchill went on to draw up a directive to the British Commanders ordering them to virtually throw themselves upon the advancing Germans. His most spectacular suggestion was for the deliberate sinking of a British battleship and cruiser across the mouth of Tripoli harbour in order to interrupt the flow of essential supplies to Rommel's forces in Libya.[24] It was a mad plan in the grand Churchill manner and it was strenuously and successfully opposed by Admiral Cunningham. Instead, Cunningham steamed his fleet close past Tripoli, caught the defenders by surprise, and subjected them to a heavy bombardment with no damage to his own ships.

The desperate measures ordered by Churchill graphically illustrate his embattled position. He stressed to his Commanders that the urgency was extreme, that the Germans would grow even stronger in the air and that the German onslaught on Greece and Yugoslavia was likely to be successful.[25] He had not only given up the Balkan front as a lost cause, but could now foresee the possible loss of Egypt with its half-million British Empire troops and mountains of stores and equipment. This would be a disaster that Churchill could not hope to survive. No wonder that, when Menzies left Cliveden for dinner at Chequers, he found that they were ''all depressed by the news of what I called the 'botch' in Libya''.[26]

The result of Menzies' Sunday visit to the Astors is to be found in the *Times* on the Monday morning. It published an editorial on ''Leaders and Peoples'' which acknowledged Churchill's public success in Bristol but also took the opportunity of describing Menzies as ''another living and worthy embodiment of the convictions of a great people'' and proposing that his ''most valuable visit to this country should certainly be prolonged...''.[27] Most of the British press now supported Menzies in his efforts for greater dominion representation in London and particularly his own retention in the British capital.

It is not clear whether Menzies' visit to Cliveden prompted his determination to prolong his stay in London. But it is clear that, by the following day, he had cabled to Fadden with just such a suggestion. He claimed that Churchill had requested him to remain in London for a further fortnight in view of the military crisis in the Middle East. For his part, Menzies expressed ambivalence on the proposal because of the political position in Australia and he asked Fadden for his urgent advice.[28] Menzies' claim that Churchill wished him to prolong his visit is doubtful. It is more likely that he prompted Churchill to make such a request just as he had earlier prompted Fadden to ask him to go to Dublin.

Churchill certainly provided the reason, if not the request, for Menzies' prolonged stay. Menzies had now lost all confidence in his handling of the war and he was desperately afraid that Churchill's "do or die" methods would further imperil the safety of Australian forces. While Churchill now fought with renewed vigour from the corner into which he had backed the Imperial forces, Menzies was stricken with feelings of unremitting gloom regarding Britain's chances.

On 14 April, Churchill took heart when Tobruk's defenders repulsed the first German attack on the town and he cabled "Bravo Tobruk".[29] Menzies' diary, recorded from a very different angle, carries a sarcastic description of that day's War Cabinet meeting with Churchill speaking as

> the Master-Strategist—"Tobruk must be held as a bridge-head or sally port, from which to hit the enemy". "With what?" says I, and so the discussion goes on. Wavell and the Admiralty have failed us. The Cabinet is deplorable—dumb men most of whom disagree with Winston but none of whom dare to say so. This state of affairs is most dangerous. The Chiefs of Staff are without exception Yes-men, and a politician runs the Services. Winston is a dictator; he cannot be over ruled, and his colleagues fear him. The people have set him up as something little less than God, and his power is therefore terrific.

Menzies' mission was now clear—remove Churchill from his position of undisputed power. Notwithstanding the tentative nature of his cable to Fadden, Menzies wrote in his diary that night that he had definitely decided to remain in London for a further fortnight to oversee the situation in the Middle East which he was determined not to have solved by Churchill's "unilateral rhetoric".[30] Menzies was worried about a military disaster, but he would also have been aware that a sufficiently serious disaster could destroy Churchill. By staying on in London, he would be in a position to influence not only the military events but also these consequential political repercussions.

NOTES

1. DRAFT REPLY BY CHIEFS OF STAFF to Memorandum by the Prime Minister of Australia, 9 April 1941, PREM 3/156/4: PRO
2. *IBID.*
3. DEFENCE COMMITTEE (OPERATIONS) MINUTES, 9 April 1941, Cab. 69/2, D.O.(41)12: PRO. See also Minute D.124/1, Churchill to Ismay, 10 April 1941, PREM 3/156/6: PRO
4. *IBID.*
5. *IBID.*
6. *IBID.*
7. CABLE M.57, Menzies to Fadden, 10 April 1941, CRS A5954, Box 617, Paper No. 19: AA. See also AA CP 290/9, Bundle 1(13) SC which has a copy of this cable dated 11 April 1941
8. MINUTES OF MEETING at Ministry of Aircraft Production, 10 April 1941, CRS A5954, Box 617, Paper No. 19: AA
9. MENZIES DIARY, 10 April 1941
10. See fn. 7
11. CABLE M.52, Menzies to Fadden, 10 April 1941, CRS A5954, Box 628, "Discussion on Brief, Part 1(iv)—Supply": AA
12. WAR CABINET CONCLUSIONS, 10 April 1941, Cab. 65/18, W.M.38(41): PRO
13. MENZIES DIARY, 10 April 1941
14. WAR CABINET CONCLUSIONS/CONFIDENTIAL ANNEX, 11 April 1941, Cab. 65/22, W.M.39(41): PRO
15. MENZIES DIARY, 11 April 1941
16. *IBID.*
17. M. GILBERT, pp. 1058–9
18. MENZIES DIARY, 12 April 1941
19. LETTER, Stevenson to Liddell Hart, 12 April 1941, 1/450, Liddell Hart Papers: KC
20. NICOLSON DIARY, 13 April 1941, Sir H. Nicolson (ed.), p. 162
21. MENZIES DIARY, 13 April 1941
22. W. S. CHURCHILL, *The Second World War*, iii, p. 185
23. M. GILBERT, p. 1061
24. W. S. CHURCHILL, iii, pp. 186–8
25. *IBID.*, p. 188
26. MENZIES DIARY, 13 April 1941
27. *TIMES*, London, 14 April 1941
28. CABLE M.58, Menzies to Fadden, 14 April 1941, AA CP 290/9, Bundle 1(13) SC: AA
29. M. GILBERT, p. 1062
30. MENZIES DIARY, 14 April 1941

9

The Military Defeats Mount

*M*enzies' request to prolong his stay in London for the third time was dispatched to Fadden late in the evening of 14 April. It called for a reply by the following day. Within 24 hours Menzies had followed up his initial request with a further cable that reviewed the critical situation in Greece and Libya and reinforced his claim to remain in London. He now confided to Fadden that his decision to remain in London arose from the "fact that I appear to be the only Minister outside the Prime Minister who will question any of his views or insist upon points being examined..."[1]

Churchill also cabled to Fadden, presumably at Menzies' request, asking that Menzies' stay be prolonged to "cover the immediate crisis in the Balkans and Libya". Churchill's cable claimed that it was a "great advantage to have him with us in the War Cabinet and Defence Committee while your troops are so much to the fore". As for the battles, Churchill did not venture to predict the outcome in Greece although, in Libya, he was hopeful that they could stem the German tide.[2]

Fadden, of course, would have been loath to order his Prime Minister to come home and Churchill's request ensured that any possible resistance crumbled. Fadden therefore readily concurred and expressed his gratification at knowing that Menzies was of assistance to Churchill. Moreover, Fadden claimed that Australia was not downhearted by the latest defeats and realised that "the temporary reverses that may beset us are but the ups and downs of war."[3]

The Australian War Cabinet was, in fact, most downhearted and nervous about the military reverses, and there was even some bitterness arising from a feeling that Australian forces were bearing the brunt of the fighting. The Australians looked enviously at their Canadian cousins, ensconced in the relative safety of Britain, and urged Menzies to press for their dispatch to the Middle East. Failing that,

Menzies should press for other reinforcing troops to be sent from Britain which, under the circumstances, was over-protected.

This incessant importuning by his distant Australian colleagues increased in intensity as the military reverses proceeded on all fronts. It put Menzies under such pressure that he apparently told Dill on 16 April that he "would hardly dare go home, and that he might as well go for a trip to the North Pole".[4]

But if the military reverses seemed to threaten the end of Menzies' political career in Australia, they did likewise for Churchill's in Britain. In considering this, Menzies was again immensely encouraged by the reaction of the British press to the further postponing of his departure.

In its editorial comment, the *Times* effusively praised Menzies' contribution in London. Not only was his longer stay welcomed, but the *Times* also suggested a more permanent role for him. Though it recognised local political difficulties in the Dominions, the paper questioned whether they should be allowed to "outweigh the immense advantage of enlisting all the best leadership of the British Empire in the decisive direction of Imperial policy".[5]

The rest of the British press also generally welcomed the delaying of Menzies' departure.[6] The *Scotsman* suggested that an Imperial War Cabinet was a "probability of the fairly near future"[7], while Kemsley's *Daily Sketch* expressed the hope that Menzies' stay be prolonged indefinitely. In line with Menzies' own thoughts, it argued that the Empire was a "single entity, and we need, we must have, at the heart of it the best talent that any part of it can provide". The paper then confidently predicted that Menzies would take an "*increasingly im- portant part in the affairs of the whole Empire*" and maintained:

> *Often before in the history of our island we have been able to say that the hour has brought forth the man. Perhaps the Empire will have a chance of saying that, too.* There is every indication that Australia has sent us a man who will be of enormous value in the sustentation of the joint effort.[8]

This clearly conjured up a major political role for Menzies in London and set no limit to the task he could be called on to undertake.

As with the first extension of his trip, the Australian press was not so enthusiastic. It had already been calling for his early return but was now confronted with Churchill's request that he remain longer. Just hours before Fadden announced the delay in Menzies' departure, an *Age* editorial argued for his immediate return. It claimed that his absence was causing "comment which becomes more pointed as the period becomes more extended'' and it doubted whether he could "contribute as helpfully to the deliberations of the British Government as he should be able to contribute to the administration of his own country''.[9]

Following Fadden's announcement, Murdoch's Melbourne *Herald* argued that Australia must fall in with Churchill's request and acknowledged that it was fortunate that Menzies could remain in London still longer to "share with the British Government decisions upon which Australia's interests deeply depend". Still, the *Herald* emphasised that his leadership was missed in Australia and that there was "need for his early return so that the knowledge he has gained in England may be translated into a greater Australian war effort. . . ''.[10] There was little solace in this for any hopes Menzies harboured to prolong his stay indefinitely.

This was made even clearer when the *Times*'s suggestion of co-opting Menzies for the War Cabinet reached Australia. Though it was publicly supported by one of Menzies' colleagues, a leading Labor member argued that Bruce "should be sufficient liaison to convey the Australian point of view" and that Menzies' continued absence caused harmful delays in government decision-making and destroyed the "cohesion that the circumstances demand''.[11]

This argument was buttressed by Fadden who emphatically denied to the press that the Australian War Cabinet had discussed the possibility of Menzies staying in London for a further six months. Fadden said that only after Menzies' return to Australia would the questions of a resident Australian Minister in London and the formation of an Imperial War Cabinet be examined.[12] It was now clear that Menzies' colleagues would not readily accede to a protracted stay in London without his first returning to Australia, while the Labor Opposition had now given clear warning that it wanted the Australian Prime Minister to be a resident of Australia, not London.

Before Menzies received notice of these foreboding comments, he seems to have been considerably heartened by his decision to remain in London. On the night that he announced it to the British press, Menzies entertained some 50 leading military and political figures at a Dorchester dinner. Menzies noted that practically all the Cabinet, except Churchill, was present. Despite the bad news on the battle fronts, Menzies gave those present a "cheery party" at which he made a "wicked speech about the Chiefs of Staff; thank God the speech is by those present, understood to be funny''.[13]

With the war situation deteriorating, talk of a replacement for

Lloyd George and Churchill in discussion at a diplomatic reception,
April 1941

Churchill became more widespread and the search for a successor intensified. Lloyd George was one of those considered and Cecil King visited him on 16 April to obtain his views on the situation. While King observed that Lloyd George was an old man, he nevertheless considered his "grasp of the requirements of the situation far beyond anything I have met with among politicians".[14]

On the question of a compromise peace, Lloyd George told him that Britain had passed up good chances for this in the past and would now have to be in a stronger position before the talks could be initiated. In the interim, if Britain were defeated in both Libya and Greece, Lloyd George predicted serious political repercussions. Though he thought Churchill could hang on as Prime Minister, Lloyd George claimed that he would be forced to "accept the guidance of a Cabinet of five or so members without portfolio". Apart from himself, Lloyd George thought other members of such a Cabinet could include Beaverbrook, two Labour MPs, Sir Stafford Cripps and Herbert Morrison, and the President of the Board of Trade, Oliver Lyttelton.[15] This idea of a small War Cabinet, freed from departmental duties, was one much touted among those seeking to neutralise Churchill's power. It involved retaining him at the head but stripping him of real power by stacking the War Cabinet with his opponents. Menzies also agreed with this solution and would soon be pushing it hard.

On the same day that Cecil King was meeting with Lloyd George, it was suggested to Menzies that he should also meet the "Welsh Wizard". The suggestion came from the Australian businessman W. S. Robinson, who liked to mix a fair measure of politics with his business. His business was base metals and it was booming and he apparently sought to ensure this continued by cultivating leading politicians. Not only in Australia, but in the United States and Britain, Robinson was adept at making the proper political contacts. In Britain, he was apparently on good terms with two Cabinet Ministers, Oliver Lyttelton and Brendan Bracken, both of whom were close to Churchill. It is therefore not clear what lay behind his suggestion that Menzies should meet Lloyd George.

In his letter to Menzies, Robinson assured him that there was "joy everywhere as a result of your decision to extend your stay" and prayed that "your friends—and enemies—in Australia have an equal appreciation of the work you have done for the Empire as the people of this dear country". Then, almost as an afterthought, he suggested that Menzies should visit Lloyd George as "I know it would be much appreciated by him and would go well in Australia".[16] This suggested that Robinson might well have had a foot in both the Churchill and Lloyd George camps. Despite his contacts in the Churchill camp, Robinson seemed to have harboured hopes for peace and perhaps expected that, by bringing Menzies and Lloyd George together, these hopes could be promoted.

Certainly in 1939, Robinson's view of war with Germany had been far removed from Churchill's. Just three days before war was declared he had written from London with dire predictions of the coming conflict. He had then claimed that the war would bring such destruction that all civilisation would be "submerged in a flood of bolshevism. . . .". With this in mind, Robinson wrote, "I hope, pray and work for peace".[17] Across the top of the letter suggesting he visit Lloyd George, Menzies had written "No Action". Ten days later, though, he did meet Lloyd George. Robinson's letter is the only evidence to date of any prior suggestion of such a meeting.

Any contenders for Churchill's position needed a military defeat of sufficient magnitude to shock the nation and cast doubt on his fitness for leadership. In mid-April, there was not one, but two such defeats in prospect for Britain. On 17 April, Yugoslavia surrendered to German forces, leaving the British Expeditionary Force to fight on alone in Greece. As Churchill later wrote, a "grim prospect now gaped upon us all."[18] Already, on 16 April, he had ordered Admiral Cunningham to prepare plans for the evacuation of British forces.[19] In the meantime, they fell back to Thermopylae.

The question of evacuation from Greece now also occupied the attention of the Advisory War Council and the Australian War Cabinet, as did the question of who was to bear the political cost. Fadden assured the Advisory War Council that Menzies had always consulted his colleagues and that the commitment to Greece was a joint one and not a special responsibility of Menzies.[20] While there was argument over who was responsible for the disaster, there was general agreement that its scale should be limited as much as possible.

On 17 April, following meetings of both bodies, Fadden cabled Menzies with an expression of their joint concern at the possible loss of their forces in Greece "in a forlorn hope, while at the same time the security of Egypt and the Suez Canal is endangered by the division of our strength in the two theatres of war". He called for a "candid re-appreciation of the whole position in the Mediterranean" and urged Menzies to take immediate steps to allay their fears.[21] Fadden also dispatched a similar cable to the British Government.[22]

Events were already moving faster than the Australian Government could anticipate. Even before Fadden's cables were sent, the Greek Government had suggested that British forces be evacuated to save Greece from devastation by the Germans. In the event of such an evacuation, Churchill decided that the troops be evacuated to Crete which would remain as an offshore British bastion.

When Fadden was informed of these latest developments, he immediately cabled back that the evacuation of Australian troops from Greece was essential and that the Australian Government trusted that "plans for their evacuation which have been prepared in advance as requested by our earlier messages may be successfully implemented in regard to our men . . .". This pointed reminder about evacuation plans and the call for only the Australians to be evacuated was not to be well received by Churchill. Fadden compounded the offence by also requesting that Australian troops not be sent to Crete, but rather to the Middle East where they could be reassembled into a single Australian corps.[23]

Fadden informed Menzies of his cables to the Dominions Office and also of public concern in Australia. He asked that Menzies keep Canberra informed on the evacuation and for Menzies' view on the general situation in the Middle East.[24] Fadden's cable revealed a certain exasperation with Menzies' failure to keep his colleagues fully informed of developments. In fact, however, while Menzies was perhaps not sufficiently attuned to the anxiety being felt at home, he was himself hampered by a lack of knowledge of what was actually happening in Greece.

The Dominions Secretary, Lord Cranborne, sent Fadden's cables on to Churchill. Cranborne pointed to Fadden's concern that evacuation be commenced promptly and informed Churchill that Bruce had also made this point to him with great force that afternoon, on the ground that adequate air protection was no longer available for British and Dominion troops in Greece. Cranborne asked Churchill what sort of reply should be sent to the Australians.[25] Churchill was furious and replied angrily to Cranborne that there could be "no question of the Australians being separately withdrawn from the fighting line". Bruce, he wrote, was "not good when things are bad".[26]

Bruce was not the only one in London with the jitters. Oliver Harvey, a confidant of Anthony Eden and soon to be his Principal Private Secretary, noted in his diary that the press was viciously attacking Eden for the Greek and Libyan debacles. But, Harvey claimed, there was also "much criticism of Winston, I hear, in City circles for bad judgement—it is an attack which really cloaks defeatism among the rich and wet of course".[27]

The following day, Harvey again referred anxiously to the rising tide of criticism lapping at the feet of Churchill's government. Harvey blamed it on the "remnants of the Chamberlainites" who were using the military defeats as the "dishonest cloak for defeatism—at the end of that road lies L.G., who, abetted by that ass Liddell Hart would readily be a Petain to us, with the support of the press barons and city magnates".[28] To give impetus to the nervousness in London, the city was subjected to a savage German bombing attack during the night of 16 April. It was one of the heaviest raids of the war with nearly 500 planes wreaking destruction on the centre of London.

Caught in the centre of the raid was Menzies. Though he was relatively secure in his Dorchester suite, he described it as a terrible experience with a dozen large bombs falling close by the hotel. He later wrote that, after going upstairs to have a drink with two elderly ladies, he had

> *scarcely sat down when a great explosion and blast shattered the windows of the room, blew the curtains in, split the door, and filled the room with acrid fumes. Twice the whole building seemed to bounce with the force of the concussion. Twice I visited the ground floor, and found it full of white-faced people.*
> *. . . It is a horrible sound to hear the whistle of a descending stick of bombs, any one of them capable of destroying a couple of five-storey houses, and to wonder for a split second if it is going to land on your windows!*[29]

Before dawn, Menzies went with others of his party to survey the damage. Many of his familiar London landmarks were damaged or destroyed and he was considerably shaken by the extent of the devastation. In his diary, he graphically wrote of the "craters and fallen masonry in the streets, and the fear of an unexploded bomb lurking around every corner". In the midst of such massive destruction, he anxiously wondered: "How can it go on for years?"[30]

Menzies' reaction to the London bombing was markedly different from his earlier reaction to the bombing in Plymouth. Both the personal danger and the surrounding devastation were much greater but Menzies himself had again changed in his view of the war. Rather than responding to the bombing with thoughts of revenge, Menzies now sought the means to end all the fighting. His experience that night, coupled with the defeats occurring around the Mediterranean, finally confirmed his pessimistic view of Britain's chances of total victory and set him even more firmly against Churchill's war policies.

In the light of day, the devastation was more apparent and the full shock effect finally hit Menzies. He wrote of people being "drawn, black under the eyes, and shaken" and admitted that he was feeling "very 'off' myself". Two days later, Menzies was still reflecting on the bombing and its destruction. Moreover, he questioned Churchill's policy of bombing Berlin when Germany could retaliate so much more heavily. He asked himself whether London's nerves could "stand three consecutive nights of such widespread and obviously terroristic bombing as that of Wednesday night".[31] His own negative answer was implicit and contrasted sharply with the attitude of the ordinary Briton.

At this time his earlier misgivings about the Commander of British forces in Greece, General Wilson, resurfaced. Menzies compared the fate of the Australians under Wilson's command with those holding out in Tobruk under Australian generalship and concluded that he must "insist upon Australians getting proper commands, for I have more confidence in them than I have in Wavell and Co., whose gross miscalculations have brought us to this pass".[32] Menzies' new-found determination was no doubt partly prompted by Fadden's pressure in the same direction and the fact that if he could secure enhanced roles for the Australians, it would help to stem the rising tide of criticism in Australia.

Menzies' determination was also bolstered by Shedden who, in a memorandum on 17 April, strongly urged that Menzies use that day's War Cabinet meeting to place on record "some emphatic views" relating to the military planning that had produced the defeats in Greece and Libya. Shedden angrily noted that they had been entitled to expect a fair measure of success and had instead been "presented with a rank failure".[33]

Shedden, and presumably Menzies, seemed to have really believed that the Greek expedition had a reasonable chance and they now felt cheated. Shedden rejected the notion of taking grave military risks for political or ethical reasons, since this "only disperses our efforts and defers the attainment of the strength necessary for decisive military action". In order to prevent any further senseless frittering away of Australian forces, as well as to mollify Australian public opinion, Shedden urged that Blamey be given command of the Western Desert (in which two Australian divisions were involved) and that the Australian forces be concentrated into a homogeneous force under Australian command.[34]

On 19 April, Menzies had a long talk with Britain's top soldier, General Dill, during which he pressed Shedden's argument that Blamey should be given a Command in the Middle East instead of "some unknown Major General with a hyphen in his name". Menzies came away from the meeting hopeful of a success that would appease those he described as the "yellow-bellies in Australia—thank God a minority, but noisy, and with access to the press".[35]

In fact, the clamour from Australia was to worsen considerably as the Greek evacuation proceeded. The principal concern was that there be adequate air cover to protect the departing troops. However, on 18 April, Churchill instructed the Air Force Commander, Air Chief Marshal Longmore, that, in dividing his scarce aircraft between the various battles, "victory in Libya counts first, evacuation of troops from Greece second . . .".[36] Though this was no doubt strategically correct since Britain had more to lose in Libya than in Greece, it was nevertheless a betrayal of the Dominion troops in Greece whose lives were now at even greater risk.

When the Australian Government received from Blamey a dispatch describing the desperate situation facing his troops, Fadden urgently cabled his concern to Menzies. Fadden's tone was now definitely strident as he informed Menzies that extreme measures must be taken to avoid catastrophe. He instructed Menzies to ensure the utmost protection for Australian troops and that Menzies give it his "personal and almost exclusive attention to ensure that in whatever possible way help can be rendered it is most definitely forthcoming".[37] The Australian War Cabinet was virtually ordering its Prime Minister to take personal responsibility for ensuring a safe and immediate evacuation.

While Australia was pressing Menzies to urge an evacuation, Churchill was being enticed by the spectre of re-creating the Spartan stand at Thermopylae. He later recalled that, in his mind: "The intervening ages fell away. Why not one more undying feat of arms?"[38] The problem was that the "undying feat" would have to be performed by mainly Australian troops who would mostly be very dead at the end of it. Churchill recognised that Australia stood in the way of realising this dream and he resented it deeply. He also felt that the evacuation was still premature and even that the military situation could be reversed in Britain's favour.

On 20 April, as Fadden pressed for an evacuation, Churchill informed Eden that he was "most reluctant to see us quit, and if the troops were British only and the matter could be decided on military grounds alone, I would urge Wilson to fight if he thought it possible".[39] However, events were moving more quickly than even Churchill anticipated and the War Cabinet meeting on 21 April was forced to approve a recommendation from Wavell favouring immediate evacuation.

In reporting Wavell's recommendation to the War Cabinet, Churchill did not fail to note that it was based on an opinion provided by Blamey. Though Churchill said some kind words about the Anzacs, he was clearly disappointed at their failure to make a stand at Thermopylae. Now, when Menzies requested additional air support for the departing troops, Churchill gave him no comfort except to promise that they would concentrate on rescuing men rather than equipment. His former instructions remained, according Greece second priority to Libya in air support.[40]

As for public discussion of the disaster, Churchill sought to limit the political repercussions by opposing any statement in the House of Commons and proposing instead that he "give a broadcast when more material was available". Menzies was feeling similarly vulnerable and urged that the public must be made to recognise that it was "impossible for us to have deserted Greece".[41]

Following the War Cabinet meeting, Menzies dispatched a cable to Fadden in an effort to placate his Australian colleagues. He assured them that, while the position was most disturbing, Australia's attitude was well understood and everything would be done to provide additional air support in Greece so long as Egypt was not endangered as a result.[42] Menzies' assurance was a considerable over-statement of the facts and he had hardly made the all-out effort that Fadden had requested he make to secure the added air support. Though recognition of the importance of maintaining air strength over Tobruk would have been a consideration, his mind was also increasingly preoccupied with another concern—seeking out and assembling the means for his transfer to Westminster.

The British effort to hold Greece was now at an end. But the trials of the British Imperial forces so wantonly committed were far from over. In the waters around Greece, German dive-bombers savagely attacked those units of the evacuation fleet caught in coastal waters during daylight. British fighter cover was almost non-existent.

In Australia, Menzies would bear much of the political cost of this debacle. But in Britain it was Churchill's reputation that suffered. There, Menzies' reputation as an alternative fount of political and military wisdom was enhanced.

NOTES

1. *DAFP*, iv, Doc. 404, Cable M.59, Menzies to Fadden, 15 April 1941
2. CABLE NO. 260, Churchill to Fadden, 15 April 1941, AA CP 290/9, Bundle 1, Item(3): AA
3. CABLE NO. 229, Fadden to Churchill, 16 April 1941, AA CP 290/9, Bundle 1, Item(3): AA
4. J. KENNEDY, p. 97
5. *TIMES*, London, 16 April 1941
6. SEE *STAR*, *Daily Telegraph*, London, *Manchester Dispatch*, 17 April 1941
7. *SCOTSMAN*, 17 April 1941
8. *DAILY SKETCH*, London, 17 April 1941, italics in original
9. *AGE*, Melbourne, 16 April 1941
10. *HERALD*, Melbourne, 16 April 1941
11. *AGE*, Melbourne, 17 April 1941
12. *AGE*, Melbourne, 18 April 1941
13. MENZIES DIARY, 15 April 1941. The following day, though, he expressed "mixed feelings" on the extension of his visit and wrote that he was "desperately homesick". Menzies Diary, 16 April 1941
14. KING DIARY, 16 April 1941, C. King, pp. 120–2
15. *IBID.*
16. LETTER, Robinson to Menzies, 16 April 1941, CRS A5954, Box 630, "Aluminium": AA
17. LETTER, Robinson to Murdoch, 31 July 1939, MS 2823/27, Murdoch Papers: NLA
18. W. S. CHURCHILL, iii, p. 198
19. CABLE (EXTRACT), Churchill to Cunningham, 16 April 1941, PREM 3/206/3: PRO
20. ADVISORY WAR COUNCIL MINUTES, 17 April 1941, CRS A2682/2/268: AA
21. CABLE NO. 232, Fadden to Menzies, 17 April 1941, AA CP 290/9, Bundle 1(11) SC: AA
22. *DAFP*, iv, Doc. 407, Cable No. 235, Fadden to Cranborne, 17 April 1941
23. *DAFP*, iv, Doc. 410, Cable No. 237, Fadden to Cranborne, 18 April 1941
24. CABLE NO. 235, Fadden to Menzies, 18 April 1941, AA CP 290/9, Bundle 1(11) SC: AA
25. MINUTE, Cranborne to Churchill, 18 April 1941, and dictated to Chequers 10.45 p.m., PREM 3/2061: PRO
26. MINUTE M.453/1, Churchill to Cranborne, 19 April 1941, PREM 3/206/1: PRO
27. HARVEY DIARY, 17 April 1941, ADD.MS.56397, Harvey Papers: BL
28. *IBID.*, 18 April 1941
29. MENZIES DIARY, 16 April 1941
30. *IBID.*
31. MENZIES DIARY, 17, 18 April 1941
32. MENZIES DIARY, 18 April 1941
33. "A.I.F. OPERATIONS", Memorandum, Shedden to Menzies, 17 April 1941, CRS A5954, Box 587, "Middle East Position": AA
34. *IBID.*
35. MENZIES DIARY, 19 April 1941

36. CABLE, Churchill to Longmore, 18 April 1941, "The Prime Minister's Private Telegrams 1941", VI/I, Ismay Papers: KC
37. CABLE NO. 239, Fadden to Menzies, 20 April 1941, AA CP 290/9, Bundle 1(11) SC: AA
38. W. S. CHURCHILL, iii, p. 202
39. MINUTE, Churchill to Eden, 20 April 1941, PREM 3/206/3: PRO
40. WAR CABINET CONCLUSIONS/CONFIDENTIAL ANNEX, 21 April 1941, Cab. 65/22, W.M.42(41): PRO
41. *IBID.*
42. CABLE M.67, Menzies to Fadden, 21 April 1941, AA CP 290/9, Bundle 1(13) SC: AA

10

The Conspiracies Begin

On 21 April 1941, Churchill ordered the evacuation of the British Imperial forces in Greece. The weight of the German tanks had quickly crushed their defences and a bloody prospect awaited the retreating troops on the beaches and off the coast of Greece. German aircraft attacked virtually unopposed and played havoc with the evacuation. From London, Menzies looked on with horror at the result of his inaction. He desperately strove to minimise the political repercussions in Australia while at the same time maximising the dissatisfaction in London and firmly focussing it upon Churchill.

News of the disaster was received grimly in Australia. Information from General Blamey made clear to the Acting Prime Minister, Fadden, the handicaps under which Australian troops had operated. Shortages of equipment, lack of reinforcements and absence of air support had made the undertaking impossible from the start. It all added up to a political catastrophe for the governing United Australia Party and it was a situation largely the result of Menzies' original decision not to consult and involve the Labor Party in making the commitment of Australian forces to Greece.

On 21 April 1941, Fadden approached Menzies with a plan to circumvent this anticipated political danger. He warned Menzies that it was "not unlikely that happenings in Greece will cause much criticism and dissension when Parliament meets...." He urgently advised Menzies to establish a form of National Government by vesting the Advisory War Council with supreme executive authority in relation to all war matters, confiding that certain Labor MPs had indicated their readiness to participate on such a body. Fadden's discussions were probably with the ambitious Evatt who was keen at any price to occupy a Government seat and perhaps saw himself leading a compromise Cabinet. The oft-repeated opposition from most Labor members to any form of National Government seems to have been overlooked by

Fadden in his haste to neutralise the criticism which he feared would follow when full information of the campaign in Greece and its heavy casualties became known.[1]

Even within the Government ranks, there was increasing disquiet about the military situation and Menzies' leadership. On the day of the dispatch of Fadden's cable to Menzies, the Army Minister, Percy Spender, submitted a lengthy memorandum to Fadden on the poor state of Australia's defences. He informed Fadden that the Australian Army was still "in no condition to face an enemy powerful enough to reach these shores in any substantial force".[2]

Spender raised the possibility of the Germans taking Egypt and the Suez Canal and bottling up the British fleet within the Mediterranean. He anxiously advised that Australia risked losing the greater part of her forces and equipment now in the Middle East and that Japan would be likely to use this to her advantage in the Pacific. To lessen the consequential risks to Australia, Spender urged that the country be progressively moved onto a total war footing.[3]

So there was now an increasing realisation that the Greek expedition was a severe setback for Australia with possibly disastrous long-term implications. Australia began to view its own security with alarm and at last to take the war seriously. This was to affect further Menzies' relations with Churchill.

Menzies reacted with only qualified approval to Fadden's plan for a unified war effort. He could not condone vesting the Advisory War Council with executive powers over the war effort. Instead, Menzies reiterated his previous support for a National Government, which would bring the Labor Party directly into the War Cabinet. He informed Fadden that he would make a statement to try and still the disquiet and pointedly reminded him that, while the battle was raging, a "public debate on such matters as the extent of our supplies or our forces can do nothing but harm". Menzies further implored, "For God's sake let us extricate ourselves from our present difficulties before we start having debates about how we got into them".[4] However, debates once begun were difficult to stop and the clumsy extrication from Greece only served to intensify them.

Menzies was trying to limit these debates with his offer of a National Government. Apart from his cable to Fadden, Menzies also dispatched a message to Curtin informing the Labor leader of his continued support for a government of national unity.[5] During the previous year, Menzies had used the idea to embarrass the Labor Party and to boost his own public support. Now, however, he latched onto a National

Government as a way out of his difficulties in Australia and as a convenient avenue to a political future in Britain. Basically, it was essential that Menzies retained his Prime Ministership long enough to make the switch from Canberra to Westminster. It was only as a Dominion Prime Minister, for example, that he could secure a permanent seat in the British War Cabinet.

Not only did the Australian reaction to Greece affect Menzies' position in Canberra, but it also had consequences in Britain. After making a press statement on 22 April to "steady the malcontents" in Australia, Menzies was contacted by Churchill who reported that he was "disturbed at the way in which reported statements in Australia are adversely affecting Australia's reputation".[6] Menzies now decided to broadcast direct to Australia to try and "stop the rot". Interestingly, Menzies noted in his diary that his broadcast was widely reported in Britain and that it would do good there, if not in Australia.[7]

On 22 April, the day Menzies met the press to justify the Australian commitment to Greece, the press throughout the world suddenly began to report seriously moves for greater Dominion representation in the War Cabinet. A news story in the *Washington Star* claimed that Menzies' visit had convinced many influential MPs that closer collaboration with the Dominions was necessary and that "much would be gained from the actual presence in London of dominion ministers." It also claimed that neither Dominion visitors to London nor the British people themselves were "deeply impressed with the ability or calibre of the British war cabinet, outside the central figure of Mr. Churchill".[8] This report carried the unmistakable stamp of Menzies and represents the first stage of his campaign to dislodge Churchill.

In London, the *Daily Telegraph* carried a report that similarly seemed to emanate from the Menzies camp. It noted that Menzies had made no definite plans to leave London and could well prolong his stay past the extra period already envisaged. A decision on his departure, the paper claimed, would depend on the outcome of the battles raging round the Mediterranean. It also suggested that Menzies might delay his departure in order to meet with the New Zealand Prime Minister, Fraser, who was to arrive in London in the near future. However, the possibility of such a meeting developing into a full Imperial Conference was judged by the paper as unlikely given the expressed opposition of Canada's Prime Minister, Mackenzie King, who did not want to leave his divided society and feared the reaction of Canada's French minority to greater Imperial integration.[9]

The Australian press representatives in London, with whom Menzies was in close touch, also reported the possibility of his extending his stay still further. The Melbourne *Age* quoted authoritative sources, claiming that he was playing a crucial role in vital war decisions.[10] This image of an indispensable Menzies at the helm in London was clearly calculated to prepare the Australian public for the indefinite absence of their Prime Minister.

The Sydney *Sun* went still further and set out clearly the means by which Menzies hoped to find a permanent place in London. The report stated that Menzies' appeal for a National Government was designed to facilitate his own prolonged stay in London as a member of an Imperial War Cabinet. The report claimed that such a Cabinet would probably "emerge from the efforts now being made to convene an Imperial Conference in London". In order to circumvent the expected criticism from those Dominions whose Premiers did not want to sit on such a body, it was suggested that the Imperial Conference could nominate representatives other than the Premiers. The Imperial War Cabinet would then be vested with executive powers and act on behalf of the entire Empire. Though Churchill would be at the head of this body, his power over policy would presumably be heavily circumscribed by any Cabinet of Menzies' making.[11]

This was Menzies' basic strategy—first to isolate Churchill and then replace him completely. Under the guise of improving communications and according the Dominions fair representation, an Imperial Conference would bring overwhelming pressure to bear on Churchill to establish a small War Cabinet in which Churchill's supporters would be replaced by those of Menzies. They would include Beaverbrook and Lloyd George. This would allow Churchill's policy of total victory to be moderated and a formula found to usher in a compromise peace.

Beaverbrook was even then beginning to distance himself from Churchill. If Churchill fell, as Beaverbrook clearly expected he would, his erstwhile supporter did not want to be caught in the wreckage. Beaverbrook had often used the threat of resignation to force concessions from Churchill but now he was adamant that he would no longer serve as Minister for Aircraft Production. Claiming health reasons, he refused a request from Sir Charles Wilson (later Lord Moran), Churchill's doctor, that he stay on. In a comment revealing the state of his relations with Churchill, Beaverbrook complained that he could not remain usefully in the War Cabinet since Churchill "does not ask my advice, nor does he need it".[12] In the event, Beaverbrook was persuaded to remain, but only as Minister of State with rather nebulous responsibilities.

While Beaverbrook was bringing his tenure of the Aircraft Production Ministry to an end, Menzies was still trying to obtain co-operation in increasing aircraft production in Australia. The exigencies of war now meant that Australia's survival might well hang on the production of her own fighters and bombers. On 14 April, Shedden had advised Menzies that Australia's defence policy must move towards that long proposed by the Labor Party. He urged that, in the likely absence of a British fleet, Australia's emphasis should be on local defence by aircraft and "all possible efforts and resources should be directed to producing as much as we are able to do, as quickly as we can". [13] The urgency of Shedden's suggestion was clear but there was little that Menzies could do without the express approval of Churchill. This he had been unable to obtain. Still, Menzies went ahead with his discussions with British and Australian industrialists.

On 21 April, Menzies had dined at Claridges with Rootes, Australian aircraft industrialist John Storey and W. S. Robinson and they discussed aircraft manufacture in Australia. After two months in London, Menzies was little further along in his attempts to get British approval for the project, but he was at pains to conceal this, at least from Robinson. Robinson apparently left the dinner under the impression that Menzies' proposal had already received the enthusiastic approval of the British Government. In such circumstances, he gave it his own full support and offered to return home to assist in its implementation.[14] It was only later, in response to searching questions from Robinson, that Storey admitted the tenuous state of the proposal. He nevertheless assured Robinson that Menzies could count on the full support of Beaverbrook and that the plan would be quickly endorsed by the British War Cabinet.[15] In fact, this was far from the case—Beaverbrook was strong on vague promises but most reluctant to give any definite undertaking that would have as its result the export of capital equipment, and thus a reduction in Britain's own aircraft production capacity.

On 21 April, Menzies also dined with Churchill, Eden and Attlee at Downing Street, where he revealed his lack of faith in the British Chiefs of Staff, and by implication, in Churchill himself. Menzies bluntly informed Churchill that the latter needed Chiefs of Staff who would tell him when he was talking nonsense. At this, Churchill exploded. But Menzies found that Churchill nevertheless shared his view of his military chiefs and described them in "terms I [Menzies] could not have equalled!".[16] Still, he had moved Churchill not a whit towards replacing the Chiefs or changing his dictatorial style of leadership. The battle lines were now clearly drawn between the two Premiers.

It was that night, after a meeting of the War Cabinet, that British forces in Greece were ordered to evacuate. Churchill, with Menzies' concurrence, ordered that Australia not be informed of the evacuation until it was either over or well under way.[17] This order made Menzies' position more difficult with his Australian colleagues, who were pressing him for news. But Menzies was neither prepared to oppose Churchill's very strong views on the subject nor to perhaps threaten the safety of the operation by cabling the news to Australia.

On 23 April, Menzies worriedly wrote that the situation in Greece was going from "bad to worse"[18] and he made his "steadying" broadcast to Australia. Apart from vigorously defending the decision to send forces to Greece, he also announced Blamey's elevation to the post of Deputy-Commander-in-Chief under Wavell.[19] This was hardly the position urged for him by Shedden and Blamey found it rather invidious. However, its value for Menzies lay in its possible capacity to appease critical opinion back home.

Menzies received a further indication of the state of Australian opinion on 23 April. Fadden cabled the results of a discussion held by the Advisory War Council, and endorsed by the War Cabinet, in which his colleagues finally came to terms with the fact that Australia could no longer count on either a British or American fleet saving them from Japanese attack. They now urged that plans be prepared to meet the possibility of Britain being forced out of the Mediterranean with the loss of much of its fleet, and its consequent inability to provide a fleet to meet a Far East emergency.[20]

With these contingencies in mind, Menzies was asked for a "candid and outspoken appreciation" which would provide a realistic outlook and an "accurate statement of the assistance that we could definitely rely on rather than hope for in the circumstances outlined".[21] Menzies too could foresee the possibility of an evacuation from Egypt and the loss of the Mediterranean Fleet. Churchill, however, was adamantly opposed to planning for any such eventuality.

While Churchill could set his face against an Egyptian evacuation, his military commanders, on the other hand, had to take cognisance of such a possibility. Wavell did draw up plans to cover what he called the "Worst Possible Case", setting out his response to the loss of Egypt and the evacuation of British forces. On 24 April, he informed General Kennedy in the War Office of his plans; Churchill remained unaware of their existence.[22] Later, Menzies and Churchill clashed bitterly over the need for such precautions.

While Menzies was being urged to plan for an Egyptian evacuation, there was a very real evacuation proceeding from Greece. This, too, produced divisions between Churchill and Menzies as each sought to determine the disposition of British air strength between Libya and Greece.

At the War Cabinet meeting on 24 April, Menzies raised the question of air support in Greece. To his diary, Menzies later confided that he was "afraid of a disaster, and understand less than ever why Dill and Wavell advised that the Greek adventure had *military merits*".[23] Churchill responded by admitting that his instructions to Cairo were to give priority to Libya but that he would now ask his Air Force Commander in the Middle East, Air Marshal Longmore, to "spare all the aircraft he could for Greece during the immediately critical days".[24] This assurance seemed to have satisfied Menzies, though in reality, it did not necessarily mean that the air cover would be provided. The priorities remained unchanged and Longmore was free to retain most of his aircraft for the battle in Libya. This is what in fact occurred.

When Menzies came to report his meagre efforts to Fadden, he omitted to mention that Libya still remained the first priority for the air force. Instead, he trumpeted that Churchill had been forced to order the maximum possible air support for the evacuation from Greece.[25] The situation did in fact pose a genuine dilemma. Australian troops were caught in dangerous positions in two separate theatres, with air support inadaquate to support both. If Menzies pressed too hard to protect the evacuation from Greece he stood the risk of imperilling just as many Australian troops in the embattled town of Tobruk. It was this desperate state of affairs to which his ready concurrence to the Greek adventure had contributed.

He showed a similar readiness to fall in with British thinking on the question of Australian exports. Despite tremendous pressure from Australia, Menzies refused to claim from Britain a greater allocation of shipping for Australia's primary products. Instead, he accepted a 50 per cent cut in the value of exports for the following year, though with an additional amount to be held in storage in Australia.[26] It was, of course, in Menzies' nature to accept British imperatives as his own, but his attention, anyway, was increasingly being diverted towards the overthrow of Churchill and away from his brief as Australian Prime Minister.

At this time, political observers in London began to sense that the political atmosphere was growing more tense, that the House of Commons was restive and that the popularity of the Government was declining. Though Churchill's position still seemed secure, Eden was being increasingly tipped to be dumped as Foreign Secretary.[27] It was in this atmosphere that Bruce found Menzies strangely unperturbed at the problems that beset him as Australian Prime Minister.

In a brief private discussion on 24 April, the Australian High Commissioner was surprised to find Menzies confident of his political position in Australia and seemingly unworried by the possibility of being ousted in favour of a National Government under a Labor Prime Minister. In fact, Bruce revealed that Menzies stayed silent for much of their meeting and allowed him to do the talking. Bruce interpreted this silence as confidence.[28] It is more likely that Menzies' silence was caused by the hypnotic prospect of ultimate Imperial power that increasingly beckoned from Downing Street. His position in Australia had become the means to an end, rather than the end itself.

Bruce intended to give Menzies the benefit of his advice as a former Australian Prime Minister on how best to secure his political position. As Australian High Commissioner, he had obviously paid a lot of attention to the stream of increasingly querulous cables emanating from Australia and he now strongly advised Menzies that it was imperative for him to be able to give his colleagues and Labor opponents a "full picture of what was in Winston's mind, both with regard to immediate problems and the eventual winning of the war".[29]

At this Menzies seems to have really opened up, claiming that Churchill had given no real thought to how the war could be won and was entirely preoccupied with the Battle of the Atlantic and the situation in the Mediterranean. Moreover, Menzies could see no way of forcing Churchill to face up to the question of how eventual victory was to be won. He argued that Churchill was a "bad man to have any real discussion with" and cited Beaverbrook as alleging that Churchill had an "unrivalled power of avoiding discussion of anything he did not want to deal with specifically".[30]

The view was now quite clearly entrenched in Menzies' mind that the British Premier had no conception of how to produce the total victory to which he was so committed and was blindly launching the British Empire into battle after battle in an exhausting fight to the finish. But when Bruce urgently counselled that Menzies confront

Churchill and risk a "first class row if he could not get what he wanted in any other way", Menzies' response, while he agreed to approach Churchill, led Bruce to believe he still had considerable private reservations.[31] This was no doubt true as Menzies' mind was now working at a tangent to the High Commissioner's.

The moves to retain Menzies in London were fast gathering pace. A Liberal National MP, Edgar Granville, announced that he would ask Churchill to form a supreme War Cabinet composed of Ministers without departmental duties, and including Dominion statesmen. The latter part of Granville's suggestion immediately received the enthusiastic support of the *Daily Mail* which, on 25 April, argued that the desirability of Menzies' retention in London was beyond dispute. The paper noted his political difficulties in Australia which threatened his future and maintained that it was therefore important to "secure now the retention of his great abilities in a position of responsibility at the head of Imperial affairs here".[32] The campaign for his retention was now very much in the open and Menzies could clearly count on most of London's press in his support.

It was fitting that the *Daily Mail* should make its call on 25 April —Anzac Day—when Australia remembered her dead of the First World War. Menzies spent the day in London laying wreaths at the Cenotaph and speaking at an Anzac Day luncheon. While Menzies was lunching at Overseas House, Shedden was lunching with Hugh Dalton at the Dorchester. Dalton noted that Shedden was "anxious to draw me (1) on how the Labour Party came to enter a National Government in this country, and (2) on how we feel about the PM's interferences in strategy". Shedden was presumably acting as an envoy for Menzies, who was anxious to achieve political stability in Australia so as to allow his prompt return to London, and as well to ascertain the strength of Labour support for Churchill in the face of the recent military disasters. Like Bruce, Dalton suggested that Menzies should resign and serve under Curtin, but found that Shedden was not much taken by the idea.[33]

It seems that Shedden was now, if not before, fully involved in Menzies' plans to return to London and rescue the Empire. He shared Menzies' reservations about Churchill's leadership and had obviously received from his old mentor, Lord Hankey, much criticism regarding Churchill's approach to the war. Later, in his diary, Shedden assessed the comparative qualities of Menzies, Churchill and Roosevelt. Shedden claimed that Menzies received greater popular acclaim in Britain than Churchill and argued that there was no-one in the British

Empire who "approaches him as the successor to Churchill". Though Shedden admitted it was a radical idea, he nevertheless asked himself "why should not a Dominion statesman lead the Empire in war?"[34]

This frank admission, from within his own camp, of Menzies' ultimate ambition, reveals the Trojan horse nature of his calls for Australian representation in the War Cabinet. Such representation was the means to a grander end. Once within Churchill's Cabinet citadel, Menzies could launch a direct attack on the position of the British Premier. Shedden's vision of Menzies as leader of the Empire obviously suggests that he was privy to Menzies' private thoughts and ambitions. In a number of other talks with leading Britons before he left London, Shedden continued playing the role of stalking horse for Menzies' political ambitions in Westminster, flushing out opposition to Churchill and building on the support for his own man.

On Saturday, 26 April, Menzies awoke to find that the *Times* had printed his Anzac Day speech verbatim on its cable page. He gleefully noted in his diary that it was "an honour hitherto reserved for Winston". His elation seems to have carried over into his Saturday morning press conference with Australian journalists. In this off-record briefing, one journalist privately recorded that Menzies had complained of the "shocking lack of guts and drive in War Cabinet", that all but Beaverbrook were "yes-men" and that Churchill needed a strong deputy who would be prepared to stand up to him.[35]

This carefully calculated attempt to fan the flames of dissension allowed the press a partial insight into Menzies' state of mind, but he held back from revealing his pessimism about the war and the appeal that a compromise peace held for him. His argument was still pitched at the level of improving the war leadership by providing Churchill with better ministers, and he played down the inevitable diminution of Churchill's power that such provision would almost inevitably entail. Menzies was particularly concerned to stack the War Cabinet with men who did not share Churchill's faith in total victory.

One such man was Lloyd George and Menzies now went from his press briefing to lunch with the elderly Welsh statesman at his country house in Surrey. Despite W. S. Robinson's suggestion that such a meeting would be good for his public relations in Australia, Menzies seems not to have mentioned it at the press briefing. Indeed it seemed to suit his purpose to keep the lunch on a semi-clandestine level. Lloyd George's views were well known and a meeting with Menzies would obviously raise questions in the minds of the journalists about Menzies' own commitment to pursue the war to the finish. It is cer-

tainly a revelation to discover that, a few hours after criticising the War
Cabinet for its general lack of guts and gung-ho, Menzies was lunching
with Lloyd George, the Welsh Pétain. It is an even greater revelation to
read Menzies' assessment of the aged leader.

The importance that Menzies attached to this crucial meeting was
indicated by the length of his diary entry which exceeds by far any
other, including those on Churchill. It is worth repeating in full.

> *Drive down to Churt to lunch with Lloyd George, who is as clear*
> *headed as ever, and has some shrewd things to say about Cabinet*
> *organisation, Winston's leadership, and the like. We found we had*
> *many ideas in common, much as follows—*
>
> 1. *Winston is acting as the master strategist, without*
>   *qualification and without really forceful Chiefs of Staff to*
>   *guide him.*
> 2. *Dill has ability, but is as timid as a hare.*
> 3. *There is no War Cabinet, since W. C. deals with conduct of*
>   *war himself, by "directives" etc, and his Ministers just*
>   *concur.*
> 4. *Beaverbrook might have some influence but he is up to the*
>   *neck in the detail of aircraft construction, and simply has no*
>   *time for general study and appreciation. No War Cabinet*
>   *Minister here should have anything to attend to except War*
>   *Cabinet.*
> 5. *War Cabinet should meet every morning. This week, this*
>   *crucial and anxious week it has met twice for an hour and*
>   *1½ hours respectively!*
> 6. *Winston should be at the helm, instead of touring the*
>   *bombed areas, as he has been doing most of the week. Let the*
>   *King and Queen do this. In any case they do it much better.*
> 7. *More food could be grown in this country, but there is*
>   *nobody finally responsible for comprehensive policy, which*
>   *must include food, agriculture, fisheries and so on. Many*
>   *ministers, many opinions. Same with* shipping. *M/Shipping*
>   *attends to the fag end—e.g. charter parties, Admiralty builds*
>   *and mends ships, Labour controls labour, Transport the*
>   *getting of goods off the wharves, Supply what can be carried*
>   *on the ships etc. etc. In brief, Churchill is a bad organiser.*
> 8. *A non-executive War Cabinet must contain a Dominions*
>   *man, for the Dominions type of mind is essential.*
> 9. *The problem of a couple of good men to prop up Churchill is*

acute. He is not interested in finance, economics, agriculture
and ignores the debates on all three. He loves war and spends
hours with the maps and charts, working out fresh
combinations. He has aggression without knowledge or at any
rate without any love for inconvenient knowledge. His
advisers are presumed to have knowledge, but haven't enough
aggression to convey it to Churchill.

10. *Foreign policy is deplorable—e.g. Japan. We never have ideas,*
    and we never beat Germany to it. Alex Cadogan is a dull dog,
    if not actually a dead dog.

11. *Eden has not [?trained] on, and John Anderson [Lord*
    President of the Council and Chairman of the Cabinet's
    Home Affairs Committee] is a bureaucrat par excellence—no
    imagination, or sweep, or fire.

L−G frankly does not see how we win the war, though he agrees
we will not lose it. But he points out that Germany has a couple
of million skilled workers now available in Italy, France and
Czecho Slovakia, who can, even if not trusted to make aircraft,
make other things such as M/T [?motor transport] and so relieve
the pressure on Germany. They must *work, if they are to live.*
Why, then, he says, should we think that USA and UK can
outbuild Hitler? And if we do, why does that end the matter?
Hitler has a vast superiority of bombers, both in numbers and
place, but though destruction here is terrific, he has not destroyed
us or deterred us! L−G. plainly thinks we are "wishfully
thinking". But L−G was equally indeterminate on the question
"If there is a stalemate and a negotiated peace, what next?"
He rates Hitler's ability very high, and comes back to the
melancholy truth that the Germans in their hearts like us much
more than the French ever did.[36]

Menzies later recalled his reaction to Lloyd George in terms that
clearly suggest that the talk was not the finish of their relationship.
Lloyd George's personal magnetism was so strong, Menzies wrote,
that ''if he said to me 'Menzies, I want you to abandon everything that
you are doing and follow me', I think I probably would''.[37] However,
Menzies was no blind apostle. Whatever the magnetism, it was Lloyd
George's view of Churchill and the war that was the real attraction for
him. Menzies could sense the possibilities of creating a cabal. Whether
the cabal was to be transformed into a Cabinet would now depend on
the fall of events.

NOTES

1. CABLE, Fadden to Menzies, 21 April 1941, CRS A5954, Box 630, "Advisory War Council—Increase of Personnel": AA
2. LETTER, Spender to Fadden, 21 April 1941, MS 4875, Box 1, Correspondence 1939–1949, Spender Papers: NLA
3. IBID.
4. CABLE, Menzies to Fadden, 22 April 1941, CRS A5954, Box 630, "Advisory War Council—Increase of Personnel": AA
5. CABLE M.72, Menzies to Curtin, 22 April 1941, CRS A5954, Box 630, "Advisory War Council—Increase of Personnel": AA
6. MENZIES DIARY, 22 April 1941
7. MENZIES DIARY, 23 April 1941
8. WASHINGTON STAR, 23 April 1941
9. DAILY TELEGRAPH, London, 23 April 1941
10. AGE, Melbourne, 23 April 1941
11. SUN, Sydney, 23 April 1941
12. LETTER, Beaverbrook to Wilson, 19 April 1941, BBK.D/141, Beaverbrook Papers: HLRO
13. MEMORANDUM, Shedden to Menzies, 14 April 1941, CRS A5954, Box 625, "Paper 7A": AA
14. "NOTES ON DISCUSSION ON MONDAY 21ST APRIL", by W. S. Robinson, undated draft, CRS A5954, Box 617, "Aircraft Production Policy": AA
15. LETTER, Storey to Robinson, 22 April 1941, CRS A5954, Box 617, "Aircraft Production Policy": AA
16. MENZIES DIARY, 21 April 1941
17. MINUTE, Cranborne to Churchill, 22 April 1941, PREM 3/206/1: PRO
18. MENZIES DIARY, 23 April 1941
19. DAILY EXPRESS, London, 24 April 1941
20. DAFP, iv, Doc. 424, Cable No. 252, Fadden to Menzies, 23 April 1941
21. IBID.
22. J. KENNEDY, p. 103
23. MENZIES DIARY, 24 April 1941
24. WAR CABINET CONCLUSIONS/CONFIDENTIAL ANNEX, 24 April 1941, Cab. 65/22, W.M.43(41): PRO
25. CABLE M.84, Menzies to Fadden, 26 April 1941, AA CP 290/9, Bundle 1, Folder 13: AA
26. DAFP, iv, Doc. 423, Cable No. 82, Menzies to Fadden, 22 April 1941
27. CHANNON DIARY, 24 April 1941, R. R. James, p. 301
28. NOTE OF CONVERSATION WITH MENZIES, 24 April 1941, CRS M103, "1941": AA
29. IBID.
30. IBID.
31. IBID.
32. DAILY MAIL, London, 25 April 1941
33. DALTON DIARY, 25 April 1941, Dalton Papers: LSE
34. "PRIME MINISTER'S VISIT ABROAD", note by Shedden, undated, CRS A5954, Box 15, "1941 Diary": AA

35. BEDNALL DIARY, 26 April 1941, in. C. Hazlehurst, *Menzies Observed*, Sydney, 1979, p. 216
36. MENZIES DIARY, 26 April 1941
37. SIR R. G. MENZIES, *Speech is of Time*, London, 1958, pp. 70–1. See also Sir R. G. Menzies, *The Measure of the Years*, London, 1970, p. 5

11

A Mission for Menzies

*B*y the end of April 1941, the evacuation of British forces from Greece was all but complete. Thousands of troops were left behind, either dead and destined for shallow graves in the rocky Greek soil or alive and headed for a long incarceration as prisoners of war. Even the evacuees were not provided with a rescue so much as a remission. Many were off-loaded on the Greek island of Crete where they would again have to face the full force of German military might and suffer another bitter defeat. During those final and bloody April days, Menzies was preparing for his departure from London but he had his heart and mind firmly set on an early return.

Churchill meanwhile was busy ensuring his political survival. Just as Menzies had taken heart from his own successful tour of the provinces, he too now set off on a tour of his own through the bombed cities of Liverpool and Manchester. Here he took the political temperature and was happy to find that he could continue to draw on the enthusiastic support of the ordinary men and women of Britain.

Churchill returned to Chequers where he broadcast to the nation on Sunday, 27 April. It was both an explanation and a justification of the British expedition to Greece. He informed the nation that he had been asked whether he was aware of "some uneasiness which it was said existed in the country on account of the gravity, as it was described, of the war situation". In order to satisfy his mind, Churchill told his audience that he had travelled to Britain's industrial heart, to "some of the places where the poorest people had got it worst" and had returned "not only reassured, but refreshed".[1] It was a pointed reminder to his detractors that he still retained the confidence of the ordinary Briton.

But to men like Menzies, Churchill's clear public support was becoming less of a consideration. The evacuation from Greece was now nearly complete and the Australian Prime Minister was finding it a terrible anxiety, though he held out "hopes of a decent percentage of evacuation".[2] The political backlash in Australia would largely depend on the extent of the losses. It would be the first major blow suffered by Australian forces and would be brought home to the Australian public by the appearance in their newspapers of the lists of dead, injured and missing. Menzies could well relate the length of these lists to the likely length of his continued tenure as Prime Minister. He had been responsible for sending Australian troops overseas in the first place, a move opposed by the Labor Party, and on their fate hung his.

On the day of Churchill's broadcast, Menzies was pleased to read what he called a wise article by the retired General Fuller in a Sunday newspaper.[3] Fuller was a well-known British military writer and advocate of mechanised warfare who had been passed over by the War Office because of his right-wing views. Menzies' admiration for Fuller's article was no doubt partly prompted by Fuller's own expressed admiration for Menzies. But he would also have approved of Fuller's other concerns. The general warned of the impossibility of Britain fighting Germany single-handed on land in Europe and emphasised the vital importance of retaining Egypt. It was, Fuller wrote, "better that we approach starvation (in Britain) than abandon that region".[4] With three divisions of Australian troops deployed there, Menzies could warmly endorse these views.

While Menzies was anxious for Egypt to be reinforced and retained for Britain, his now reflex pessimism encouraged a desire to see plans prepared for the eventuality of Egypt needing to be evacuated. By nature, Churchill was unwilling to admit that this might be a possibility and he had the advantage of knowing, from intercepted German communications, that Rommel was hard pressed to maintain the momentum of his attack in Libya. In his eyes, those who now concentrated their attention on preparing for the evacuation of Egypt were firmly in the camp of the defeatists.

On 27 April, following his broadcast to the British people, Churchill now learned for the first time that plans actually existed for the evacuation of Egypt. He was informed of this by the Director of Military Operations, General Kennedy, in the course of a dinner discussion at Chequers. The discussion quickly turned into a shouting match, Kennedy arguing that an evacuation of Egypt would not necessarily be a disaster for Britain. He later recalled that Churchill "fairly exploded" and accused him of "pure defeatism".[5]

The following day, Kennedy was told by his superior, General Dill, that he had "raised a terrific storm" which was exacerbated by

Menzies who "spoke in the Cabinet on the same lines as you did at Chequers".[6] It was increasingly apparent that Churchill was now facing his first determined opposition as Prime Minister. And his Dominion counterpart was in its vanguard.

At the War Cabinet meeting on 28 April, Churchill met his opponents head-on by turning the prospective parliamentary debate on Greece into a vote of confidence in his leadership.[7] Whatever the unease felt in the lobbies, there was still a shared belief that Churchill's leadership was necessary to inspire and unify the nation. Few would therefore be prepared to vote a lack of confidence in Churchill, and this meant that the critical edge of the debate would be blunted. Churchill would not only be likely to survive but his hold over policy would be maintained.

As for the Greek debacle, Churchill told his War Cabinet that it should congratulate itself on the numbers evacuated and suggested that the losses would be between 5000 and 10,000 men. The British campaign, he continued, had resulted in Yugoslavia becoming an open enemy of Germany and an improvement in the American attitude to the war. He further claimed that German losses almost certainly exceeded Britain's and that it had been a "glorious episode in the history of British arms".[8]

Churchill's attempt to picture Greece as a success failed to impress Menzies. In his account of the meeting, he noted sourly that Churchill's estimate of the losses in Greece was grossly over-optimistic and that, while he might be a great man, he was becoming "more addicted to wishful thinking every day".[9] Then followed bitter exchanges during which Menzies urged a greater flow of news from Britain. This was really an indirect attack on Churchill, who was largely responsible for keeping the tight hold that existed on the flow of war news. Menzies argued that this had badly affected public opinion in America and had caused the "dissatisfaction of Australian opinion...".[10] Despite his arguments, Menzies found little support in the War Cabinet. Only Beaverbrook and the Information Minister, Duff Cooper, were prepared to stand with Menzies against Churchill on this issue.[11]

He was not surprised at the lack of support he received. He had already judged most of the members of the War Cabinet as worthy of nothing other than replacement, and it was not to them that he looked for support. It was, rather, to men passed over for position by Churchill and now strongly critical of his policies. Among them was the aged Lord Trenchard, retired chief of the RAF, and a man touted by the press for possible inclusion in a refurbished War Cabinet.[12] Menzies met Trenchard over lunch on 28 April and found him very critical of Churchill's policies, especially the bombing of military targets in France, since "the bombs that miss kill Frenchmen, whereas the ones that miss in Germany kill Germans".[13] It is not clear how far Menzies went in his talk with Trenchard, but it further spread his contacts with the critics of Churchill.

Another such passed-over politician was Oliver Stanley, the former Secretary of State for War, who that day was also deep in discussion on the matter of Churchill's shortcomings. Stanley used a quiet corner of the Lansdowne Club to dine with Hugh Dalton, upon whom he launched an anti-Churchill diatribe. Dalton was unshaken in his support of Churchill and he was shocked to hear Stanley attack Churchill over the Greek expedition. Stanley claimed the defeat in Greece could cause Britain to be thrown out of the Middle East and the Mediterranean. He argued strongly for a public Parliamentary debate on Greece and threatened to criticise the whole affair in his own speech. He also reminded Dalton of Churchill's responsibility for the fiasco in Norway in 1940 and of the irony of his coming to power as a result of it.[14] The implication was that Churchill should not now escape unscathed from another fiasco of his own making.

While Stanley and Dalton were engaged in their private talk, Menzies was airing views similar to Stanley's in another part of London. He had taken over a room at the Savoy to dine with Australian press representatives and push his own case for preferment. One of the correspondents, Colin Bednall, wrote in his diary of this most remarkable dinner, with Menzies pressing his case onto a group of increasingly inebriated journalists. Bednall confided that Menzies repeated his condemnation of the British Government, stated that he had "decided to come back to London" and finally convinced the journalists to tell the "public of Australia that Menzies is wanted in London—as if it was their own idea".[15]

Another journalist at the dinner later reported to Bruce that the dinner was obviously organised to persuade the journalists to "cable to their respective papers urging the absolute necessity of his, Mr. Menzies, return to London and entering the War Cabinet". Bruce was surprised at Menzies' activities, but not at his intentions. He admitted that, from his own talks with Menzies, it was "so clearly exactly the programme that the Prime Minister has in mind".[16]

Menzies' attempt to pressure the journalists provoked antagonism from some. But, more importantly, it reached the ears of Churchill. A

confidential report on the dinner by one of the journalists was intercepted by the British censor and passed on to Downing Street.[17]
Churchill would now be in no doubt as to Menzies' designs. According
to one report noted by Shedden, "so deep were Churchill's suspicions
of Menzies' intentions, the censors had instructions to submit any of
Menzies' correspondence to him."[18] The accuracy of this allegation
and the extent to which British censors had access to Menzies' communications remains unclear, but Shedden certainly took the report
seriously. But then, he was privy to Menzies' views and activities and
the report would have accorded well with his view of events.

As well as dealing with the political intrigue surrounding him,
Churchill had also to try and stabilise the deteriorating military situ-
ation around the Mediterranean. On 28 April, Churchill learned that
Crete was soon to be faced with a German attack. Contrary to an
Australian request, much of the British force in Greece (including
Australian troops) had been evacuated to this ill-defended island.
Churchill enjoined them to stoutly resist the expected attacks, though
he admitted to his War Cabinet that their chances of success were not
great.[19]

On the same day, Churchill issued a directive calling for a "do or
die" effort to defend Egypt. He pointedly informed his military commanders that he expected that British forces would not "wish to
survive so vast and shameful a defeat as would be entailed by our
expulsion from Egypt...". Churchill further ordered that all plans for
the evacuation of Egypt should be rescinded and advised that no
surrenders would be "considered tolerable unless at least 50 per cent.
casualties are sustained...".[20] He had the advantage, by now, of
knowing of Rommel's supply problems in Libya and coolly calculated
that a stout British defence could well produce reverses for the daring
German general. Menzies was not so well informed and Churchill's
directive can only have added to his gloom with its prospects of another
costly defeat.

This directive of Churchill's also ordered that there be no further
reinforcement of Malaya and Singapore "beyond those modest
arrangements which are in progress...".[21] So, the repercussions of the
Middle East situation meant further trouble for Menzies, undermining
his efforts to boost Far East defences against Japan. Churchill had
ensured that Menzies would have little to show his Australian colleagues in justification of his long absence. Menzies was already preparing them for the bad news. On 27 April, he informed Fadden that
the Chiefs of Staff could not immediately provide the candid military

appreciation requested by Australia and that he had been further advised that it would be impossible to obtain a statement of specific dispositions to cover the event of a Japanese attack.[22]

Given the likely absence of British air and naval reinforcements to the Far East, Menzies made some attempt to extend an independent peace feeler in the direction of Japan. As a follow-up to his controversial "Peace in the Pacific" speech, Menzies had talks with prominent Britons sympathetic to Japan and anxious to produce a lasting settlement. Among them was Lord Sempill who had, in 1940, enlisted Bruce's support in his efforts at appeasement.[23] Sempill had lunched with Menzies on 31 March and they apparently dined together at a later date.[24] On 23 April, Sempill advised Menzies that Lord Hankey had been consulted and given his backing to Menzies' plan to meet privately and quietly with the Japanese Ambassador. Sempill offered to set up such a meeting for Menzies, arguing that it would "fill out the very useful remarks that you made touching these matters which were so seriously misconstrued by a minority in Australia".[25]

It seemed that Menzies dallied with the idea of making a Munich-type mission to Tokyo to force the pace of British diplomacy and hopefully produce a Pacific settlement that would remove the risk of war with Japan.[26] As it happened, the memory of Chamberlain's fate, and the pressure of events, caused him to abandon the project. On 30 April, he was forced to inform Sempill that his "hope of seeing the Japanese Ambassador has vanished into thin air".[27]

On 28 April, Menzies cabled Fadden informing him of his forthcoming departure for America and asking whether he had any objection to him now leaving London. He also enquired whether Curtin had reacted to his invitation to join a National Government.[28] Fadden immediately agreed to Menzies' leaving London and assured him that the furore over Greece was fast dying out. However, he also informed Menzies that the chance of a National Government was hopeless, since Curtin was opposed to any change in the political position.[29]

While the political changes necessary for Menzies to secure his position in Australia still seemed out of reach, the pressure for changes in London had increased. The military situation around the eastern Mediterranean, together with Menzies' impending departure, gave rise to more moves to change the British War Cabinet. As far away as America, reports were circulating of Menzies' great political stature in London[30] and of the support he could count on as Prime Minister of Britain.[31] In London itself, the *Star* reported that the "trend of thought in political circles'' was tending to favour an Imperial War Cabinet. On 30 April the paper eulogised Menzies' ''unqualified success'' in London and suggested he be retained.[32] The *Manchester Guardian*'s political correspondent suggested the inclusion of Lloyd George and Menzies, among others, in the War Cabinet,[33] while a columnist in the *Daily Herald* expressed regret at Menzies' departure and supported his inclusion in the War Cabinet as the representative of the Dominions.[34] Churchill, however, firmly resisted this pressure and refused to consider forming a smaller War Cabinet with Menzies among its members.

On Tuesday, 29 April, Menzies completed his second year as Australian Prime Minister. Apart from a note in his diary, there is nothing to indicate that he felt moved to mark the event in any way. Even if he had been so inclined, there was little time for celebration. He spent part of the day preparing his London speeches for publication.[35] Their publication was a further indication to Menzies of the impact he had made in Britain and their appearance in the bookshops would carry this impact further.

Menzies was further occupied by a cable from Fadden, who had misinterpreted a routine Dominions Office communication to indicate that there was increasing support in Britain for a compromise peace. Fadden asked Menzies whether the reference to ''increasing temptation to conclude peace with Germany actually represents state of mind of any section of British Government''.[36] Fadden's cable had actually been sent six days earlier, but had been delayed by an oversight in Sydney. Bearing in mind Menzies' activities at that time and his links with Lloyd George and Beaverbrook, Fadden's question may well have taken him aback. Certainly Menzies was a little too vehement in his reply, claiming that there was ''*no* section of the United Kingdom Government which has in mind possibility of concluding peace with Germany''.[37] Even if Menzies' denial was only referring to the War Cabinet, it was false and he well knew it from his contact with Beaverbrook. However, it was crucial that the reality be concealed from his Australian colleagues who were generally stalwart in their support for total victory.[38]

If Menzies was startled by Fadden's cable, he could take some heart from a talk that Shedden had with General Ismay, Churchill's right-hand man. Ismay was an ardent admirer of Churchill but even he was forced to admit that neither his Ministers nor the Chiefs of Staff had the wherewithal to stand up to Churchill and that Churchill's disappearance would leave the nation leaderless.[39] This was further confirmation for Menzies that his attack was well directed. His aim was to use the dissatisfaction with Churchill's dictatorial methods to ensure his own elevation to the War Cabinet. Once in place, Churchill could be removed at the appropriate time leaving the predicted vacuum that Menzies confidently expected to fill.

During the afternoon of 29 April, Menzies managed to attend one of the meetings of the vital Defence Committee (Operations). Here he raised the latest Australian request for a new, candid appreciation of the military situation in the Middle East in the event of certain contingencies occurring. The Chiefs of Staff were unwilling to consider such hypothetical situations. As this would put Menzies in an invidious position on his return to Australia, he argued strongly that it should be possible to "frame the general lines which our strategy would follow if such a situation arose". Churchill strenuously discounted any threat from Japan and resisted the formulation of plans for the Middle East "which might tend to distract the minds of those conducting the battle to a consideration of their line of retreat...". Instead, Churchill suggested that Menzies merely meet once more with the Chiefs of Staff during which "the method of meeting various contingencies could be touched upon...".[40]

Although Menzies apparently fell in with Churchill's suggestion, his diary indicates that he was far from satisfied. He wrote bitterly that he had gone to the Defence Committee to discuss

"what next" if Egypt falls. The answer is a lemon i.e. Winston says "Let us keep our minds on victory*". I argue a great deal, and nobody else says anything.*[41]

That evening Menzies and Shedden dined with General Dill at his flat in Westminster Gardens. Though Menzies had been highly critical of the failure by Dill and the other Chiefs of Staff to stand up to Churchill, Dill was apparently not the "mere cipher" that Menzies alleged. In fact, Dill had his own serious misgivings about Churchill and his conduct of the war, misgivings that were similar to those of Menzies.[42] Against the backdrop of the mounting disaster in the Middle East, Menzies' anxiety must have reached new heights with the knowledge that Britain's senior soldier shared his concern about Churchill. There was now overwhelming pressure on Menzies to seek to directly curb Churchill's power in the effort to inch the Empire back from the brink of defeat.

On 30 April, just three days before Menzies' departure, Beaverbrook chose finally to resign from the Ministry of Aircraft Production, ostensibly on the basis of ill-health.[43] It is more likely that he could sense impending political changes. He was also apparently convinced that a tremendous German attack on Britain was imminent.[44] He agreed to remain in the War Cabinet with the vague title of Minister of State, thus managing to distance himself from Churchill while retaining a springboard from which he could later launch an attack on his leadership.

Shedden had another lunch that day with the embittered Hankey, who again delivered his litany of complaints regarding Churchill. He told Shedden that Churchill had excluded the Chamberlainites from effective power, criticised Churchill for being jealous of the knowledge of others and argued that the War Cabinet did not work as well as Lloyd George's during the First World War. As for Greece, Hankey maintained that Churchill should not have undertaken a commitment Britain could not fulfil.[45]

In Shedden, Hankey found an eager audience. The Australian informed Hankey of Menzies' gradual estrangement from Churchill during the period of his visit and told him that Menzies now admitted it was "dangerous to go to Chequers and spend an evening because Churchill was so persuasive". Hankey noted that Shedden had "seen through the humbug of the present regime and is absolutely shocked".[46] Both men were buttressed in their beliefs as a result of their talk. Shedden was more than ever convinced that Menzies should replace Churchill, while for his part, Hankey proceeded to approach his old colleagues from the Chamberlain government in an attempt to increase the number of voices demanding political changes.

While Shedden lunched with Hankey on 30 April, Menzies flew in the King's plane to Wales. There he visited Cardiff, which had been heavily bombed the previous night, and then went on to a rousing reception at Swansea, where he received the freedom of the city. This was a strange interlude at the end of his visit to Britain. At a time when the military campaigns in the Middle East were moving fast on all fronts and Menzies was still presumably involved in achieving the original objectives of his visit, it is curious that he felt able to absent himself from London and engage in another public relations exercise. Taking his campaign to Wales gave further emphasis to Menzies' new priority—to firmly establish a popular constituency in Britain that would be willing to accept him at its head.

In Menzies' absence, Churchill used a late night meeting of the Defence Committee to approve an American proposal that part of the US Pacific Fleet be moved to the Atlantic. Churchill regarded the

Americans' move as another hopeful sign of their increasing involvement in the war. It could also ease the problems of the Royal Navy in the Atlantic and Mediterranean. However, the repercussions in the Pacific and for Australia could be disastrous if Japan interpreted the move as providing *carte blanche* for her own expansion.[47]

The following morning, 1 May, Menzies discovered what had occurred in his absence. Apparently, Churchill had been strongly advised to inform the Australian as a matter of form. But the *fait accompli* was not so lightly taken by Menzies. He recognised the enormous potential for political embarrassment for himself contained in the proposal. It was extraordinary that such a major change of policy affecting Australia could be decided without any form of consultation with the Australian Prime Minister.

At noon, Menzies attended his final War Cabinet meeting where he "made a stink" about the Defence Committee decision of the previous evening.[48] As a result, the War Cabinet resolved itself into a meeting of the Defence Committee (Operations) and proceeded to discuss the question anew. In his diary, Menzies angrily recorded his view of the events:

> Great argument in War Cabinet. I protest against W.C. deciding
> what advice to offer USA regarding moving Pacific fleet (or a real
> section of it) to the Atlantic without reference to Australia,
> though I was in London![49]

In the Defence Committee discussion, Menzies presented strong arguments for consulting the Dominions "from the point of view of procedure...". After a stout defence of the decision from Churchill, Menzies expressed agreement with the argument that "whatever helped to bring the United States of America into the war would help to keep the Japanese out." Still, he pressed the point that the Dominions had to be consulted on such matters. He assured the meeting that if it was "put to them in the right way, they would probably agree; but they would feel very badly about it if they were presented with a *fait accompli*". Eden was alone in arguing against the move and argued the Foreign Office view that the US Pacific Fleet was the sole barrier to a Japanese advance southward.[50]

Menzies cabled to Fadden urging that Australia fall in with the American proposal, taking the position that the "entry of the United States of America into the war as a belligerent transcends in importance every other present issue...".[51] Australia's Minister in Washington, Richard Casey, taking a view similar to that of the

Foreign Office, argued that Australia support a much-reduced proposal that would leave most of the US fleet in the Pacific. The larger proposal, Casey warned, would "leave British countries and interests in the Pacific in considerable peril".[52] However, the Australian War Cabinet accepted the arguments of its Prime Minister who was presumed to be actively protecting the national interest at the helm of the Empire.[53] Little did they realise that from Menzies' vantage point, general interests of Empire, and tied up in them personal interests, loomed larger than the threat to his distant charge.

The sudden eruption of this new issue on the eve of Menzies' final departure from London obscured the War Cabinet's post mortem on the Greek expedition. Though the evacuation was now complete, there was much in the account of the campaign that could cause trouble for Menzies in Australia. The War Cabinet was informed that an estimated 43,000 troops out of 56,000 had got away, with 500 being subsequently lost at sea.[54] Despite the assurances that Churchill had given, the Chiefs of Staff now reported that the lack of fighter protection had caused the evacuation to be "carried out under constant bombing attack . . . ".[55]

Admiral Cunningham, whose ships suffered severely, was more direct in his criticism. Writing to a colleague on 1 May, he said:

> *We have now fallen on rather evil times. Having landed a large army in Greece we have just finished taking it off again under direful conditions. About 400 bombers attacking troops and ships all day and not a plane of our own to defend them.*[56]

Though Churchill felt able to congratulate Wavell on a "successful evacuation" on the basis that Britain had paid her "debt of honour with far less loss than I feared",[57] Menzies could not be so satisfied. The grisly details of the campaign had yet to percolate fully through to Australia.

The long War Cabinet/Defence Committee meeting on 1 May caused Menzies to be late for a lunchtime engagement with the Iron and Steel Institute. Apparently still angry from his argument with Churchill, Menzies opened his speech with an explanation of his late arrival. It was caused, he said, by "a thing called the War Cabinet, which in my experience observes the most irregular hours". This was a direct stab at Churchill and his penchant for wearying, late night meetings. It was a common complaint in London that these meetings were unnecessarily tiring for those in attendance (other than Churchill, who slept most afternoons) and that it allowed Churchill to browbeat proposals past his exhausted ministers. If the point was lost on any among his audience, Menzies gave it further emphasis by inviting those with complaints to "address them in writing to the Prime Minister of this country".[58]

Among the audience was Hankey, who had come straight from a secret talk with the military operations head, General Kennedy. Kennedy had implored Hankey to wrest the control of the war from Churchill's grasp before Britain was defeated and claimed that General Dill shared this view.

The pressure on Hankey to act against Churchill was increased tremendously by Menzies who approached him in the street after the luncheon and proceeded to "burst out at once about Churchill and his dictatorship and his War Cabinet of 'Yes-men'". He urged on Hankey the immediate calling of an Imperial War Cabinet with one Dominion Prime Minister remaining afterwards as a permanent, full member.[59] Over the next four months, Menzies would push this plan to its limit.

Hankey had had a succession of approaches from people who shared his concern about Churchill, and his reaction was to try to rally the old Chamberlainites to stand up to Churchill. On leaving Menzies, Hankey met with the Lord Chancellor, John Simon, at the House of Lords, where they discussed the whole problem. Simon advised Hankey to use Menzies to confront Churchill. He argued that Menzies had become a "great Imperial figure, has attended the War Cabinet and the Defence Committee for some weeks, has a big stake in the war, and is entitled to speak his mind . . .". Hankey took Simon's advice, telephoned Menzies and "begged him to urge Churchill to drop his dictatorial methods and to use his military and political advisers properly". Menzies assured Hankey that he was already determined to tackle Churchill and he promised to press the points that Hankey had raised.[60]

During the evening of 1 May, Menzies' last night in London, he met with Churchill for their final confrontation. In his diary, Menzies noted only that he had a "Long talk with Winston regarding the help he needs in Cabinet".[61] This bald statement, scribbled in the rush of departure, concealed the details of what was apparently a meeting marked by considerable acrimony.

Shedden provided more details of their confrontation when he reported to Hankey the following day that Menzies had "got no change out of Churchill" who had argued that his advisers were devoid of ideas and so he had to run things single-handed.[62] Much later, Churchill recalled that Menzies had accused him of being too autocratic to which he had retorted that he believed Menzies was "something of the same sort in Australia". Churchill saw through Menzies' argument and stoutly maintained that he was "prepared to be thrown out, but he was not prepared to have his powers as Prime Minister whittled away".[63]

Menzies' approach to Churchill was probably more a tactical matter of form than anything else. He could not really have expected that a talk in Downing Street would cause the British leader to change his ways and cede part of his power to others. By throwing Menzies' charges back in his face, Churchill gave Menzies unequivocal notice that he would not step aside without a struggle. This last meeting between the two Premiers served as a bitter farewell. That night, Churchill took a train to Plymouth where he was due to spend 2 May inspecting the bomb damage to the city and its Royal Naval Dockyard.

Before leaving London himself, Menzies received more stimulus for his campaign to return at an early date. In a farewell message to Shedden, General Kennedy supported Menzies' permanent retention in London, arguing that his "right place is at the central control".[64] Kennedy had been mightily impressed with Menzies and later recalled that the Australian Prime Minister had made "no secret of his downright opinions". He claimed that Menzies had expressed "what many of us felt in our hearts, that only Churchill's magnificent and courageous leadership compensated for his deplorable strategic sense". What Kennedy and his fellow officers wanted was a leader with "more balance and less brilliance" and their support for Menzies must have weighed heavy with the Australian Premier. Not only had Churchill lost Menzies' confidence but it must have seemed to Menzies that he no longer retained the confidence of his generals.[65]

Hankey was not content to let matters lie. Even before he heard the results of Menzies' meeting with Churchill, he had written a letter to Britain's Ambassador in Washington, the former Chamberlain supporter, Lord Halifax, and he entrusted the letter to Menzies for delivery. He counted on Halifax to add his weight to the pressure on Churchill for change.

In this secret letter, Hankey recounted his private worries about Churchill running the war as a "complete dictatorship". He informed Halifax that these worries had been heightened by independent approaches from four senior officers, a top civil servant and Menzies. Hankey complained that there was little he could do alone to effect the necessary changes especially as Churchill "still maintains his hold over public opinion and parliament, and has a wonderful gift of persuading them to put up even with bad tidings''. Though Hankey claimed Churchill to be the only possible leader he nevertheless wrote that he was confiding in Halifax because he considered him as the "only alternative leader if anything happens to Churchill''.[66]

Hankey's rather disjointed letter does not make plain exactly what he expected Halifax to do. Halifax occupied a seat in the War Cabinet when in London, but his distant appointment to Washington was not calculated to help the application of his influence on British politics. Perhaps Hankey hoped that the prospect of possibly replacing Churchill would draw Halifax back from his American exile. More likely it was just a simple appeal from a now relatively powerless man for Halifax to do something, no matter what. For Menzies, though, carrying Hankey's letter to Halifax must have conjured up the prospect of securing another powerful ally in his battle to return to London.

With Menzies' impending departure in view, the British press renewed efforts to have him retained or returned for inclusion in the War Cabinet. The *Times* strongly suggested that he be made deputy to Churchill with control over the Home Front.[67] The *News Review* reported rumours of the likely formation of an Imperial War Council under pressure from a "powerful section of the Conservative Party, backed by opinion in the Dominions''. Menzies was "freely mentioned as a likely member of the Council''.[68] The *New Statesman* similarly touted Menzies as a member of the War Cabinet,[69] while the *Daily Mail* described him as "this brilliant first citizen of the Commonwealth'' who would make a welcome addition to the War Cabinet.[70] Across the political spectrum the British press was practically unanimous in its support for Menzies' retention.

Menzies' lobbying of the Australian journalists in London was also producing some favourable results. A report in the Sydney *Daily Telegraph*, headed "Britain Wants Menzies'', was obviously a direct outcome of the dinner Menzies had provided for the press two days earlier. The report claimed that there was quite a campaign in London to secure Menzies' retention and it set out the reasons behind the moves and the method by which it could be achieved. The suggested members for the Imperial War Cabinet were Churchill, Menzies, Lloyd George, Smuts, Mackenzie King and Fraser (Prime Minister of New Zealand). The report claimed that such a Cabinet was urgently needed and that all its members should be free of departmental responsibility. These were Menzies' very criticisms of the British War Cabinet and the report canvassed exactly the method by which Menzies planned to achieve such changes—an Imperial conference should be called from which Dominion representatives could be appointed to the War Cabinet.[71]

The Brisbane *Telegraph* also noted the campaign for Menzies' retention and came out in support of it. The paper argued that Menzies should have "some definite advisory capacity" and that his "enthusiastic keenness" should be made available to the British Government for the war's duration.[72] On the other side, however, Murdoch's Melbourne *Herald* took a firm line against any suggestion that Menzies remain in London and urged instead that a "Minister for the Pacific" be immediately appointed and dispatched to take Menzies' place.[73]

As for the reaction of his colleagues, Fadden made no mention of the mounting campaign for Menzies' retention when he dispatched a final cable to Menzies in London. Instead, Fadden used the cable to set Menzies' mind at rest as to the reception he could expect in Australia. He assured Menzies that, while he may not have done as much as he would wish to do, the Cabinet was very happy with the results and he would receive a cordial welcome from the Parliament and the country as a whole.[74]

Menzies, though, seemed to have no illusions about his return to Australia and was looking forward with distaste to his return to the rough and tumble of Australian politics. In a final cable from London, markedly less gracious than that from Fadden, Menzies pointedly noted that there had been only one direct reply to the many cables he had sent reporting his discussions in London. Now that he was leaving, Menzies tersely informed Fadden that "Copies have been furnished to High Commissioner to whom any replies should now be addressed".[75]

Menzies' complaint was not exactly accurate, nor was it particularly justified. Despite his long cables, there was little to which the Australian War Cabinet could usefully reply. Menzies had not managed to achieve the large-scale transfer of British productive resources to Australia, nor secured definitive answers to the many defence questions facing Australia. As for the issue of Britain's cutback in imports from Australia, Menzies had fallen in with British needs at Australia's cost. Fadden had certainly replied to Menzies' report on this issue but in terms that Menzies had apparently found best to ignore.

Fadden had given Menzies belated instructions to settle the principles of how Britain could soften the blow to Australia's primary industries. He had rejected Menzies' argument that the cutback was forced on Britain by shipping losses and suggested that the figures supplied by Menzies were exaggerated. While accepting Menzies' argument that Britain's food needs were paramount, Fadden nevertheless maintained that "we do not consider that a programme that preserves Australia's interests need be inconsistent with such an objective".[76] Menzies apparently reacted to this merely by shunting it across to Bruce for action following his departure.

In general, Menzies could now feel satisfied that his plans to return to London were receiving widespread support in London and at least partial support in Australia. An important pillar of the London support was Beaverbrook, who had a long final talk with Menzies. Afterwards, Menzies noted with satisfaction that Beaverbrook "approves of me, and thinks absurd that I should go back to Australia!".[77]

Beaverbrook's approval quickly found expression in his *Daily Express*, which published frequent calls for Menzies' return. The subject of Menzies' long talk with Beaverbrook was not otherwise revealed, but its nature was obvious and Menzies' parting diary note said a lot. Menzies wrote anxiously that he was "desperately afraid of the future in Great Britain".[78] This, then, was Menzies' mission—to return and rescue the Empire from Churchill's mad excesses.

Over the next few months, Menzies would make persistent and increasingly desperate attempts to achieve this return to London. The war in the Mediterranean would look even blacker for Britain and the impetus for political changes in London would grow apace. But Churchill was now aware of Menzies' intentions and would bend all his energy to thwart the Australian's designs on his own position. Beneath the epic battles being played out across Europe, Britain provided the focus for a bloodless battle over the future of the Empire. Both Menzies and Churchill threw themselves into this struggle with a will.

NOTES

1. R. R. JAMES (ED.), *Winston S. Churchill: His Complete Speeches 1897–1963*, vi, New York, 1974, p. 6379
2. MENZIES DIARY, 27 April 1941
3. *IBID.*
4. *SUNDAY PICTORIAL*, London, 27 April 1941
5. J. KENNEDY, p. 106. See also "Notes on My Life" by Lord Alanbrooke, p. 270, 3/A.14, Alanbrooke Papers: KC
6. J. KENNEDY, p. 108
7. WAR CABINET CONCLUSIONS, 28 April 1941, Cab. 65/18, W.M.44(41): PRO
8. WAR CABINET CONCLUSIONS/CONFIDENTIAL ANNEX, 28 April 1941, Cab. 65/22, W.M.44(41): PRO

9. MENZIES DIARY, 28 April 1941
10. WAR CABINET CONCLUSIONS, 28 April 1941, Cab. 65/18, W.M.44(41): PRO
11. MENZIES DIARY, 28 April 1941
12. *MANCHESTER GUARDIAN*, 29 April 1941
13. MENZIES DIARY, 28 April 1941
14. DALTON DIARY, 28 April 1941, Dalton Papers: LSE
15. BEDNALL DIARY, 28 April 1941, in C. Hazlehurst, *Menzies Observed*, Sydney, 1979, p. 217
16. TALK WITH T. HOLE, 22 May 1941, CRS M100, "May 1941": AA
17. TALK WITH T. HOLE, 3 July 1941, CRS M100, "July 1941": AA
18. "The Political Atmosphere on the Return of the Prime Minister to Australia", ch. 40 of Shedden's draft memoirs, pp. 6–7, CRS A5954, Box 767: AA. Shedden had crossed out this section of the chapter
19. M. GILBERT, p. 1072
20. DIRECTIVE BY CHURCHILL, 28 April 1941, PREM 3/156/6: PRO
21. *IBID.*
22. *DAFP*, iv, Doc. 435, Cable M.87, Menzies to Fadden, 27 April 1941
23. LETTER, Sempill to Bruce, 19 August 1940, AA 1970/559, Box 2, Miscellaneous Papers of S. M. Bruce: AA
24. MENZIES ENGAGEMENTS, CRS A5954, Box 612, "Prime Minister's Engagements": AA
25. LETTER, Sempill to Menzies, 23 April 1941, CRS A5954, Box 625, "Far Eastern Defence": AA
26. *TATLER*, London, 14 May 1941
27. LETTER, Menzies to Sempill, 30 April 1941, CRS A5954, Box 625, "Far Eastern Defence": AA
28. CABLE M.92, Menzies to Fadden, 28 April 1941, CRS A5954, Box 630, "Advisory War Council—Increase of Personnel": AA
29. CABLE NO. 266, Fadden to Menzies, 29 April 1941, CRS A5954, Box 630, "Advisory War Council—Increase of Personnel": AA
30. *CHRISTIAN SCIENCE MONITOR*, Boston, 26 April 1941
31. *DAILY MIRROR*, New York, 27 April 1941
32. *STAR*, London, 28, 30 April 1941
33. *MANCHESTER GUARDIAN*, 29 April 1941
34. *DAILY HERALD*, London, 30 April 1941
35. MENZIES DIARY, 29 April 1941
36. CABLE NO. 274, Fadden to Menzies, 29 April 1941, AA CP 290/9, Bundle 1, Folder 12: AA
37. CABLE M.95, Menzies to Fadden, 1 May 1941, AA CP 290/9, Bundle 1, Folder 3: AA
38. See SPEECH by Army Minister, Percy Spender, 26 April 1941, MS 4875/2/6, Spender Papers: NLA
39. "ISMAY 29/4", CRS A5954, Box 15, "1941 Diary (Visit to London)": AA. There is some confusion over when this talk occurred since, in his Engagement Book, Shedden was listed as lunching with Ismay on 28 April
40. DEFENCE COMMITTEE (OPERATIONS) MINUTES, 29 April 1941, Cab. 69/2, D.O.(41)20: PRO
41. MENZIES DIARY, 29 April 1941
42. HANKEY DIARY, 1 and 13 May 1941, S. Roskill, iii, p. 500

43. LETTER, Beaverbrook to Churchill, undated but probably 30 April 1941 according to a pencilled note to that effect, BBK D/416, Beaverbrook Papers: HLRO
44. M. GILBERT, p. 1074, fn. 1
45. "HANKEY 30/4", CRS A5954, Box 15, "1941 Diary (Visit to London)": AA
46. HANKEY DIARY, 30 April 1941, in S. Roskill, iii, p. 500
47. DEFENCE COMMITTEE (OPERATIONS) MINUTES, 30 April 1941, Cab. 69/2, D.O.(41): PRO
48. CADOGAN DIARY, 1 May 1941, D. Dilks (ed.), p. 375
49. MENZIES DIARY, 30 April 1941. The meeting was actually on 1 May and Menzies apparently wrote up this entry some time later, mistakenly putting the wrong date on it
50. DEFENCE COMMITTEE (OPERATIONS) MINUTES, 1 May 1941, Cab. 69/2, D.O.(41)22: PRO
51. DAFP, iv, Doc. 443, Cable M.97, Menzies to Fadden, 2 May 1941
52. DAFP, iv, Doc. 445, Cable No. 328, Casey to Department of External Affairs, 2 May 1941
53. DAFP, iv, Doc. 446, Cable No. 269, Fadden to Cranborne, 4 May 1941
54. WAR CABINET CONCLUSIONS, 1 May 1941, Cab. 65/18, W.M.45(41): PRO
55. WEEKLY RESUME OF THE NAVAL, MILITARY AND AIR SITUATION, 1 May 1941, Cab. 66/16, W.P.(41)95: PRO
56. LETTER, Cunningham to Rear Admiral Hugh England, 1 May 1941, CUNN 5/3, Cunningham Papers: CC
57. CABLE T.127, Churchill to Wavell, 1 May 1941, PREM 3/206/3: PRO
58. DAILY TELEGRAPH, London, 2 May 1941
59. HANKEY DIARY, 1 May 1941, S. Roskill, iii, p. 501
60. IBID., pp. 501–2
61. MENZIES DIARY, 1 and 2 May 1941
62. HANKEY DIARY, 2 May 1941, S. Roskill, iii, p. 502
63. TALK WITH EVATT, 18 May 1942, M100, "May 1942": AA
64. LETTER, Kennedy to Shedden, CRS A5954, Box 630, Miscellaneous Correspondence 9/5/41–11/6/41: AA
65. J. KENNEDY, pp. 114–15
66. LETTER, Hankey to Halifax, 1 May 1941, A4/410/4/5, Halifax Papers: CC
67. TIMES, London, 30 April 1941
68. NEWS REVIEW, London, 1 May 1941
69. NEW STATESMAN, London, 3 May 1941
70. DAILY MAIL, London, 3 May 1941
71. DAILY TELEGRAPH, Sydney, 1 May 1941
72. TELEGRAPH, Brisbane, 2 May 1941
73. HERALD, Melbourne, 1 May 1941
74. CABLE NO. 277, Fadden to Menzies, 2 May 1941, CRS A5954, Box 613, "American and Canadian Itinerary": AA
75. CABLE M.99, Menzies to Fadden, 2 May 1941, CRS A5954, Box 616, "Cabled Reviews to Australia": AA
76. CABLE NO. 275, Fadden to Menzies, 30 April 1941, CP 290/9, Bundle 1(12) SC: AA
77. MENZIES DIARY, 1 and 2 May 1941
78. IBID.

12

Menzies in America

*D*uring April 1941, German Panzer divisions had again thrown British forces from the European continent. Their expulsion from Greece and Rommel's recapture of Libya marked one of the lowest points in the war for Britain. Worse was to come. Australian and other Imperial troops, with the remnants of the Greek Army, were occupying Crete as a bastion against the further flow of German forces south towards Egypt, and during May 1941 the island would see a bloody repeat of the Greek campaign. On 2 May Churchill was advised that the troops on Crete were expecting an attack from some 800 German planes, with them having only six modern fighter planes to put up in defence. That afternoon, a very worried Menzies bid farewell to Beaverbrook at London's Paddington station and boarded a train on the first stage of his journey back to Australia.

Throughout his stay in London, Menzies had watched with mounting horror as the British Empire steadily slipped towards defeat. His overwhelming impression on his departure was of an inexorable slide to destruction so long as Churchill retained the guardianship of the Empire. The forthcoming battle for Crete would prove further confirmation of Menzies' fears. But Menzies had left London ignorant of Rommel's supply problems in the vastness of the Libyan desert. This secret information, revealing that Rommel was now relying more on bluff and bravado than on weight of armour, enabled Churchill to realise that Egypt and the embattled fortress of Tobruk could be defended. Moreover, there was the strong possibility that Rommel could be stopped in his tracks and thrown back across the desert. Menzies was never made privy to this vital information and continued to sink into a sea of unremitting pessimism.

Menzies' departure from London signalled the beginning of a broad campaign to achieve his early return to the Imperial capital. Beaverbrook's *Daily Express* was the most prominent voice in this campaign and its pressure was relentless. On 5 May, the paper called, "Come back, Menzies!" It claimed that Menzies had made a great impression in Britain and called for a national government in Canberra that would permit his return to London. This, the paper argued, would make the British people rejoice.[1]

The following day, the *Daily Express* reiterated the call for a national government in Australia which could release Menzies for London. This, it claimed, would be "of the maximum assistance in the battle against Germany" since the British War Cabinet needed the "foremost, ablest, most competent brains that the Empire can produce". The paper demanded a post for Menzies "right at the top".[2] Other newspapers similarly sang Menzies' praises and openly asserted his desire to return.[3]

One report that went perhaps a bit too far for Menzies' comfort was published in the *People* on 4 May. It reprinted parts of an article written by an Australian journalist present at the Savoy dinner on 28 April. The article was due to be published in Australia's *Truth* newspaper and it provided a frank statement of Menzies' complaints about Churchill. It supported Menzies' call for an Imperial War Cabinet and claimed that the British Government was a "mere one-man band, in which there is no chance of dissentient voices being raised". It revealed that there had been strong words between Menzies and Churchill over the conduct of the war.[4] This was not something that Menzies would have wished to be publicly known. His campaign for inclusion in the War Cabinet was not based on open opposition to Churchill but on his ability to add strength to Churchill's leadership. That dinner with the journalists in London was beginning to cost Menzies dear.

While the British press was calling for his return, Menzies was in North America actively pursuing the same end. American material support was crucial for Britain, so the endorsement of the Americans would be a considerable asset to him. The American press had already begun to notice his impact in London and its reaction had been favourable. *Time* magazine had heralded his arrival in New York with an article surveying his visit to London and his political problems in Australia. It portrayed Menzies as a sharp critic of Churchill who had nevertheless made a great impression on the British Premier and was being openly touted as "Mr. Churchill's most likely successor if anything happened to the Prime Minister".[5]

On his arrival, the New York *Mirror* devoted a large article to Menzies, calling him the "Empire's Strong Man". On another page, the paper accompanied a photograph of Menzies with the claim that he had been a great success in Britain and was "perhaps the biggest man in the British Empire, second in strength and wisdom not even to Mr. Churchill". It also alleged that the British Foreign Office had tried to play down his trip to America and limit its public impact. The paper claimed that Menzies' friends had to approach the national radio networks directly to arrange for the broadcast of his main speech in the United States.[6]

Menzies' message to the Americans was for them to "produce the goods", to go all out to produce the wherewithal which Britain needed to fight the war. This message was a boost for those elements in America seeking to draw their country closer to the conflict. But Menzies' stirring message had a sober side and laid more stress on quickly finishing the war than decisively defeating the Germans. Very much in the tone of his talk with Lloyd George, Menzies warned the Americans that "No part of the world can escape from a world war, and a long drawn out war ruins every part of the world".[7] He could still see no quick end to the war and still greatly feared that ruin was to be the destiny of the British Empire.

While Menzies' first port of call was New York, it was really a transit stop on the way to Canada. His first concern was to get to his fellow Dominion leader to press the case for an Imperial Conference. So, after meeting the American press and the Mayor of New York, Menzies boarded a Canadian bomber for the flight to Ottawa. There on 7 May, he was met by the Canadian Prime Minister, Mackenzie King, who later accompanied him to a luncheon at the Canadian Club. In his luncheon speech, Menzies emphasised the gravity of the war situation and urged an all-out effort by the Dominions. If Menzies hoped by his visit to gain the support of Mackenzie King, this speech was of no assistance. In fact, it was taken up by sections of the Canadian press as a stick with which to beat Mackenzie King for not having already geared Canada up to maximum effort.[8]

Later that afternoon, Menzies had the rare honour of addressing a meeting of the Canadian House of Commons. He was given a rapturous reception, with one Canadian paper describing his presence as a "freshening inspiration from the distant horizon" with a "message of determination and courage". Canadian MPs were united in a "standing, desk-pounding group which seemed to have refreshed its resolve that 'this is the war we must win' ".[9] The *Ottawa Journal* printed a full report of his reception as well as the complete text of Menzies' speech which ran to 84 column inches.[10] Menzies' own reaction was to note once again the great contrast between the reception accorded him overseas with that in Australia.[11]

It was presumably Menzies' formidable presence, rather than the speech itself, which gave rise to such unalloyed admiration. Menzies certainly cut a much more vigorous and striking figure than Mackenzie King, Churchill or Roosevelt and his power of oratory was considerable. However, his speech to the Canadian House of Commons concentrated on the rigours and crippling cost of the fight yet to come, rather than painting a picture of certain victory. Menzies claimed that Britain could not be said to have begun winning the war, and that to date the "greatest triumphs have been in extricating ourselves from utter defeat". He called for greater production of munitions to ensure that "this war is to be shortened and brought to an end on such terms as this suffering world demands". Again he conjured up a vision of the world made bankrupt by the war with everyone sharing an "honourable poverty".[12] Throughout this long speech Menzies did not once refer to the leadership of Churchill, concentrating instead on the bravery of the ordinary Briton.

It was all well and good for the Canadian MPs to applaud his speech, but it was Mackenzie King whom Menzies needed as an ally. Fortunately for us, the Canadian Prime Minister has left a lengthy account of Menzies' one-day visit that further clarifies much of Menzies' purpose, and makes clear Mackenzie King's rejection of it. The Canadian admitted that Menzies had taken Ottawa by storm and that he had many of the qualities of a great leader. Nevertheless, Mackenzie King observed shrewdly that Menzies was "thinking pretty much of Menzies most of the time, and likes very much the environments of high society, palaces, etc., which will cost him, perhaps, dearly in the end".[13]

As for Menzies' purpose in Canada, Mackenzie King concluded that his primary aim seemed to be the promotion of "a conference of Prime Ministers—some kind of an Imperial Cabinet". Menzies pushed his case hard in private talks with Canadian leaders, claiming that there was "no British Cabinet, no War Cabinet—that Churchill was the whole show, and that those who were around him were 'yes men', and nothing else". He praised Beaverbrook as the "one man doing things" and cited Lloyd George as being equally critical and in support of Menzies' campaign for change. Mackenzie King observed that Menzies' ambition to join the British War Cabinet was painfully obvious and the Canadian perceptively "sensed the feeling that he would rather be on the War Cabinet in London than Prime Minister of Australia".[14]

Menzies may have taken Ottawa by storm, but he failed miserably with Mackenzie King. While the Canadian Premier claimed to admire Menzies on a personal level, he was not convinced by his arguments for Dominion representation. Instead, he countered with the suggestion of periodic visits to London by Dominion Ministers. The Canadian was painfully aware of leading a society divided between its English and French sections and similarly divided on its reaction to the war. French-speaking Canadians would be liable to react angrily to the close identification with Britain that such Dominion representation would entail. On a more lofty level, Mackenzie King saw his continued presence in Canada as necessary to preserve the unity of the nation. Additionally, as he warned Menzies, he foresaw political danger to the position of any Dominion Prime Minister too long absent from his post.

In his diary account, Mackenzie King presumed that Menzies' ambition was limited to gaining a seat in the British War Cabinet. Menzies did not, of course, canvass the future possibility of himself replacing Churchill in Downing Street. Still, there was more than a hint of the direction of Menzies' ambition when he stressed the necessity of deciding on a successor to Churchill.[15] Menzies knew there was no obvious successor to Churchill and that with a seat in the War Cabinet he would be better placed than any of the possible contenders.

His intentions once in the War Cabinet were also hinted at in his talks with Mackenzie King. Far from his public stance of maintaining that Britain would win, he privately informed the Canadian War Cabinet that he was pessimistic about the Middle East and the Mediterranean and "outspoken as to no certainty of victory thus far, and certainly no victory without U.S. co-operation. . . ".[16] This openly pessimistic view of the war and the doubtful prospects for victory, was a clear indication of how Menzies wished to apply any power he might obtain in Britain. That is, towards the winding down of a war that was ruinous to the Empire.

Menzies seemed to have not fully realised that Mackenzie King's opposition to greater Dominion representation was implacable. Perhaps he was overawed by the personal adulation he received in Ottawa and failed to appreciate the Canadian political realities that would override his arguments. Indeed, there is even a suggestion of an implicit understanding between Churchill and Mackenzie King to block any moves that Menzies might make. The survival of each depended on Menzies' hopes being frustrated.

Before Menzies left Ottawa for Washington on 8 May he had

breakfast with Malcolm MacDonald, the British Minister whose "exile" by Churchill to the High Commissionership in Canada Menzies had earlier bemoaned. MacDonald was identified with the policies of Chamberlain, and Menzies had enjoyed a friendship with him. Their meeting gave Menzies a chance to unburden himself about Churchill and his own hopes for change. After the Australian Prime Minister's departure, MacDonald added his voice to the calls for an Imperial Conference.

At the same time, Mackenzie King sent to Churchill a full account of his own meeting with Menzies. The Canadian informed Churchill that Menzies did not, in fact, favour an Imperial War Cabinet containing *all* the Dominion Prime Ministers, and that their joint presence in London would have to be "confined to some special occasion when some definite practical question might necessitate joint consideration".[17] Whether the canny Canadian was aware of Menzies' intended use for such a conference is not clear, but Churchill was certainly aware that Menzies hoped to use it to impose a specifically designed War Cabinet on him—one where Menzies would sit as Dominion representative. Mackenzie King's cable alerted the British Premier to the fact that Menzies was still pursuing this aim.

On 15 May, Mackenzie King was visited by a fellow countryman, Sir Campbell Stuart, who acquainted him more fully with the scope of Menzies' plans. Stuart was a director of the London *Times* and prominent in the organisation of Imperial communications. But his influence went further than his position suggested. As one observer noted, Stuart was a man worth knowing as he was "very much somebody 'behind the scenes' ".[18] Stuart now confided to King that "Menzies' ambition was to be Prime Minister of England, and that there were perhaps in England some who would be prepared to accept him."[19] Stuart was not simply repeating idle London gossip but had come from a private meeting with Menzies in Washington[20] and may well have been enlisted in Menzies' crusade. Whatever Stuart's purpose in Ottawa, the effect of his information was merely to confirm Mackenzie King's own suspicions and provide him with a clearer justification for thwarting Menzies' attempts to call an Imperial Conference.

While Menzies proceeded with his tour of North America, military events around the Mediterranean continued to look grim for Britain and the voices in Britain calling for peace rose several decibels. The parliamentary debate on the Greek campaign was set for 7 May and Churchill made it a test of will with his opponents by calling for a vote of confidence in his leadership. Two days prior to the debate and after a talk with the Health Minister, Ernest Brown, Hugh Dalton noted the uneasy political atmosphere in London. Brown warned Dalton that there would soon be a titanic struggle between "those who wanted to make a premature peace and those who . . . intended to fight this thing out to the end".[21]

That same day, Dalton was also informed by Churchill's assistant, Major Morton, of a conversation with the former War Minister, Leslie Hore-Belisha. Hore-Belisha had sounded out Morton on the chances of his return to the Cabinet and had made it "clearly understood that, in the event of his not getting a job, he would join up with L.G. [Lloyd George] and form a really powerful Opposition".[22] In the debate on 7 May, Lloyd George and Hore-Belisha provided the spearheads for the attack on Churchill.

In a strong defence of his leadership, Churchill used the Commons debate to lash out at his critics and stop their attack in its tracks. Churchill particularly rounded on Lloyd George and described his speech as the sort with which the "illustrious and venerable Marshal Pétain might well have enlivened the closing days of M. Reynaud's Cabinet".[23] This was damning criticism indeed and hit Lloyd George hard. Though Lloyd George supported a negotiated peace, he did not favour a Pétain-like solution with German occupation of Britain.

If the image of Vichy France was not enough to still the hand of his opponents, Churchill pointedly reminded them that they were answerable to their constituents. Given Churchill's continuing public popularity, this might well have made many MPs consider the consequences of becoming associated with Churchill's critics. Churchill also reminded them that evidence of criticism in the British Parliament would only give comfort to Germany and threaten the flow of material support from the United States.

This was one of Churchill's great inspirational speeches and it at least partially dispelled the doubts of his critics. He argued that he had never promised anything but "blood, tears, toil and sweat" and that Britain could hope for nothing other than this for a very long time, but he reiterated that at the end there would be "complete, absolute and final victory". But, he warned, this victory would depend on Britain staying united, and he reminded the House that the National Government had been formed to "fight this business to the end".[24]

Churchill won his vote of confidence by 447 to 3 but the bare figures are misleading. The underlying unease remained. The day after the debate, Harold Nicolson confided to his diary his sense of the latent support in Britain for a negotiated peace and of his fear that "people will jump at any escape which makes cowardice appear respectable . . . ".[25]

Churchill was fortunate in the timing of his vote of confidence. There was a slight lull in the fighting following the fall of Greece and he was able confidently to claim that Crete and Egypt would withstand the German blows. Later, after the fall of Crete and the flight of Hitler's deputy, Rudolf Hess, to Britain, the issues of Churchill's continued leadership, and of a general settlement in Europe, were once more to become matters of much discussion.

Menzies' ability to influence these issues would be largely determined by events in Australia. He was relying on being permitted to once again leave for London. But already there were growing signs that this permission would not be easily given. On 5 May, the Melbourne *Age* called for his speedy passage across North America and opposed his recall to London. The paper forcefully argued that, when Australia's "very existence is challenged, and far-reaching decisions must be taken without delay, the place of the nation's responsible leader is in our own midst".[26]

Menzies arrived in Washington from Ottawa on 9 May and began four days of dinners and discussions. Due to Roosevelt's illness, it was not until his last day in the American capital that Menzies called on the American President and later met the U.S. Chiefs of Staff. The bedside meeting with Roosevelt was more in the nature of a courtesy call than anything else. Menzies had to admit to the press that, despite his claimed close association with Churchill, the British Prime Minister had not entrusted him with a message to Roosevelt on any of the pressing issues of the war.[27]

In his public comments, Menzies concentrated on the need for America to produce weapons of war for Britain at a faster rate. His own pessimism sometimes broke through the confident veneer. While Churchill was relying on the build-up of British air strength and the bombing of German cities to defeat Hitler, Menzies called the whole strategy into question. He admitted that "air superiority might not after all settle the war in Britain's favour". He also raised the possibility of the war lasting as long as 20 years and told the Americans that a quicker victory depended on the level of their support being increased.[28] In a national radio speech to the American people, Menzies was similarly equivocal on British prospects, telling the Americans that, if Britain won, "we shall take years to recover from the strain".[29]

Despite his sober pronouncements, Menzies was still hailed by those Americans anxious to involve their country more fully in the war. Though at least one newspaper rejected Menzies' call for a greater American effort,[30] most of the press seem to have supported his call and to have found in Menzies the essence of an inspirational leader.[31] An Australian diplomat in Washington was rather taken aback by the response evoked from the Americans, but reflected that his Prime Minister's London experience must have increased his stature to the extent that he "seemed a more vigorous Menzies, seized of the need to make the maximum effort towards winning the war".[32] Menzies was certainly showing plenty of vigour, but his eyes were more firmly fixed on winning a seat in the British War Cabinet than on winning the war.

Back in Australia, the Labor Party had won a resounding victory in the New South Wales State election. Federally, Menzies was on a tightrope with a by-election due in June to fill a vacancy left by the death of one of his supporters. The Labor Party was now in a good position to force a general election on Menzies and to have a better than even chance of winning it. If this happened, as London's *Daily Herald* noted, "the plot to make him a member of our War Cabinet would end".[33]

Menzies' colleagues were now decidedly jittery and, on 11 May, Fadden advised him that the New South Wales result could encourage a "frontal attack" from the Labor Party. In an implicit criticism of his long absence, Fadden informed him that the Australian public was waiting for a lead from the Government on the war and that he had "refrained from comprehensive statement of Governmental policy pending your return so as not to cut across anything you have in mind". Fadden now urged that he be allowed to make some statement to "stabilise public opinion, leaving bigger aspects and drive for you".[34]

Menzies agreed to Fadden's proposed statement and expressed annoyance at the criticism in Australia. In his reply, Menzies strongly defended the Australian war effort which he claimed was universally regarded as the world's best, relative to population, and warned Fadden that his defeat by Labor would "astonish and depress Britain" and be seen there as "defeatist and destructive of unity". He promised that on his return to Australia he would make a call to "put everything on a complete war basis".[35]

By the time this cable reached Canberra on 14 May, Fadden's concern about the political situation had increased. He immediately cabled back urging that Menzies should address a public meeting in Sydney at the earliest possible date after his return. He warned that the

Labor Party was "intoxicated with success" and that Menzies' presence in Sydney was vital to bring a "healthy breath of reality into such party excesses in war time". Menzies immediately agreed to this suggestion.[36]

That the political atmosphere in Australia was working against Menzies' interests was nothing new, but now the situation in London also began to deteriorate. On 11 May, Churchill had replied to Mackenzie King's report on Menzies' visit to Ottawa. He claimed to be delighted with Menzies' success and described him as a "staunch comrade". As for Menzies' pressure for an Imperial Conference, Churchill appeared to agree and suggested to Mackenzie King that "July or August for a month or six weeks would be most desirable if it could be arranged". It was more than probable that Churchill was being particularly crafty in suggesting a six-week conference, knowing very well Mackenzie King would be reluctant to attend. To emphasise the point, Churchill concluded the cable by congratulating the Canadian on the "way you have carried Canada forward in such perfect unity".[37] This unity, they both knew, depended on Mackenzie King's continued presence in Canada and militated against his attendance at a lengthy Imperial Conference.

As a matter of course, Churchill's cable was passed on to the Dominions Office where the Minister, Lord Cranborne, took fright at Churchill's apparent concurrence to an Imperial Conference. He immediately advised Churchill that the proposal for such a conference "clearly emanates from Mr. Menzies" who had "come strongly to the conclusion, during his visit here, that there should be permanent representation of the Dominions on the War Cabinet by an outstanding Empire personality, preferably himself". Cranborne warned Churchill that Menzies hoped to achieve this by means of an Imperial Conference. The anxious Dominions Secretary claimed that it was important for Churchill to have the background to the proposal, "in case you have not already got it". However, Churchill was well aware of Menzies' designs and tersely wrote on the bottom of Cranborne's note: "I have got it."[38]

Unlike Cranborne, Churchill was not panicking but steadily diverting threats to his position as they appeared. Now that Menzies was on his way to Australia, he would ensure that he stayed there and that all his attempts to return would be thwarted.

At this time, Churchill was also tackling the problem of Rudolf Hess, Hitler's deputy, who had flown to Britain with the aim of settling the war in the west before Germany turned east against Russia.

Like Menzies and Lloyd George, Hess was convinced that there could be no victory for Britain given the prevailing circumstances and that, with Churchill deposed, Britain was sure to sue for peace.[39] Hess has always been portrayed as being mad or suffering from delusions. However, his basic premise—that Britain was ripe for a negotiated peace—was not so far removed from reality if attention is concentrated on the British elite rather than the public at large.

On 12 May, Hugh Dalton noted that some of the Peers were beginning to lack resolve on the war and even to openly suggest suing for peace in the autumn.[40] On 10 May, the Duke of Bedford proposed to the Labour MP R. R. Stokes that Lloyd George should make a public statement setting out possible peace terms to which Germany could respond. Lloyd George, the Duke wrote, was "so *obviously* the one man who could save the country!".[41] Four days later, after news of Hess was released, Stokes wrote to Lloyd George claiming that there was

> *much more support for the views you expressed (during the*
> *Commons debate on 7 May) than was apparent. Many people feel*
> *the whole strategical control a tragic farce. As one of the Chiefs*
> *of Staff said to me—"There is a great deal too much cigar stump*
> *strategy!"*
> *What many of us hope therefore is that the criticisms of last week*
> *should not be allowed to fade out and that if the Hess visit holds*
> *out any opportunity of bringing the war to an early conclusion*
> *that opportunity should not be lost.*[42]

On 10 May, 24 hours prior to the arrival of Hess, the Germans launched their last and most severe bombing attack of the Blitz on London. Many familiar London landmarks were hit, including the House of Commons and Westminster Abbey. Whether by coincidence or design, this attack should have helped Hess in his pursuit of peace.[43] However, there was little comfort for him in the public British reaction to his arrival. He had seriously misjudged the mood of the ordinary Briton and the strength of Churchill's hold on the country. Though there were those who yearned for peace, few were prepared to propose such a course publicly.[44]

Still, Hess had put Churchill in a quandary and for a time he simply kept him under wraps and said nothing. Apparently, Churchill was not sure of the reaction of his countrymen to the knowledge of a German peace emissary. Beaverbrook stepped in at this stage with the apparent intention of boosting peace speculations. On 15 May he convinced Churchill not to issue a statement of the official British attitude to Hess. Such a statement could have immediately quashed the rumours and supposition that were rife throughout the world. The following day, Beaverbrook invited all the editors and political correspondents to lunch and informed them that "Hess had come over to explain that we are beaten and had better give way".[45] Cecil King, one of the editors present, wrote in his diary that Beaverbrook urged them to create "as much speculation, rumour, and discussion about Hess as possible". He now claimed that Churchill was keeping silent on Hess so as to keep the speculation boiling over.[46] It seems clear that Beaverbrook wanted to create in the public mind a strong sense of the possibility of peace, perhaps with the aim of gauging public reaction.

Even Churchill acknowledged that now was the time if Britain were to sue for peace. Though he was not prepared personally to negotiate with Hitler, he recognised that their realisation "that the British Empire could at this time get out of the war intact, leaving the future struggle with a Germanized Europe to the United States" was the "master key" to greater American involvement.[47]

Hess represented a complication to Menzies' own plans. He was now far from the centre of power in London and even if everything went well it would probably be some months before he could secure his return. If, in the meantime, Britain should come to terms with Germany all Menzies' plans would be forfeit. At first, he refused to speculate about Hess when questioned by reporters in New York.[48] He also refused to discuss British war aims, claiming that "it would be fruitless until the war was won".[49]

The following day in Chicago, Menzies told reporters that, in relation to Hess, "he would be disposed to be on guard for a Nazi trick".[50] Two days later, Menzies was interviewed in Salt Lake City, where he now "emphatically voiced his opposition to any type of negotiated compromise" and claimed that a stalemate would be "a calamity for every country in the world for many years".[51]

Menzies' underlying intentions were revealed more clearly during his visit to Chicago on 15 May. His main public engagement was to address 1000 members of the Council on Foreign Relations in the Grand Ballroom of the Stevens Hotel. He reiterated his call for maximum US co-operation and received a standing ovation for his trouble.[52] However, before his speech, Menzies met in his hotel suite with the British Ambassador, Lord Halifax, who had interrupted a tour of the American mid-west to come especially to meet the Australian. A local paper speculated that their discussion "presumably . . . concerned

Lord Halifax's observations on his nine day tour of the area".[53] This was well wide of the mark.

Menzies met with Halifax to pass on Hankey's secret letter and to enlist Halifax's support in his campaign to return to a position of power in London. This support he received in ample measure. Halifax later reported to Hankey that he had been very disturbed by his letter and that Menzies had "opened up very freely" at their Chicago rendezvous. Presumably, Menzies set out his plan to return to London by way of an Imperial Conference resolution. Halifax pledged his personal support for Menzies' return since the "whole trend of events—and what one may expect to be coming—seems to me to make it of very great importance to have someone a) of that calibre and b) of the Dominions, in at Cabinet discussions".[54] Whatever boost this may have given to Menzies' plans, the support of Halifax was necessarily diminished by his distance from London.

Just as Menzies had captured the imagination of the people, or at least of the press, in Britain and Canada, so also was the case in the United States. His visit was very much aimed at newspapers, with numerous press conferences, off-the-record briefings and intimate lunches with executives. All this effort bore fruit. *Life* treated him well, with a full-page photograph and a description of Menzies as being "Forthright as a Churchill, tireless as a Willkie" and claimed he was talked of by Englishmen as "a possible future Empire Prime Minister".[55] The New York *Herald-Tribune* similarly ranked Menzies among the "most powerful figures of the English-speaking world".[56] The backing of the American press was no mere ego-booster for Menzies, though it doubtless also served that purpose. It was extremely useful to be able to claim US support in any bid for power in Britain.

While the press in Britain and America was practically unalloyed in its praise of Menzies and backed his bid for an Imperial role, its Australian counterparts took a different view. Menzies' own methods may well have been partly to blame for this. His indiscreet talk to Australian journalists had smacked of intrigue and back-stabbing.[57] These journalists might also have found it difficult to justify a Prime Minister leaving his post in wartime for service elsewhere. In fact, less than favourable stories were already being circulated about Menzies' London activities.

In mid-May Bruce had to move very quickly to prevent a minor scandal over Menzies' indiscretions. Scotland Yard attempted to have a radical journalist interned for trying to sell a report which alleged that Menzies had violently quarrelled with Churchill over his preference for "Yes-men" and that Menzies had accused Churchill of "drinking far more brandy (than) was good for his brain". When Bruce was approached by the police for his opinion he advised that it would be extremely dangerous to try to intern the journalist, as it would give him "the opportunity of claiming that he was being interned for saying very much less than the Prime Minister of Australia had said to the Press Correspondents".[58]

For its part, the Australian press was already alive with rumours and reports of Menzies' supposed future plans. On 17 May, Smith's Weekly suggested that it would not take much to persuade Menzies "that his future is in Westminster and, perhaps, Downing Street".[59] Murdoch's Melbourne Sun reiterated its previous stand against Menzies' return to London while supporting the dispatch of an Australian Minister. However, the Sun did leave open the possibility of Menzies being that Minister if he first resigned the Prime Minister-ship.[60] The Melbourne Argus also suggested that Menzies might realise his ambition of returning to London by resigning as Prime Minister and going as a special envoy with Ministerial status.[61]

The Sydney Sun noted these rumours and claimed that they were politically inspired by Menzies' enemies eager for his removal. The paper argued instead that Menzies' trip had given him the "greatest possible authority to speak and act for Australia as its war leader" and "if it is found necessary for him to return to London, he should go as Prime Minister".[62] Other papers ignored this aspect and instead stressed the vital necessity for him to provide the leadership and unity that Australia lacked.[63]

Menzies left Los Angeles by air on 17 May on the final leg of his journey back to Australia. Despite the pressing necessities of war, for the past two years he had steadfastly resisted American pressure for a direct air route from the United States to Australia. Because of his own policies, he was therefore forced to take a convoluted route by Pan American plane through Hawaii and New Zealand where he could meet a Tasman Empire Airways flying boat for the trip to Sydney. While this further delayed his arrival in Australia, it had the advantage of allowing for talks with the New Zealand government. These talks presumably followed the by now familiar course, with Menzies pressing hard for his planned Imperial Conference and underlining his disquiet with Churchill's leadership.

As he prepared to leave New Zealand he wrote privately of a "sick feeling of repugnance and apprehension" that grew on him as he neared Australia and wished that he could "creep in quietly into the bosom of the family and rest there".[64] He well knew the political storms into which he was flying and now looked on his homecoming as something to be endured before he could grasp the grander destiny that awaited him in London. There, the survival of the Empire was at stake and Menzies was naturally reluctant to re-enter the atmosphere of Canberra's relatively petty politics.

The sick feeling at the thought of the political storms was no doubt made more real by violent weather during the approach to Sydney. Menzies' flying boat was forced to battle against strong headwinds and had to fly dangerously low over the sea for much of the way. The Melbourne *Herald* noted that, in the approach to Sydney, "streaks of lightning flashed through the murk and loud above the roar of the motors hailstones rattled against the fuselage".[65] Though Menzies survived, looming political storms would prove much more difficult to ride out.

NOTES

1. DAILY EXPRESS, London, 5 May 1941
2. DAILY EXPRESS, London, 6 May 1941
3. SCOTSMAN, News Chronicle, Glasgow Herald, 6 May 1941
4. THE PEOPLE, London, 4 May 1941
5. TIME, New York, 5 May 1941
6. MIRROR, New York, 7 May 1941
7. TIMES, London, 8 May 1941
8. EVENING CITIZEN, Ottawa, 8 May 1941; Farm Journal, Ottawa, 9 May 1941; Amherst News, Nova Scotia, 13 May 1941
9. EDMONTON JOURNAL, 8 May 1941
10. OTTAWA JOURNAL, 8 May 1941
11. MENZIES DIARY, 7 May 1941
12. NEW YORK TIMES, 8 May 1941
13. MACKENZIE KING DIARY, 7 May 1941: CUL
14. IBID.
15. IBID.
16. IBID.
17. CABLE, Mackenzie King to Churchill, 10 May 1941, PREM 4/43A/12: AA
18. Comments of the Australian Governor-General, Lord Gowrie, as reported in the War Journal of Gerald Wilkinson, 22 December 1942. WILK 1/1, Wilkinson Papers: CC
19. MACKENZIE KING DIARY, 15 May 1941: CUL
20. "Prime Minister's Visit Abroad, 1941—List of Official Engagements", CRS A5954, Box 612: AA
21. DALTON DIARY, 5 May 1941, Dalton Papers: LSE
22. IBID.

23. SPEECH BY CHURCHILL, 7 May 1941, R. R. James, *Winston Churchill: His Complete Speeches*, p. 6389
24. IBID.
25. NICOLSON DIARY, 8 May 1941, Sir H. Nicolson (ed.), p. 165
26. AGE, Melbourne, 5 May 1941; see also *Sun*, Sydney, 8 May 1941
27. SUN, New York, 12 May 1941
28. DAILY NEWS, New York, 10 May 1941
29. EXAMINER, Los Angeles, 14 May 1941
30. REGISTER, New Haven, Conn., 14 May 1941
31. WASHINGTON POST, 11 and 13 May 1941; See also *New York Times*, 15 May 1941; *Star*, Indianapolis, 13 May 1941
32. (SIR) A. WATT, *Australian Diplomat*, Sydney, 1972, p. 40
33. DAILY HERALD, London, 12 May 1941
34. CABLE, Fadden to Menzies, 11 May 1941, CRS A5954, Box 630, "Correspondence with Australia—Political and General": AA
35. CABLE, Menzies (in Washington) to Fadden, 13 May 1941, AA CP 290/9, (15) SC: AA
36. CABLE NO. 307, Fadden to Menzies, 14 May 1941; Cable, Menzies to Fadden, 14 May 1941, CRS A5954, Box 630, "Correspondence with Australia—Political and General": AA
37. CABLE, Churchill to Mackenzie King, 11 May 1941, W. S. Churchill, *The Second World War*, iii, Sydney, 1950, p. 680
38. NOTE, Cranborne to Churchill, 12 May 1941, PREM 4/43A/12: PRO
39. M. GILBERT, p. 1087
40. DALTON DIARY, 12 May 1941, Dalton Papers: LSE
41. LETTER, Duke of Bedford to R. R. Stokes, MP, 10 May 1941, copy sent to Lloyd George by Stokes, 5 June 1941, G/19/3/26, Lloyd George Papers: HLRO
42. LETTER, Stokes to Lloyd George, 14 May 1941, G/19/3/27, Lloyd George Papers: HLRO
43. SEE: Lockhart Diary, 17 May 1941, K. Young (ed.), ii, pp. 99—100
44. C. ROLPH, *The Life, Letters and Diaries of Kingsley Martin*, London, 1973, p. 240
45. NICOLSON DIARY, 16 May 1941, Sir H. Nicolson (ed.), pp. 166—7
46. KING DIARY, 15 May 1941, C. King, p. 129
47. MINUTE, Eden to Churchill, 13 May 1941 with note by Churchill, 15 May 1941, PREM 3/476/10: PRO
48. NEW YORK TIMES, 14 May 1941
49. CHRISTIAN SCIENCE MONITOR, Boston, 15 May 1941
50. NEWS, Chicago, 15 May 1941
51. TRIBUNE, Salt Lake City, 17 May 1941
52. NEWS, Chicago, 16 May 1941
53. TRIBUNE, Chicago, 16 May 1941
54. LETTER, Halifax to Hankey, 25 May 1941, HNKY 5/4, Hankey Papers: CC
55. LIFE, 16 May 1941
56. HERALD TRIBUNE, New York, 15 May 1941. See also *Time*, 19 May 1941; *Tribune*, Salt Lake City, 20 May 1941; *News*, Chicago, 16 May 1941
57. One freelance Australian journalist in London recalled that Menzies had privately told the reporters that "Churchill talked too much." This journalist

was not impressed with the contrast between Menzies' private criticisms of Churchill and his public protestations of loyalty and friendship. Menzies, the journalist wrote, was "just a politician, insincere and fond of the sweets of office and the patronage associated with it . . . A four-flusher—that's what Mr. Menzies is. . ." Letter, John Hughes to his daughter, 22 July 1942, HUGHES 75/9/1, John Hughes Papers: IWM

58. NOTE of meeting with Sir Philip Game, 15 May 1941, CRS M100, "May 1941": AA

59. *SMITH'S WEEKLY*, Sydney, 17 May 1941

60. *SUN*, Melbourne, 21 May 1941. See also *Herald*, Melbourne, 23 May 1941

61. *ARGUS*, Melbourne, 23 May 1941

62. *SUN*, Sydney, 22 May 1941

63. *SUNDAY SUN*, Sydney, 18 May 1941; *Telegraph*, Brisbane, 21 May 1941; *Courier-Mail*, Brisbane, 23 May 1941

64. MENZIES DIARY, 23 May 1941

65. *HERALD*, Melbourne, 24 May 1941

13

Menzies Aims for London

A ustralia anxiously awaited Menzies' return. He had been away for four months and had returned almost empty handed. He had not managed to arrange for the transfer of manufacturing facilities; reinforcements of aircraft for Australia and Singapore were still vague promises; Australian troops in the Middle East had been mauled in Greece while others remained trapped in Tobruk; the British guarantee to send a fleet to the Far East in the event of war with Japan was looking extremely suspect; the transfer of part of the US Pacific Fleet could well prove instrumental in encouraging Japanese expansion in the Pacific; Australian—British relations had been soured by Menzies' attempts to undermine Churchill's power; and Australia's primary industries faced ruin as a result of his acceptance of British cutbacks. The one clear advantage for Australia was that she could no longer harbour any illusions about Britain springing to her defence in case of attack. Thus, a new sense of purpose and urgency could be instilled in the Australian war effort.

Fortunately for Menzies, Australia was so taken aback by the impression he had created overseas that the country took some time to realise that his trip had been an abysmal failure so far as national needs were concerned. The Australian press generally welcomed his return and called for him to provide unity and leadership.[1] The Boothby by-election was won by the UAP candidate so that Menzies retained his one-seat majority in Parliament. It should therefore have been possible for him once more to take up the reins of power and establish himself in a way that he had not previously been able to do.

Once again, Menzies was his own worst enemy. A comment made on landing in Sydney did much to arouse the political enmity which seemed always to surround his person in Australia. In a broadcast to the nation, Menzies said that it was "diabolical that anyone should have to return to Australia and play party politics...in this great national crisis''.[2] Though he was probably referring more to some of his own colleagues who were conspiring for his removal,[3] the comment was pitched in such a way that it upset the Labor Party. Fadden was also upset by Menzies' attitude on landing in Sydney. After acting in Menzies' stead for four months, Fadden was virtually ignored by the returning Premier. And then, as if to add insult to injury, Menzies commandeered Fadden's car for the trip into Sydney, leaving Fadden to make his own arrangements.[4]

Also waiting to greet Menzies at the Rose Bay landing stage was Labor's ambitious Dr Evatt. Evatt gave him a long letter which surveyed the aimless Australian war effort and called for Menzies to form some kind of national administration. Evatt claimed to be ''worried to distraction about the disillusionment and the defeatism which are evident in so many places''. He then made an implicit suggestion for Menzies to invite him and several others into a coalition administration that would provide political stability by increasing Menzies' parliamentary majority.[5] There is no evidence that Menzies made any attempt to take up Evatt's offer. He might well have reasoned that such an administration would still be too shaky to permit his return to London and that the power-hungry Evatt was simply using him as support to allow himself to climb into the Prime Ministerial office.

On this first day back in Australia, Menzies also received a cable from Beaverbrook which confirmed his backing for Menzies' early return to London. He assured Menzies that he would welcome him back to London with ''much more enthusiasm than any other visitor from any other part of the Empire'' and he hoped that Australia would ''decide to send you soon and keep you here for as long as the war lasts''.[6] This was just what Menzies wanted to hear. His three weeks in transit to Australia had largely cut him off from his British contacts and it was reassuring to know that his plans for London remained viable. It was with considerable warmth that he replied to Beaverbrook, informing him that their association was one of the highlights of his journey and that he would ''ask for nothing better than to renew it''.[7]

The same day that Beaverbrook dispatched his cable, his *Daily Express* urged that Menzies ''should be relieved of political anxieties so that he can come to Britain and work in the cause of democracy and freedom''.[8] Two days later, after the Boothby by-election, the *Daily Express* called for a national government in Australia that would ''enable Menzies' great gifts to be put at the service of the War Cabinet here in London, where the swift war decisions have to be made''.[9] Again, on 30 May, the paper argued against Labor objections to a national government and urged that one be formed which would "release Menzies for a post in the War Cabinet in London. . .where the whole Empire wants to see his abilities used".[10]

This support from Beaverbrook was useful for keeping Menzies' name before the British public and establishing an overwhelming claim to a seat in the War Cabinet. In Australia, though, these continual reports of a British destiny awaiting Menzies helped to further unsettle his position as Prime Minister. Apparently, Menzies' plan was to establish himself firmly as a dynamic and forthright war leader of a national government before making the switch to Westminster. Too much press talk of a likely London post hampered this plan.

On Monday, 26 May, two days after his return, Menzies addressed a large public meeting in Sydney. This was the meeting Fadden had organised to stabilise public opinion and stop the drift to Labor. Menzies' speech, which was broadcast nationally, called on Australians to unify behind his leadership and push their war effort to the limit. As for the war itself, Menzies denied that he had ever anticipated defeat for Britain but he stressed that, "if there is one year in the history of the British people that can be described as a year of Fate it is 1941. . . . I tell you I pray to God we shall go through 1941 to safety."[11]

Menzies' speech was widely welcomed as being the "speech of a leader determined to leave Australians under no further possible illusion as to the necessity for a greater war effort and increased personal sacrifices".[12] However, the value of the speech was quickly depreciated by the continual rumours of his wish to return to London.

On 28 May, Menzies reported to the Advisory War Council on the results of his trip. All the rationale for making the trip was now forgotten as he regaled the Council with a long diatribe on the lack of proper leadership in London. He described the British War Cabinet as not "an effective Cabinet as ordinarily understood" and that the Cabinet system simply did not operate in the United Kingdom. He blamed this solely on Churchill, who dominated his fellow members. Menzies claimed that *he* was the only one who offered criticism within the War Cabinet or, apart from Churchill, originated discussions on strategy. He informed the Council that the really effective organ was the Defence Committee, but it too was dominated by Churchill's strategical views. Menzies had little good to say of any of the Cabinet except Beaverbrook, whom he described as the one man able to stand up to Churchill.[13]

Menzies' solution for the failings of this body was the familiar one spelt out in his discussion with Lloyd George. Menzies now tried to press this onto his Advisory War Council, arguing:

> the ideal War Cabinet should consist of five or six Ministers without departmental responsibilities. This body should hold daily meetings and review the military situation with the Chiefs of Staff. They would be able to devote their entire energies to the higher direction of the war. A War Cabinet constituted on these lines functioned in the later stages of the last war. Mr. Lloyd George informed the Prime Minister that no War Cabinet can be effective which does not include a Dominion representative.[14]

Menzies stressed the importance of having such a Dominions representative and claimed in justification that Churchill had "no conception of the British Dominions as separate entities" and that "the more distant the problem from the heart of the Empire, the less he thinks of it".[15] It was obviously important for Menzies to try to convince his Council colleagues of the need for someone, such as himself, to push the Dominion viewpoint in London and limit Churchill's unbridled power over strategy. However, the more Menzies pursued this argument, the less convincing was his appeal for a greater Australian war effort under his leadership.

The attraction of London was so obviously reflected in Menzies' eyes that his report to the Australian parliament was overshadowed by speculation about his plans to return there. Menzies kept the rumours going by refusing to either confirm or deny their substance. On 31 May, the *Age* reported that both Menzies and the Government favoured direct representation on the British War Cabinet but that "Menzies himself would not return except in the capacity of Prime Minister, holding essential authority".[16] While Menzies tried to secure his Australian base preparatory to returning to London, Churchill was just as assiduously trying to sidetrack his efforts.

Malcolm MacDonald, Britain's High Commissioner in Canada, reported on Menzies' visit to Ottawa and his efforts to muster support for an Imperial Conference. Menzies' breakfast talk with him had paid dividends and MacDonald's report praised Menzies' personal triumph in Ottawa and claimed that Mackenzie King would support a proposal for a shorter Imperial Conference of two to three weeks. It is likely that MacDonald rather than Mackenzie King had been convinced by Menzies of the need for such a conference and was doing what he could to bring it about. Certainly, his report of Mackenzie King's view was a considerable overstatement.[17]

MacDonald's report reached Churchill in late May just as the terrible Crete campaign came to a close. The island was massively attacked by German airborne troops on 20 May and within a week, the Royal Navy was carrying out yet another evacuation without the vital assistance of air support. For four nights from 28 May, the small ships of the Royal Navy repeatedly anchored off the beaches of Crete to take on survivors of the battle. Barely a third were snatched from the clutches of the Germans and the navy suffered grievously for its efforts. Three cruisers and six destroyers were sunk by German dive bombers, while many more ships were badly damaged. One sailor died for every eight troops rescued.

The pursuit of Churchill's "Balkan front" had cost Australia dear in dead and captured troops. But as well the combined effect of the evacuations from Greece and Crete had hit the Royal Navy hard. The Mediterranean Fleet was now seriously depleted and any reserve capacity Britain may have had to dispatch a large naval force to the Far East had been destroyed. Menzies' support for that policy had played a crucial part in demolishing the 150-year-old edifice of Australian defence. Even had she been willing to, Britain could no longer protect Australia with the guns of the Royal Navy.

The loss of Crete, following hard on the defeats in Libya and Greece, was a severe blow to Churchill. It increased the political pressure on his leadership and renewed the calls for an Imperial War Cabinet. Facing this situation Churchill now appeared to consent to the call for an Imperial Conference. On 28 May he informed Cranborne that he was "quite agreeable" to a conference and he proposed July as a possible time to hold it.[18] It would soon be clear that Churchill was merely playing for time and that he was strenuously resisting the idea.

The position in Crete also meant more trouble for Menzies. Australian troops caught on the island were sent there against the express wish of the Australian Government and their predicament was again marked by a lack of air support and proper equipment. There was also a force of Australian troops on Cyprus which seemed set to share the fate of their fellows on Crete. On 29 May, Menzies cabled to Churchill to impress upon him the depth of the Australian concern and he urged Churchill to send "large and urgent reinforcements of fighter planes" to the Middle East. He emphasised that a "defeat around the Suez would be a calamity of the first magnitude, and it appears to us that the most effective counter is in the air".[19] Menzies' vision of losing Suez was hardly calculated to endear him to Churchill who was trying desperately to stiffen the British resolve to defend the area.[20]

On the same day that Menzies dispatched his querulous cable, Churchill saw fit to acknowledge Menzies' success in North America and congratulated him on the "powerful, moving addresses you have delivered in Canada, the United States, and above all on your return home" which had "confirmed all the goodwill you gathered from our people".[21] In his reply, Menzies informed Churchill that he was "not without hopes of reducing such political difficulties as exist here".[22] Churchill well knew that the reduction of Menzies' political difficulties in Australia could launch him straight back at London. However, even then, Churchill was moving to ensure that this would not happen.

On 30 May, Churchill followed up his earlier agreement to an Imperial Conference with a proposal that there be a simultaneous inter-Allied Council. In a minute to Cranborne and Eden, Churchill noted that the Dominion Prime Ministers might well be in London in July and suggested it would be a good time for a "rally of all the Allied powers whose representatives are here".[23] Churchill's proposal was presumably an attempt to create, during a difficult time, a picture of overwhelming support for Britain and hence for his own leadership. It would be difficult in such a situation for Dominion Prime Ministers, either separately or together to question this leadership.

In Cranborne, Churchill had a ready ally for his plans. In fact, Cranborne suggested that the Imperial Conference need not be held in the immediate future. He pointed out that a July meeting would mean bringing Menzies back almost immediately and that while Menzies would be delighted, Cranborne asked Churchill whether he would "want him back quite so (soon)". He also advised Churchill that Mackenzie King was "clearly very wobbly about coming". Instead Cranborne suggested an individual invitation to the South African Prime Minister, Smuts, to come to London. In the midst of all his military worries, Churchill was unwilling to decide between the various proposals and instructed Cranborne to submit the matter to the War Cabinet.[24] No doubt Churchill was also very wary of being seen to be too vigorous in his own opposition to a Conference. It was much more preferable that the whole War Cabinet be seen to kill the proposal for purely practical reasons.

Meanwhile, the fall of Crete had again spurred Churchill's critics into activity. On 29 May, Hankey met with Lloyd George for the first time since the war began and found a broad basis for agreement on Churchill's failings. Hankey noted in his diary that they then discussed the possibility of Lloyd George joining a re-formed War Cabinet with Lloyd George suggesting that he might be willing to enter a War

Cabinet with Churchill and Beaverbrook. Hankey was surprised to find Lloyd George very well informed on both military and political developments. He concluded that it was "quite clear that one of his main sources of information was Beaverbrook...".[25] Though Lloyd George apparently did not raise Menzies' name in connection with the War Cabinet, Hankey was certainly determined that both Lloyd George and Menzies should be included among its number.

While Hankey was seeking out Lloyd George, he himself was being sought by others equally concerned at the military situation. Leading military figures as well as the influential Conservative peer Lord Salisbury, used Hankey as a sounding board for their criticisms of Churchill.[26] On 6 June, Hankey met Salisbury and talked at length over tea. Hankey later confided in his diary of his plan to "get Ll. G. into the Govt. with Menzies" and that Salisbury had agreed that Menzies would be "useful".[27]

It was at this time that Churchill tried to entice Beaverbrook back into a closer association by offering him the Ministry of Food. Beaverbrook refused, presumably preferring to await the outcome of the rising dissatisfaction.[28] On 2 June, the same day that Beaverbrook refused the Food Ministry, Oliver Harvey noted the extent of the dissatisfaction that was blossoming following the fall of Crete. In his diary he plaintively asked who could take the place of Churchill. Harvey concluded that there was only Beaverbrook and Lloyd George in the public mind, and "goodness knows where they would lead the country to—to Berchesgarten [sic] probably".[29] Similarly, the Conservative MP Paul Emrys-Evans advised Harvey that Churchill must either explain Crete or be overturned and that Churchill needed "good vigorous 'No men'".[30]

The stridency of Menzies' cables to Churchill likewise increased apace with the deteriorating military situation. On 4 June, Menzies sent his very strong view that Cyprus was more threatened than the British Chiefs of Staff cared to admit and that the island must be "either abandoned or reinforced to the point at which it can be held". Menzies warned that public opinion in Australia would be greatly strained by "what would be regarded as a useless sacrifice of an inadequate force". And, despite Churchill's earlier cable, Menzies repeated his call for greater air reinforcements.[31] Churchill was hardly likely to be impressed with the argument that he should fashion his military moves to suit public opinion or by the implication that he could be accused of a wanton waste of manpower.

As the impact of Crete hit home, Menzies helped to stimulate the

criticism and give it a political direction that was aimed squarely at
Churchill. In London, Menzies was reported as saying that it was
"tragic to think that our forces in Crete suffered so much through the
lack of proper equipment, and a full and adequate Air Force". He
pointedly warned that this must be the "final lesson".[32] This was
obviously a direct hit at Churchill's involvement in three consecutive
military disasters—Norway, Greece and Crete—all ones where troops
were slaughtered after being sent into the field with inadequate air
support.

At the same time, Menzies further promoted his own inclusion in
the British War Cabinet as a solution to past ills. Beaverbrook's *Daily
Express* reported on 5 June that Menzies was "more than ever convinced today of the need for Australia to be represented in the British
Cabinet" and was urging that he be sent to London to "press Commonwealth interests and to help in stimulating the war effort".[33] This
was considerable cheek from Menzies, since the Greek and Cretan
disasters had arisen during and despite his presence in London. Still, the
call was echoed widely in Australia and Britain.

On 5 June, the Melbourne *Age* reacted to the reported losses of
Australian soldiers in Greece and Crete (some 8000 in all) by criticising
the reactive war strategy of Churchill and calling for "more direct and
continuous Dominions representation in Britain's war councils".[34] In
Britain, the *Manchester Guardian* also maintained that, in the wake of
the Crete defeat, the "presence of a leading Dominion representative
all the time in London must be assured" and proposed the calling
together of an Imperial War Cabinet to "review the general strategy
and future of the war".[35]

Though there was increased support for an Imperial War Cabinet,
or some variation thereof, the practical problems of calling all the
Dominion Premiers together remained difficult. In a memorandum for
the War Cabinet, Cranborne surveyed the difficulty of obtaining the
simultaneous presence of Smuts and Mackenzie King. Both had
pressing political problems at home and were reluctant to become too
closely identified with London. As for Menzies, Cranborne reminded
his colleagues that the Australian Premier had "only just arrived in
Australia, and would have to start back almost at once". Cranborne
did admit that this would not be impossible as Menzies' "public
utterances since his return make it clear that he is quite ready to
come".[36]

Before the War Cabinet could consider this memorandum, Cranborne and Eden advised Churchill that, in view of Mackenzie King's

reluctance, the proposed conference should be postponed until later in the year. In the interim, Smuts should be invited to visit London. To this, Churchill readily agreed.[37] And, when the memorandum did come before the War Cabinet on 9 June, the decision was made formally to sound out the Premiers on the possibility of a summer conference. If the replies were negative, as could be expected, the War Cabinet would continue with their plan of a succession of visits to Britain by Dominion leaders.[38]

With an Imperial Conference now apparently blocked, Churchill proceeded with the proposed meeting of Allied representatives to provide a picture of solidarity built around his leadership. On 7 June, the day after Churchill agreed to postpone the Imperial Conference, Cranborne cabled to Australia with a proposal for an Allied meeting on 12 June. Cranborne argued that the time was "opportune for a declaration of allied solidarity in view of present German Peace propaganda offensive".[39] Though Menzies agreed to the meeting, he did so on condition that any public declaration arising from the meeting would not go beyond the vague principles previously outlined.[40] He also declared that the "conference should not be designated or constitute itself as Supreme War Council. . ."[41] Menzies was apparently anxious that he not be outmanoeuvred by Churchill, that the chance for peace not be foreclosed and that the Allied meeting should not substitute for an Imperial Conference.

Churchill also cabled to Menzies on 7 June. With an Imperial Conference averted, Churchill proposed instituting a private channel of communication between himself and Menzies for personal cables.[42] The rationale for this is not quite clear. Perhaps Churchill thought this simple expedient could partly assuage Menzies' desire to partake in the war's direction. Then again, Churchill may have wanted to restrict the circulation of Menzies' increasingly critical views. If the latter was his intention, he was to be disappointed, since Menzies repeated the criticisms of his first private cable to Churchill in a similar cable to Bruce.

Menzies' cable to Churchill and Bruce again concerned the Australian troops on Cyprus who, he feared, were clearly facing a similar disaster to Crete. He warned that the Australian reaction to a further disaster could topple the Government, and he again urged that the island be either adequately reinforced or abandoned.[43] Menzies was anxious to limit the political repercussions from any more defeats and his efforts continued to drive the wedge deeper between himself and Churchill.

Meanwhile, the calls for Menzies' return to London increased in intensity. On 8 June, the *Sunday Graphic* printed a full-page article by Beverly Baxter MP, a close associate of Beaverbrook, who nominated four men to direct the war—Churchill, Smuts, Menzies and General McNaughton, Commander of the Canadian troops in Britain.[44] That same day, Kemsley's *Sunday Chronicle* called for an Imperial War Cabinet to be immediately introduced and noted that Menzies' visit had been a tonic with public and politicians impressed by his eloquence and statesmanship.[45] The following day, the call was echoed in the *Times*, which criticised the war's direction, urging that some of the burden be removed from Churchill and that Menzies should return as a member of an Imperial War Cabinet.[46]

Much of this press criticism was probably directed at influencing the Commons debate on Crete scheduled for 10 June. Still Lloyd George held back from a frontal assault on Churchill. Perhaps he was still smarting from Churchill's "Pétain" jibe during their previous confrontation but, whatever the reason, he judged that Churchill could not be toppled by Crete alone.[47]

While Lloyd George awaited his opportunity to strike, Hankey continued his efforts to boost both Lloyd George and Menzies for the War Cabinet. On 9 June, the day of the *Times* editorial, Hankey discussed the situation with Bruce. Hankey noted in his diary that Bruce "let himself go about Churchill, and said he was sending a long telegram to Australia about it".[48] It is not clear how far this cable was a personal initiative by Bruce. Certainly the cable was in line with Hankey's own feelings.

In his cable, Bruce predicted that, in the Commons debate on Crete, Churchill would "face a House nearly as critical in temper as one Chamberlain confronted after Norway". The difference, though, would be that there was now no obvious successor waiting in the wings. If there were such a successor, Bruce claimed that the Commons would try to force a small War Cabinet onto Churchill and, if he refused to accept it, would "record a vote similar to that after Norway". Since there was no successor, Bruce correctly predicted that the debate would "probably lead to nothing with possibly a debating triumph for the Prime Minister".[49]

Despite the probable failure of the debate to effect political changes, Bruce argued that there was an overwhelming case for drastic alterations. He was already aware of Menzies' own views and his cable was presumably designed to prompt Menzies to further efforts. Bruce informed him that, in the absence of anyone strong enough either in the War Cabinet or outside of it, the only way to force the necessary changes on Churchill was for the Dominion Prime Ministers to act as one.[50]

Bruce urged that the four Dominion Prime Ministers should go immediately to London as "time is the essence of the contract". He advised Menzies that Fraser, the New Zealand Prime Minister, was due in London shortly and that Menzies could "get here in three to four weeks and Smuts and Mackenzie King in a shorter period". If this assembly was not practicable, Bruce proposed that the four Premiers should make joint representations to Churchill from their respective countries to achieve a smaller War Cabinet comprised of

(1) the Prime Minister; (2) a Dominion Prime Minister if one could be found who could stay here. . . . (3) the Secretary of State for the Dominions who should be the best man available after the Prime Minister. . .; (4) the best representative of Labour available; (5) Possibly one other.[51]

As the fifth representative, Bruce suggested that he would not "exclude the idea of Lloyd George notwithstanding his age and all that can be said against him". Though Bruce left the final composition as a "matter for consultation with Churchill", he suggested to Menzies that the Dominions were "entitled to insist on the inclusion of the Dominions Secretary and . . . only someone acceptable to them should be appointed as Dominions Secretary".[52]

If Bruce's suggestion were put into operation, Churchill could well be faced with a hostile War Cabinet composed of Menzies, Lloyd George and a Dominions Secretary not necessarily of his own choosing. Churchill's power over policy would effectively end and the way would be open for his replacement. No wonder, then, that Menzies was greatly encouraged by Bruce's cable. Stuck in Australia and operating under wartime censorship, he must have begun to feel isolated from the political storms raging in London.

In his reply to Bruce, Menzies cabled that he had received his views with "great interest and with approval" and that they were "substantially identical with those I had just previously put before my colleagues as a result of my experiences in London". Menzies advised Bruce that his political problems were considerable but that he hoped soon to make a major statement on the war effort which might well ease his difficulties and allow a further trip to London.[53]

From Canberra, the war situation looked black everywhere. From London, at least for Churchill, it was brighter. He knew of Rommel's problems in Libya and, by now, of Hitler's plans against Russia. He therefore could entertain a much more optimistic view of Britain's chances in the Middle East. With these differing views of the military scene, further conflict between Menzies and Churchill was inevitable. During this time, Menzies relentlessly harried Churchill about the Middle East and the adequacy of his plans to defend it. This was partly at the behest of his Labor critics, but also as a result of his own jaundiced view of Churchill as a military strategist.[54]

Menzies' importuning over the fate of his troops was further confirmation for Churchill that the Australian was an inveterate defeatist. On 11 June, after yet another cable of concern from Menzies about Cyprus, Churchill replied sharply that the risks facing the Australians were reasonable and that the only alternative was "immediate evacuation, inviting unopposed landing". Nevertheless, Churchill claimed that he was "anxious to help you in your difficulties, and, if you wish it, I will see that Australian troops are withdrawn from Cyprus with or without relief".[55] Churchill's view was clear—Menzies was running from a fight for purely political reasons. Though he offered to withdraw the Australians, it would obviously only be done under duress and with much bitterness. For the time being, Menzies took the point and let the matter lie.

On 11 June, Churchill contacted Mackenzie King to propose formally the Canadian's presence at an Imperial Conference at the end of July.[56] He presumably hoped that the latter would reject the invitation and put an end to the proposal. This supposition is given force by the fact that Churchill did not offer a general invitation to all the Dominion Prime Ministers. Had he done so, he could have been faced with the prospect of acceptances from Fraser, Menzies and Smuts, which would have made a conference practically unavoidable. In the House of Commons, Churchill continued to divert calls for an Imperial War Cabinet, while claiming that he would welcome an Imperial Conference. At the same time, he prepared his critics for disappointment by pointing to the different circumstances facing each Dominion and the difficulty of arranging for all the Premiers to be simultaneously present.[57]

Bruce was informed by Cranborne on 11 June that Churchill was planning an Imperial Conference for the end of July but that Mackenzie King's reluctance to attend had first to be overcome. It is likely that Cranborne was consciously assisting Churchill here in trying to shift responsibility for aborting the conference onto Mackenzie King. Bruce argued with Cranborne that a conference was imperative and that objections from Canada should not be permitted to impede it.[58] However, Bruce's efforts were in vain.

With Mackenzie King staying put in Ottawa, Churchill issued a personal invitation to Smuts on 13 June to visit London in the summer. He asked the South African to provide him with the "support of your presence and advice".[59] Churchill clearly hoped that the presence of Smuts, in seeming re-creation of his role in the First World War, would neutralise much of the criticism. But for Menzies, who Churchill knew was willing to come and who was well regarded and even demanded in London, no invitation was forthcoming. In fact, Churchill bent all his efforts to ensure that Menzies would never return to London during the war.

While Churchill forestalled the calling of a conference, the British press increased its calls for just such an event. On 12 June, the *Daily Telegraph* claimed it was necessary in order to "consider what system of direction will concentrate the maximum of Imperial energy most effectively".[60] Beaverbrook's *Daily Express* reported on Menzies' continued desire to resume his seat in the British War Cabinet,[61] while the *Sunday Times* and *Manchester Dispatch* argued that "an Imperial Conference must not be long delayed . . . "[62]

With the war raging, critics of Churchill necessarily had to be circumspect in their public utterings for fear of affecting morale or giving comfort to the enemy. But calls for greater Imperial co-ordination and control over the war were difficult to slur as unpatriotic and they allowed an outlet for those seeking to change the policies or personnel of the War Cabinet. Within the Parliament an opportunity for more candid expression was provided by the committees of backbench MPs which met to argue privately the debates of the day.

In 1940 what was known as the Conservative Watching Committee—a self-appointed group of backbenchers—had been instrumental in directing criticism at Chamberlain and was at least partially responsible for his resignation from the Prime Ministership and for the elevation of Churchill. This committee remained in existence under Churchill and continued to keep a watching brief over his handling of the war. On 17 June, one week after he had supposedly defused the parliamentary revolt over Crete, the Watching Committee met to consider the situation. Chaired by the elderly but influential Lord Salisbury, the 17 MPs revealed that their criticisms of the Crete debacle had been far from satisfied. More importantly, the meeting revealed these men to be of a similar mind to Menzies in their view of Churchill and the conduct of the war. One member received broad

agreement from his fellows when he bitterly attacked Crete as a
"stupendous blunder" and laid the blame firmly at the feet of
Churchill who was "acting as Commander-in-Chief rather than as
Prime Minister". He also linked Menzies with "the Generals",
claiming that they were all "very perturbed".[63]

The strength of the criticisms in the Watching Committee, and
the disquiet felt among the upper echelons of the Army meant that
Churchill's position was still insecure. In this instance he was helped by
coincidence and circumstance. Lord Salisbury managed to adjourn the
discussion of the committee, before agreement as to any course of
action could be reached, until a later date. As it happened, Salisbury
was the father of Lord Cranborne, and a successful attack on Churchill
could well have produced the downfall of his son. Whether this was the
reason for Salisbury heading off the attacks on Churchill quickly
became as irrelevant as the attacks themselves. The massed German
armour on the Russian border would soon rivet the attention of everyone—diverting it from Churchill—when it was released in a headlong
rush across the steppes of the Soviet Union.

On 17 June, Menzies broadcast to Australia and overseas, setting
out his plans for an "all-in" war effort in Australia. This was the
speech that Menzies hoped would send him back to London. It met
with a good reception in Australia, where it had been long awaited. In
London it carried a different dimension and greatly stimulated the calls
for his return. Kemsley's *Daily Sketch* greeted the speech with .
a call for Menzies' brains and energy to be harnessed for the
benefit of the Empire as a whole.[64] Kemsley's call was repeated in
various forms throughout the British press.[65]

Meanwhile, Churchill's attempt to use a visit by Smuts as a means
of appeasing his critics came to naught. On 17 June, the British High
Commissioner in South Africa advised that it would be most unwise for
Smuts to leave South Africa in the near future while the fate of his
forces in Libya remained unclear.[66] With Smuts unable, and Mackenzie
King unwilling, to go to London, Cranborne now asked Churchill what
was to be done about Menzies. Specifically, should Menzies now
receive an invitation to visit London alone? In the margin of Cranborne's note, Churchill wrote tersely, "*No*."[67]

With nothing to appease the calls for greater Dominion representation, Cranborne warned that the agitation by the Parliament and the
press would go on and might prove a serious embarrassment. Still,
Churchill was prepared to weather the political storm rather than have
Menzies return. He informed Cranborne that he would announce in

the Commons that "Smuts and MK cannot come; Fraser is arriving and Menzies has just gone home" and that it did not "therefore seem possible to have much of a conference!".[68]

On 21 June, the London correspondent of the Melbourne *Age* openly reported on the need for political changes in the War Cabinet and aired the major criticism of Churchill's administration—that he was surrounded by "Yes-men". The correspondent revealed that Churchill had refused to invite Menzies to remain as a permanent member of the War Cabinet despite Menzies' obvious willingness to do so. This, the report claimed, was because Churchill feared that Menzies might pose a political threat to himself, that Menzies had "already attracted a great deal of public attention, and, as a member of the War Cabinet, he would automatically have become a spectacular figure".[69]

The *Age* report was a reflection of the continuing unease in London that was marked by ceaseless rumours of imminent political changes. In fact, on 21 June, Churchill was sufficiently moved by one such report, in the *Observer*, to issue an official denial that it had any substance. That report had noted, among other things, "the persistent support for the return to this country of Mr. R. G. Menzies... either as Minister of Defence, or some other responsible position in the War Cabinet".[70]

Churchill also acted that day to confirm finally to Menzies that the latter's hopes for an Imperial Conference were shattered. Churchill informed him that neither Smuts nor Mackenzie King would be available for a conference in July and that the question of such a meeting would therefore have to be dropped.[71]

Churchill's cable reached Menzies just at the time when his view of the war reached its nadir. On 20 June, Menzies had been informed that Wavell's much-vaunted counter-attack against Rommel had ended in failure. Though Churchill assured Menzies that Egypt was still secure, he refused to make any promises or give any guarantees "except that we will do our best".[72]

Menzies was apparently devastated by this news and immediately suspected that Wavell had been forced into a premature attack by pressure from Churchill. There was much truth in this, and Menzies cabled to Blamey in Cairo for confirmation. He refused to accept Churchill's assurance on the security of Egypt and asked Blamey for his own assessment, particularly regarding Tobruk where the Australian troops remained trapped by Rommel's tanks. He also queried Blamey about the "plans for contingencies, including the evacuation of Egypt". Menzies claimed that he had understood in

London that these were in hand and he now wished to be "assured that possible moves have been adequately provided for".[73]

Menzies personally judged that the succession of German victories gave the British position in the Middle East "new elements of doubt-fulness". Tobruk could not now be relieved for some months and Menzies warned that its fall "might have far-reaching effects on public opinion in Australia", while a reverse in Egypt itself would cause "incalculable difficulties" for him.[74] The war was now going much as Menzies feared and he put the blame squarely on Churchill's shoulders. If the Empire were to be saved, Menzies had to find a means of returning to London.

There could have been some solace for Menzies in the *Sunday Times*, which on 22 June again trumpeted his virtues and predicted a big future for him in London.[75] However, even before the paper reached the streets of London, Hitler had intervened to transform the whole situation with the German Army's massive onslaught on Russia. The focus of conflict shifted from the deserts of the Middle East to the vast plains of Russia.

Menzies had now been back in Australia for four weeks. He was little nearer any of his aims. His leadership was still being disputed in Australia, while every path to power in London seemed blocked. The military situation in the Middle East appeared hopeless for Britain. Even the German attack on Russia was seen by Menzies as merely the prelude to a decisive, two-pronged German attack on the British outpost in Egypt.

The British Empire had been given a breathing space by the attack on Russia and Menzies was determined to use it to change the direction of the war and bring it to an end. The war was "do or die" for the Empire; over the coming weeks, it would be "do or die" for Menzies politically as he threw himself desperately into a last attempt to breathe life into his deflating dream of becoming the Imperial saviour.

NOTES

1. *SYDNEY MORNING HERALD*, 24 May 1941, *Sunday Sun*, Sydney, 25 May 1941; *Daily Telegraph*, Sydney, 24 May 1941; *Age*, Melbourne, 26 and 27 May 1941
2. *AGE*, Melbourne, 26 May 1941
3. *SUNDAY SUN*, Sydney, 25 May 1941; C. Hazlehurst, p. 230
4. A. FADDEN, *They Called Me Artie*, Melbourne, 1969, p. 60
5. LETTER, Evatt to Menzies, 24 May 1941, Evatt Collection, "War—ALP Government, Formation of, 1941": Flinders University Library

6. CABLE, Beaverbrook to Menzies, 24 May 1941, BBK D/408, Beaverbrook Papers: HLRO

7. CABLE, Menzies to Beaverbrook, 28 May 1941, BBK D/408, Beaverbrook Papers: HLRO

8. DAILY EXPRESS, London, 24 May 1941

9. DAILY EXPRESS, London, 26 May 1941

10. DAILY EXPRESS, London, 30 May 1941

11. SPEECH BY MENZIES (EXTRACT), 26 May 1941, C. Hazlehurst, pp. 234–5

12. SUN, Melbourne, Courier-Mail, Brisbane, Sydney Morning Herald, Daily Telegraph, Sydney, 27 May 1941

13. ADVISORY WAR COUNCIL MINUTES, 28 May 1941, CRS A2682/2/346: AA

14. IBID.

15. IBID.

16. AGE, Melbourne, 31 May 1941. See also New York Times, Scotsman, Yorkshire Post, Times, 31 May 1941; K. Perkins, Menzies, London, 1968, p. 116

17. NOTE, Cranborne to Churchill, 26 May 1941, enclosing report from Malcolm MacDonald, 14 May 1941, PREM 4/43A/12: PRO. For Mackenzie King's view, see Cable, Mackenzie King to Churchill, 26 May 1941, D. R. Murray (ed.), Documents on Canadian External Relations, vol. 7, 1974, Doc. 563

18. IBID.

19. DAFP, iv, Doc. 475, Cable No. 2649, Menzies to Churchill, 29 May 1941

20. In his reply, Churchill rebutted Menzies' criticisms and claimed that Britain was sending as much air reinforcement to the Middle East as the supply routes could stand. DAFP, iv, Doc. 478, Cable No. 386, Churchill to Menzies, 31 May 1941

21. CABLE (DRAFT), Churchill to Menzies, 29 May 1941, PREM 4/50/15: PRO

22. CABLE NO. 331, Menzies to Churchill, received 31 May 1941, PREM 4/50/15: PRO

23. MINUTE, Churchill to Cranborne and Eden, 30 May 1941, PREM 4/43A/12: PRO

24. MINUTE, Cranborne to Churchill, 30 May 1941, PREM 4/43A/12: PRO

25. HANKEY DIARY, 29 May 1941, S. Roskill, iii, pp. 510–2

26. HANKEY DIARY, 1–9 June 1941, S. Roskill, iii, pp. 512–5

27. HANKEY DIARY, 6 June 1941, S. Roskill, iii, p. 514

28. K. YOUNG, Churchill and Beaverbrook, London, 1966, p. 191

29. HARVEY DIARY, 2 June 1941, ADD.MS.56397, Harvey Papers: BL; see also, Letter, Harvey to Emrys-Evans, 3 June 1941, ADD.MS.58235, Emrys-Evans Papers: BL

30. LETTER, P. Emrys-Evans to Harvey, 5 June 1941, ADD.MS.56402, Harvey Papers; see also Channon Diary, 6 June 1941, R. R. James (ed.) p. 307; Letter, P. J. Grigg to his father, 7 June 1941, PJGG 9/6/14, Grigg Papers: CC

31. DAFP, iv, Doc. 483, Cable No. 344, Menzies to Churchill, 4 June 1941

32. DAILY SKETCH, London, 6 June 1941

33. DAILY EXPRESS, London, 5 June 1941

34. AGE, Melbourne, 5 June 1941

35. MANCHESTER GUARDIAN, 6 June 1941

36. "MEETING OF DOMINION PRIME MINISTERS", Memorandum by Cranborne, 4 June 1941, Cab. 66/16, W.P.(41)121: PRO

37. MINUTE, Cranborne to Churchill, 6 June 1941, PREM 4/43A/12: PRO
38. WAR CABINET CONCLUSIONS, 9 June 1941, Cab. 65/18, W.M.58(41): PRO
39. *DAFP*, iv, Doc. 492, Cable D335, Cranborne to Commonwealth Government, 7 June 1941
40. For details of the principles see *DAFP*, iv, Doc. 205
41. *DAFP*, iv, Doc. 495, Cable No. 2904, Menzies to Bruce, 10 June 1941
42. *DAFP*, iv, Doc. 491, Cable, Churchill to Menzies, 7 June 1941
43. *DAFP*, iv, Doc. 493, Cable No. 2855, Menzies to Bruce, 8 June 1941
44. *SUNDAY GRAPHIC*, London, 8 June 1941
45. *SUNDAY CHRONICLE*, London, 8 June 1941
46. *TIMES*, London, 9 June 1941; see also *Picture Post*, London, 7 June 1941
47. LETTER, Frances Stevenson to Oxford don, Thomas Balogh, 9 June 1941, G/2/1/12, Lloyd George Papers: HLRO
48. HANKEY DIARY, 9 June 1941, S. Roskill, iii, p. 515
49. CABLE NO. 422, Bruce to Menzies, 10 June 1941, CRS M100, "June 1941": AA
50. *IBID*.
51. *IBID*.
52. *IBID*.
53. CABLE NO. 2982, Menzies to Bruce, 13 June 1941, CRS M100, "June 1941": AA
54. SEE CABLE NO. 347, Menzies to Churchill, 6 June 1941, PREM 3/281/10: PRO; Cables No. 363 and Gordon 2, Menzies to Churchill, 12 June 1941, *DAFP*, iv, Docs 500 and 501
55. *DAFP*, iv, Doc. 497, Cable 409, Churchill to Menzies, 11 June 1941
56. CABLE NO. 99, Churchill to Mackenzie King, 11 June 1941, PREM 4/43A/16: PRO
57. Bruce reported to Menzies on Churchill's Commons comment, Cable No. 427, Bruce to Menzies, 11 June 1942, CRS A1608/H/33/1/2: AA
58. *IBID*.
59. CABLE T.290, Churchill to Smuts, 13 June 1941, PREM 4/43A/16: PRO
60. *DAILY TELEGRAPH*, London, 12 June 1941; see also *Sussex Daily News*, 13 June 1941; *Western Mail*, 14 June 1941
61. *DAILY EXPRESS*, London, 13 June 1941
62. *SUNDAY TIMES*, London, 15 June 1941; *Manchester Dispatch*, 14 June 1941
63. "MINUTES OF WATCHING COMMITTEE", 17 June 1941, ADD.MS.58270, Emrys-Evans Papers: BL
64. *DAILY SKETCH*, London, 20 June 1941
65. See *STAR*, London, 19 June 1941; *Glasgow Herald*, 20 June 1941; *Scotsman*, *Liverpool Post*, 18 June 1941; *Daily Telegraph*, London, 19 June 1941; *Times*, London, 19 and 25 June 1941; *Daily Mail*, London, 20 June 1941
66. CABLE NO. 669, UK High Commissioner in South Africa to Dominions Office, 17 June 1941, PREM 4/43A/16: PRO
67. MINUTE, Cranborne to Churchill, 17 June 1941, with attached note by Churchill, 18 June 1941, PREM 4/43A/12: PRO
68. *IBID*.
69. *AGE*, Melbourne, 21 June 1941
70. *OBSERVER*, London, 22 June 1941

71. CABLE NO. 429, Churchill to Menzies, 21 June 1941, PREM 4/43A/12: PRO
72. *DAFP*, iv, Doc. 511, Cable No. 316, Churchill to Menzies, 20 June 1941
73. *DAFP*, iv, Doc. 514, Cable No. 13, Menzies to Blamey, 21 June 1941
74. *IBID.*
75. *SUNDAY TIMES*, London, 22 June 1941; see also *Empire News*, London, 22 June 1941

14

Defeat and Despair

The attack on Russia transformed the whole scope of the war and there can be little doubt it was largely responsible for the eventual German defeat. However, the ramifications of the attack were not generally realised at the time. Russia was not expected to be able to withstand the might of the German armour for more than a few months. After the anticipated Russian defeat, Britain and her forces in the Middle East were predicted as the next target for Germany. The attack on Russia was therefore merely seen as providing a fleeting opportunity for Britain to reinforce her positions at home and abroad.[1] For Menzies, the shift in the direction of the war brought a certain softening in his criticism of Churchill. The Middle East was now not so immediately threatened and Menzies' rising crescendo of criticism, based on fear of losing Egypt, was interrupted for a time.

To Churchill, the German attack was a godsend which shifted attention from the series of British failures in the Mediterranean and North Africa and temporarily released the pressure on his leadership. For those of his critics wanting a negotiated peace, the *de facto* Anglo-Russian alliance opened up the possibility that eventual victory might yet be Churchill's. By attacking her former ally, Russia, Germany also provided clear evidence that a peace settlement would be no guarantee of peace as such.[2] Lloyd George, who had made an alliance with Russia one of the prerequisites for a British victory, now closeted himself away and became completely absorbed in the great battles raging in the East.[3] Beaverbrook was almost alone in foreseeing no early defeat for Russia and turned his energies towards providing her with war materials and general economic succour.[4]

At the time of the German attack, Menzies had been desperately afraid for the Australian forces in the Middle East and was preparing to confront Churchill over his handling of strategy in that area. Given the invasion of Russia, he now merely expressed disappointment at the failure of Wavell's attack against Rommel and advised Churchill to grab the opportunity of bolstering the Middle East. In particular, Menzies pointed to the lack of air support for the beleaguered garrison of Tobruk and asked that it be attended to by Churchill. Menzies' prognosis for the Middle East was still one of gloom and he predicted to Churchill that the Germans would follow their victory in Russia with a massive onslaught against the British Imperial forces in the Middle East.[5]

As for Menzies' return to London and the issue of an Imperial Conference, the pressure continued both in Australia and Britain. The Melbourne *Age* reported that the German attack on Russia would increase the support for the dispatch of an Australian Minister to London and that "leading Government supporters" considered it urgently necessary.[6]

In London, Churchill continued his efforts to prevent Menzies' return, particularly in the context of an Imperial Conference. He prepared to announce in the House of Commons that an Imperial Conference was not practical given the inability of Smuts and Mackenzie King to attend. Before he made the announcement, Mackenzie King requested that Churchill make a fuller explanation in order to assuage those Canadians who were intensely pro-British.

While neither Churchill nor Mackenzie King wanted the conference, neither wanted to be seen as responsible for its abandonment. Therefore, Churchill refused to make a fuller explanation that could picture himself, rather than Mackenzie King, as being the stumbling block. As he informed the Canadian, there was "undoubtedly strong pressure here for a Conference and I would not myself like to argue against it, apart from the practical difficulties involved". Furthermore, Churchill reminded him of the "position of Menzies who as you know has strongly advocated this course . . . ".[7] The following day, 24 June, Churchill made his announcement and based it on practicalities. In order to defuse the criticism, he held out the possibility of a conference in August and, to the cheers of the Commons, expressed the hope to see Menzies in London "before long".[8]

Churchill may well have felt satisfied by the results of his announcement. He had still managed to shift the onus onto Smuts and Mackenzie King, while effectively neutralising the calls for an Imperial Conference. As the London *Daily Telegraph* argued, Churchill's reasons were "decisive and must be accepted". The paper concluded that the difficulty of bringing all the Dominion Premiers together "disposes of any proposal to establish an Imperial War Cabinet" while an Imperial War Conference "could not undertake the direction of the war, as a War Cabinet exists to do".[9]

Menzies now made a bold effort to retrieve the situation. Taking up Bruce's suggestion of 10 June, he cabled to Smuts and Mackenzie King on 3 July arguing the crucial importance of a "short meeting of Dominion Prime Ministers". While Menzies professed the greatest admiration for Churchill, he argued that his visit to London revealed that Churchill carried "far too great an individual burden" and that the existing War Cabinet system was not providing for adequate consideration of long-range war policy. Menzies complained of the direction of Britain's economic and foreign policies, which he urged should be brought under the control of an authoritative Cabinet.[10]

Menzies was still, in these last hours, desperately pushing a range of measures that would secure his inclusion in the War Cabinet and severely restrict Churchill's power. And by forcing an examination of long-range policy, he would be able to open up the possibility of Churchill's "total victory" policy being abandoned in favour of a realistic compromise with Germany. Menzies urged on his Dominion counterparts that there should be a "War Cabinet in the real sense . . . in which Churchill would have constructively critical colleagues" including a Dominion Prime Minister.[11]

To achieve his aim, Menzies suggested that they meet in London where they could "jointly exercise a powerful influence in the re-shaping of the machinery of central control. . . ". He dismissed the idea of an Imperial War Cabinet as impractical and urged instead an "effective Dominions representation in a British War Cabinet, reduced in size and so constituted as to bring about the results of which I have written above".[12]

It would obviously have been preferable for an Imperial Conference to have been called at Churchill's invitation, acting under the influence of domestic political pressure. With this option apparently foreclosed, Menzies' cable to his fellow Premiers was a last-ditch attempt to out-flank Churchill's blockade. In approaching the Premiers, Menzies was careful to assure them that his proposal was not calculated to weaken the position of Churchill. This was obviously quite untrue but Menzies seemed past caring. He had only one aim—to make his mark in London and rescue the Empire—and all his energies were directed to this goal. As he informed Smuts and Mackenzie King, his political difficulties were considerable but he was "prepared to take any political risk at home if by going to London for the suggested conference I could contribute to what I feel is an essential change". Menzies asked that they reply quite confidentially to himself.[13]

Smuts replied on 10 July, reiterating his support for an Imperial Conference, but claiming that he would not be able to attend until later in the year. He also refused to support the idea of permanently including a Dominion Prime Minister in the British War Cabinet and maintained that the composition of the Cabinet was the prerogative of Churchill alone.[14]

Mackenzie King took nearly a month before he replied, and it was in much the same vein as Smuts. He stated that the other Dominions would not accept an Australian Prime Minister as their collective representative in the British War Cabinet and that Menzies' criticisms of Churchill's War Cabinet were ones which the "British Cabinet, parliament and people must remedy themselves".[15]

It is uncertain whether Mackenzie King's long-delayed reply was designed to hinder Menzies' manoeuvrings or was simply a reflection of his indecision on the issue of an Imperial War Cabinet. His political instincts impelled him to oppose it but, at the same time, he was anxious not to be seen publicly as the main impediment to greater Imperial integration. In mid-July, Malcolm MacDonald had urged King to take Menzies' cable seriously and go to London in August. MacDonald had confided that he and Halifax were both intending to travel to London during that month. This held out the prospect of London being deluged with Churchill's critics and possibly by the combined weight of their numbers and influence being able to force the pace of political change.[16] For a time, King seems to have dallied with this notion but by the end of July he had rejected it totally. Whether by divine light or by a more simple calculation of his political interests, the devout Canadian Premier finally resolved not to meddle in British politics and to oppose Menzies' plans for greater Dominion control of war policy.[17]

Menzies' approach to Smuts and Mackenzie King had been a sign of increasing desperation. Given the political situation in South Africa and Canada, it is difficult to understand how he could have entertained hopes of achieving his objective through the intercession of his Dominion counterparts. Perhaps the magnitude of his goal overwhelmed his political judgment. Meanwhile, in Australia, Menzies was in increasing difficulties. The Sydney press was never very favourably disposed towards him, and now Murdoch's press in Melbourne joined the ranks of his outright critics and began to back Fadden as an alternative Prime Minister.[18]

Following the dispatch of his cables to Smuts and Mackenzie King, there was, nonetheless, a renewed outbreak of speculation about Menzies returning to London. The Melbourne *Age* noted on 5 July that there had been a revival of reports in Canberra that Menzies might soon go to London, but commented that there was "no substantial justification for these reports".[19] In London, the *Economist* also reported that Menzies was likely to return to Britain for another visit.[20]

In the House of Commons, Churchill was asked again whether he would appoint a smaller War Cabinet including men of the calibre of Menzies. He again refused and denied any intention to call an Imperial War Conference.[21] Once more, Churchill had defused the issue. It was still, however, far from the end of the matter.

Churchill's intransigence in the face of criticism was a reflection of his strengthened position following the German attack on Russia. After the successive defeats in Greece and Crete, and the failure of Wavell's June offensive against Rommel, it was a relief for Churchill to find attention riveted on the titanic struggle between Hitler and Stalin. The expanses of Russia soaked up the German military like a sponge and did allow a respite of sorts for the overtaxed British forces in the Middle East. Though Britain was not yet strong enough to regain the initiative against Rommel, there were no more disastrous defeats immediately in prospect. The loss of Crete and Greece had failed to dislodge Churchill, so his critics now settled down to await the expected German victory against Russia. Churchill, like Beaverbrook, well realised that Britain's fate hung on Russia's and he bent his will to provide Stalin with the wherewithal for victory.

At home Menzies was being increasingly distracted by mounting unrest among his own party colleagues. Some of his more bitter critics openly called for his replacement by Fadden. On 28 July, Menzies confronted his critics at a special party meeting and he was able to have the party reaffirm its support for him. At the meeting, Menzies announced that he would begin a tour of Australian States that would take up much of his time during August. It was suggested that this tour was designed to recover some of the Government's popularity in case of an early election.[22] Having spent much of July in forestalling his political demise, he now sought to spend August rebuilding his political support among the Australian people. Meanwhile, the Japanese Army spent its time taking over bases in French Indo-China that would soon be used to launch attacks into Burma and Malaya.

In London, Menzies once more captured the attention of the British people when his book of British speeches was published in late July. It received widespread and favourable reviews in most of the British press. More importantly, it reaffirmed in no uncertain manner the British regard for Menzies. One newspaper wrote gushingly that

Menzies "touches nothing that he does not adorn with splendidly virile patriotism, passionate devotion to the Mother Country, and a deeply impressive conviction in the righteousness of our cause".[23] Another was likewise heavy in its praise and issued the Scottish invitation: "Will ye no' come back again? And soon."[24] This was an invitation to which Menzies desperately wanted to respond. At the end of July, conditions for his return to London were made more favourable by a resurgence of concern about Churchill's leadership within British political circles.

This time, Churchill was attacked for supposed instances of bungling in the production of war *matériel*. On 29 July, he replied to his critics during a debate in the House of Commons. Churchill's reception was again cool and Harold Nicolson later noted that there was a "sense of criticism in the air".[25] Another Conservative MP, Victor Cazalet, went further, assessing Churchill's speech as very bad and predicting that "things must blow up".[26] This was confirmed for Cazalet on 5 August when he lunched at the House of Commons and was surrounded by "Tremendous anti-Winston talk and feeling".[27]

At the Foreign Office, Eden's Principal Private Secretary, Oliver Harvey, similarly noted the decline in Churchill's stocks and questioned whether he could survive the course. Harvey wrote in his diary that Churchill's "headstrong qualities may outweigh his great abilities and he may have to go if we are to win the war".[28] This resurgence of criticism could be related directly to military events. The Germans were pushing at an alarming speed into the Russian heartland and were widely expected to be able soon to turn their attention on Britain's Middle East position or even on Britain itself.[29] Churchill's dictatorial methods could be tolerated when Britain was enjoying military success, but they created severe problems when times turned tough.

Churchill chose this time to meet Roosevelt for their first conference, in a battleship off the coast of Newfoundland. It took him away from London for 16 days from 3 to 19 August. In his absence, criticism blossomed, as his Ministers discovered that Churchill's presence was not indispensable to the running of Government or the prosecution of the war. One observer confided to his diary that Churchill was "growing increasingly unpopular with his ministers" and that "some go so far as to call him an old fool at times."[30] Even Churchill's Private Secretary, John Colville, was moved to write privately of the "rising annoyance in the House of Commons at the PM's personal resentment of criticism . . . and the offence which has been given to many people, including Ministers, by his treatment of them".[31]

On 7 August, Menzies met with his full Cabinet in Melbourne and that day dispatched a querulous cable to Churchill on the Middle East situation. Menzies requested from Churchill more information on the armoured and air strength in the Middle East and pointedly noted that Churchill's promised reinforcements had not eventuated. This, Menzies indicated, "fills us with great concern" and he pressed for definite and adequate reinforcements which he claimed pointedly were necessary "in the light of recent experience by the Australian Imperial Force. . . ".[32] That evening, Menzies left Melbourne by train for Adelaide, the first stop on his projected two-and-a-half-week tour of Australia.

As Menzies' train trundled through the night towards Adelaide, he had time to reflect on his political position and his hopes and fears for the future. That day, Menzies had received news from London of Churchill's meeting with Roosevelt. This was the first wartime meeting between the two leaders and it presumably caused Menzies alarm on several points. Bruce had cabled his own concern that Churchill would not stress sufficiently to Roosevelt the need for US action in the Far East to forestall the Japanese.[33] Of more importance to Menzies was the probability that the meeting would see a cementing of the bonds between Britain and America at the expense of those with the members of the Empire. This did in fact occur, with Churchill agreeing to end the economic integration of the Empire and to throw it open to economic penetration by America. Apart from this momentous agreement, the meeting was sure to establish Churchill's relationship with Roosevelt and so help to ward off threats to his position. Menzies therefore had much to mull over as his train carried him further from the centre of power in Australia and even further from Downing Street.

The political atmosphere in Australia was continuing to worsen for him. Three Labor members of the Advisory War Council pronounced on Labor's willingness to govern, with one, Norman Makin (Secretary of the Labor Party) claiming that Curtin had "stronger justification for leadership of the nation at this time" and that Menzies had "failed to consolidate the national effort".[34]

Meanwhile, the prominent Country Party member and Minister of Commerce, Sir Earle Page, again proposed a National Government for Australia. Claiming a new sense of urgency, Page implored that "not a moment should be wasted, otherwise events in the Pacific might outrun our ability to offer a bold united front". He stressed that it was now time for "blasting away the dangerous bottleneck".[35] To many people in Australia, Menzies was that dangerous bottleneck and he would have been in no doubt that his leadership was facing a fresh challenge.

By the time of his first speech in Adelaide, Menzies was obviously both depressed and frustrated. The *Age* correspondent reported that Menzies made no attempt to gloss over the troubles besetting Australia and the Empire but was rather "at pains to emphasise them". He told his Adelaide audience that it was the most vital hour in the history of Australia and that the country might soon find itself "thrown into an attitude of defence we never expected to be thrown into, and one which may call for the utmost ounce of our moral and physical courage".[36] No doubt part of Menzies' troubled mind was caused by the recent arrival of Mackenzie King's cable refusing to support an Imperial War Conference or the proposal to include Menzies in the British War Cabinet.

Despite Mackenzie King's cable, it may have occurred to Menzies that he had a chance to achieve at least an informal Imperial Conference. Mackenzie King would soon be in London, while the New Zealand Premier was also visiting the Imperial capital. If Menzies happened to time a return visit to coincide with his fellows', Churchill would find it difficult to resist a call for some form of Imperial consultation. And even if he did ignore such a call, there was the prospect of having three Dominion Premiers attending the meetings of the War Cabinet and thereby achieving an Imperial War Cabinet in substance if not in name. Halifax was also due to visit London from Washington and, from his seat in the War Cabinet, was likely to join in any chorus for political change. Bearing in mind the wartime censorship of news, it is not possible to determine the extent to which Menzies was aware of this coincidental convergence on London and whether it entered into his calculations over the next few dramatic weeks.

On 10 August, two days after making his Adelaide speech and while still in the South Australian capital, Menzies dramatically announced that he was abandoning his tour of the States. The reason was given as being Japanese moves in Indo-China, and Menzies proceeded on the overnight train back to Melbourne for a Cabinet meeting scheduled for noon on 11 August.

One can only speculate on Menzies' motives at this time. Perhaps he hoped that the dramatic cancellation of his tour would sufficiently stir both his colleagues and the population at large to allow him the chance to return to London to represent Australian interests during the apparent emergency. It is interesting in this connection that the

Age representative with Menzies should link the tour's cancellation with a possible return by Menzies to London.[37] And this was just the proposal that came from the Cabinet meetings on 11 and 12 August.

In recalling the events, the Army Minister, Percy Spender, claimed that the proposal that Menzies go to London did not come from Menzies but from Earle Page, although Spender admitted that Menzies "very willingly adopted it".[38] Earle Page may well have raised the idea at the Cabinet meeting but he would have done so only in the certain knowledge that it accorded with Menzies' private ambition. Menzies had made it plain that it was vitally necessary for Australia to be represented in the British War Cabinet and that only the Prime Minister could adequately represent Australia's interests.

At the end of the first day's meeting, Menzies met privately with Curtin, presumably to obtain his endorsement for the plan. The following day, Cabinet met again and further talks were held with Curtin and, in the afternoon, between Fadden, Curtin, Menzies and the former Labor Prime Minister, J. H. Scullin. Despite this series of talks, Menzies was unable to secure definite endorsement of his proposal to leave for London. While Curtin was sympathetic, he was unable to commit his colleagues. In the absence of a definite commitment of Labor support, Menzies bravely announced that the Cabinet had asked him to proceed to London and that he would call Parliament together on 20 August to seek its endorsement.[39] It was to be crash through or crash.

When news of Menzies' plan reached London, it received the enthusiastic backing of the British press. Beaverbrook's *Daily Express* was in the forefront once again, taking Menzies' return as an accomplished fact and warmly greeting it as "good news". The paper described him effusively as one of the "clearest minds and most invigorating personalities of the Empire" and confidently predicted that the "war machine will run more briskly when he is at the centre of things".[40]

The *Times* was also forthright in its support for Menzies. Ironically, the day that it announced Menzies' plan, the *Times* also printed an article written earlier by its Australian correspondent. The article was an accurate representation of all Menzies' arguments for a Dominion representative in the War Cabinet and set out his plan to achieve it by way of an Imperial Conference. It is likely that the article was inspired by Menzies in the aftermath of receiving Mackenzie King's refusal to support him and was designed as a means of circumventing that opposition.[41]

Other newspapers were similarly supportive.[42] At the same time, Menzies' projected return became linked with dissatisfaction over Churchill's leadership and was seen as a chance to refashion the War Cabinet. On 14 August, the *Daily Mirror* called on Churchill to "Open the door of Downing-street to Mr. Menzies and put out the mat marked 'WELCOME' ''. The paper assured its readers that Menzies would "help to win the war—which is something one cannot be quite so sure of, in the case of three or four tired and ineffective men who today have the ear of the Prime Minister".[43]

The following day, the *Daily Mirror* returned with an article that perhaps surpassed any other in its unadulterated praise for Menzies. Boldly headed, "We need this man here...", the article claimed that Menzies left one outstanding impression both in Britain and America —that he was "*without doubt one of the finest Empire statesmen ever produced*". Then, after extolling his physical attributes, the paper claimed that he had the ability to "guide Empire affairs from the very highest post" and that, in an Empire War Cabinet he would "rate second to Churchill in ability, overshadowing the renowned General Smuts by his youth and directness and the crystal clear logic of his mind".[44]

The lure of Imperial power still beckoned enticingly, but there were enormous hurdles to be overcome. He had first to obtain the concurrence of his Parliamentary colleagues on 20 August. Even if this were achieved, there still remained the question of how he was to be assured of a permanent place in the British War Cabinet.

On 13 August, Menzies sounded out Bruce in London. In a cable marked "Most Immediate, Urgent Confidential and Personal to Mr. Bruce Himself Only", Menzies set out his predicament. He noted that Smuts and Mackenzie King were both opposed to his plans and that a section of the Australian press suggested he should resign and go to London as an ordinary Minister. This suggestion, he argued, was "fatal" since he could scarcely hope to carry real authority or weight in the British War Cabinet if he had been just rejected in Australia. Still, Menzies' aim was to get in the War Cabinet and he would not dismiss any avenue out of hand. He therefore set out four questions for Bruce to explore and answer. In obtaining the answers, he suggested that Bruce should have "a confidential chat with Beaverbrook as well as going through ordinary channels".[45]

Menzies' questions to Bruce were:

(1) If a Minister other than Prime Minister were sent to London

would he be given a seat in the War Cabinet.

(2) If I went to London not as Prime Minister but as an ordinary Minister would I be given a seat in the War Cabinet.

(3) If I went as Prime Minister but after a month or two felt my indefinite absence from Australia was creating embarrassment here and then resigned Premiership what prospect would there be of my being asked or allowed to continue to sit in the British War Cabinet.

(4) What is your own opinion on the business generally.

Menzies' intention was certainly clear in the framing of these questions—how to reconcile his position as Australian Prime Minister with his overriding ambition to strike out for himself in London. He informed Bruce that he believed he was more effective in London than in Australia where a "hail-fellow-well-met technique is preferred to either information or reason".[46] Despite the clarity of his intention, there remained a hesitancy in his actions. Menzies was apparently apprehensive of arriving in London to find himself unable to turn his presence to political account. Distance and absence from London had probably taken a certain toll on Menzies' self-assurance regarding his likely reception.

Any hesitancy on Menzies' part was doubtless dispelled by a cable from Bruce, also on 13 August. It is not clear whether this was in response to Menzies' cable or was rather an individual initiative by Bruce to stiffen Menzies' resolve. Whatever its origins, the message was unmistakable. Bruce urged Menzies to "get here as soon as it is physically possible to do so" and advised him that "the next two or three months will be of transcending importance in which fundamental questions concerning the war and the post war world will be determined." As well, Bruce held out the prospect that their shared hope for an Imperial Conference might yet be achieved. He informed Menzies that Mackenzie King was in fact to make a visit to London on 17 August; that New Zealand's Prime Minister, Fraser, was in London and intended to delay his departure in order to meet Mackenzie King; and that Smuts was in Cairo and that pressure was being put on him to proceed to London.[47] This last point must surely have stiffened Menzies' resolve to pursue his goal. Once again everything seemed within his grasp.

Bruce was obviously in touch with certain of Churchill's critics and his note about the pressure on Smuts seems to imply some inside knowledge of War Cabinet discussions. In fact, on 14 August, the

British War Cabinet considered the question of a Dominion Prime Ministers' meeting and gave it their support.[48] This, though, was in Churchill's absence and his deputy, Attlee, was appointed to put the proposal to Churchill who was still meeting with Roosevelt off Newfoundland.

In his cable, Attlee informed Churchill that Mackenzie King was proceeding to London and was agreeable to a meeting of Dominion Prime Ministers at the end of August; that Fraser was in London and agreeable to staying on for a meeting; that Smuts was in Cairo and could go on to London; and that Menzies had announced he was going to London once Parliamentary approval was obtained. In view of all this, the British War Cabinet view favoured a "brief meeting for purposes of general consultation as to the war position with particular reference to Far East". Attlee then asked whether Smuts, whose position was the determining factor, should now be requested to travel on from Cairo for such a meeting.[49]

If Attlee was under any illusions as to the purpose Menzies intended for such a meeting, Churchill most certainly was not. Despite the fact that three Dominion Premiers could be in London simultaneously and Smuts had felt able to leave South Africa for Cairo and was therefore half way to London anyway, Churchill came down firmly against any meeting. With the reasoning behind his objections becoming increasingly strained, Churchill replied that he did not think Fraser should be asked to stay longer and that he doubted whether Smuts could be absent from South Africa for that long and whether Britain should "press him to dangers of flight through Mediterranean".[50]

The bulk of Churchill's reply, though, was devoted to Menzies, who was meant to be going anyway. Churchill argued:

> *Menzies has only recently returned Australia, and I cannot think we should be justified in summoning him half round the world by air for only 3 or 4 days conference in a fortnight's time. He would no doubt like invitation to join War Cabinet but this raises many complications about other Dominions and size of the War Cabinet.*
>
> *Although he is unhappy in Australia there is no other man of comparable eminence and knowledge there.*

Churchill went so far, in fact, as to urge that the Premiers be kept isolated from one another, and that it was "much better to let Mackenzie King come alone . . .".[51]

Churchill was not alone in suspecting Menzies' motives, and doing everything possible to frustrate his ambitions. Menzies had freely criticised the members of Churchill's War Cabinet and they not unnaturally resented the description of being uncritical "yes men". On 15 August, Oliver Harvey noted Eden's concern at the idea of Menzies returning to London. Rather perceptively, Harvey claimed that Menzies was "in league with the Beaver (who is boosting him) and would like to get into English politics via the War Cabinet".[52]

So, it was not only the political monolith, Churchill, who had to be toppled; most of his ministers could be relied on to buttress his position rather than see the Australian raised to a position of power over them. Menzies would have been much wiser simply to attack Churchill's dictatorial methods and not impute minion status to his ministers. They may well then have been more willing to withdraw their support from Churchill at those times when there appeared to be sound reasons to do so.

It was not only in London that Menzies faced opposition. On 14 August, he met with the Advisory War Council and found that most of the Labor members would not condone his departure for London. Menzies argued strongly that Australia needed representation in the War Cabinet if her voice was to be heard and that only the Prime Minister could satisfactorily provide this representation. But despite the support of Curtin, Menzies' plan was firmly opposed by Forde, Evatt and Makin who stressed that the primary duty of an Australian Prime Minister was to provide leadership in Australia. Evatt himself regarded it as a means by Menzies to prevent deposition and block his own rise to power.[53]

In the face of Evatt's opposition, Curtin suggested a compromise whereby Menzies went to London, not for the war's duration, but "for the purpose of establishing the representation necessary". The result was apparently inconclusive, with Evatt simply reiterating that "he was not prepared to act on the assumption that the present Government would continue for the duration of the war".[54] Menzies could not leave Australia without the concurrence of the Labor Party and this was now looking extremely doubtful.[55]

In Britain, the climate of opinion was certainly receptive to Menzies' presence and might well have been prepared to accommodate his ambition. Criticisms of Churchill were increasingly common as was indicated by Sir James Grigg, the Permanent Under Secretary at the War Office, who wrote that the "general tendency of informed opinion is to be very critical and growingly so".[56] Even Eden, while being wary of Menzies, counted himself among Churchill's critics. He informed

Oliver Harvey that "so far as conduct of the war itself goes, he (Churchill) is now a nuisance...".[57] As for the British press, it was still practically unanimous in wanting Menzies' presence in London as a member of the War Cabinet.[58]

On 18 August, Menzies was informed by Bruce that Churchill was opposed to Smuts going on to London from Cairo.[59] This meant that an Imperial Conference was now less likely. Still, the possibility remained of Menzies gaining his War Cabinet seat by the force of his own presence. Bruce addressed himself to this question in a cable to Menzies on 19 August. This was in the way of a reply to Menzies' list of questions in his cable of the previous week. Bruce informed Menzies that he had not made any direct inquiries, but advised that it would be difficult for an ordinary Australian minister to be accorded a seat in the British War Cabinet. If Menzies resigned and went as such a minister, Bruce suggested that the public and press would probably demand a War Cabinet seat for Menzies. But, Bruce warned, there would be "a section here who would be bitterly opposed to it and who would use every spurious argument and underground method to prevent it".[60]

As for the possibility of Menzies going to London as Prime Minister and later resigning and remaining in the War Cabinet, Bruce held out more hope, advising that it would "entirely depend on the position you had created for yourself in the War Cabinet while sitting as Prime Minister of Australia". Lastly, Bruce emphasised that the Prime Minister of Australia could do great work in London but that the "efforts of anyone else would be frustrated".[61]

Bruce's advice was fairly unequivocal—if Menzies were to succeed in London he had to come as Prime Minister of Australia. The possibility of Menzies coming as an ordinary minister was firmly opposed by Bruce for reasons that he had only hinted at to Menzies. However, that same day, Bruce spelt out his principal objection during a private conversation with an Australian journalist. He confided to the journalist that Menzies' return to London as a minister would raise the suspicion that he was using it as a "jumping off point for entry into British politics" with all the "consequent antagonisms and apprehensions".[62] Of course, such suspicion was already rife and the antagonism was apparent.

On 20 August, Oliver Harvey confided in his diary that Churchill was

not at all anxious for Menzies to come back here. He has sent him a stiff telegram accordingly. The truth seems to be that

Menzies would like to get out of Australian politics and many in Australia would like him to go. . . . We had a good dose of Menzies early in the summer.[63]

The "stiff telegram" referred to by Harvey was sent by Churchill on 19 August, his first day in London following his conference with Roosevelt. That Churchill should have seen fit to devote part of this important day to blocking Menzies provides a further indication of the threat Churchill apparently felt the Australian posed.

In his cable, Churchill professed to extend a warm welcome to Menzies going to London as Australian Prime Minister. However, the cable made plain that Menzies would simply receive the treatment accorded him on the previous visit. That is, like all Dominion Premiers, he could sit in the War Cabinet but he would not be able to remain there if he resigned as Prime Minister, nor would there be any chance of him representing, in the War Cabinet, the four Dominions. Churchill closed his cable with a pointed reminder for Menzies to "bear these points in mind when making your plans".[64]

As the day of the decisive meeting of the Australian Parliament drew near, it became increasingly obvious that opposition from the Labor Party could be relied upon. Although Curtin supported Menzies' plan, many of his colleagues did not and they widely broadcast their opposition in the press and on the radio. Curtin, with his own position none too secure, was apparently stunned into silence. The *Age*, which also supported Menzies, tried vainly to restore the situation for him and argued for his mission.[65] The suspense was ended on 21 August when the Labor Party overruled Curtin and came down firmly against Menzies leaving for London, although supporting the idea of greater Dominion representation in London.

Menzies responded to Labor's rejection by once again offering to form a National Government with either himself, Curtin or a third person as Prime Minister. Menzies reportedly told his Government colleagues that he would serve in any position under an alternative Prime Minister and "would be ready to go abroad in any capacity if it were the desire of the new Government".[66] A National Government, even under another Prime Minister, was therefore seen by Menzies as still allowing for his mission to London. Curtin agreed to put this proposal before his colleagues on 26 August.

Meanwhile Mackenzie King had arrived in London on 21 August and lunched with Churchill in Downing Street that same day. The Canadian Premier was relieved to find that Churchill's paramount con-

Churchill greets Canadian Prime Minister, Mackenzie King,
on his arrival at Downing Street, 21 August 1941

cern was to enlist him in his campaign against an Imperial Conference
or War Cabinet. Before the other luncheon guests were admitted,
Churchill privately and forcefully attacked the practicality of Menzies'
plan, arguing that an Imperial Conference was not possible at that time
and making clear his opposition to ordinary Dominion ministers
attending the British War Cabinet. The two Premiers immediately
found themselves in happy agreement on these questions and each was
reinforced in his determination to stop Menzies' apparent ambition
achieving fruition.[67]

Mackenzie King already had received some reassurance when he
had met earlier that day with his New Zealand counterpart, Peter
Fraser, who had privately expressed his own opposition to Menzies'
plans and denied that there was any need for an Imperial Conference.[68]
With this triumvirate firmly established in opposition to Menzies, the
Canadian went further and immediately denounced the idea of an
Imperial War Cabinet when he met representatives of the world's
press.[69]

At a meeting with British Ministers on the following day, he argued, as well, against the need for an Imperial Conference and was reinforced by ministers resentful at Menzies' push for power in London. They told him that Menzies had "made it only too obvious that he wished to get away".[70] An observer at the meeting later noted that Churchill and his colleagues were "all enthusiastic" over Mackenzie King's rejection of an Imperial War Cabinet which was "really only promoted by those who want to use it as a means to reorganize the War Cabinet here".[71]

Despite this apparent unanimity against Menzies, he still retained some influential supporters in London. One such person was Lord Astor, who now intervened to try and change Mackenzie King's publicly expressed opposition to greater Dominion representation. Unfortunately for Astor, his attempt came 36 hours too late, for the Canadian was now steadfast in his opposition after having heard the views of Fraser and Churchill. Still, in the privacy of King's Dorchester suite, Astor persisted with his attempt to alert the Canadian Premier to the dangers of Churchill's almost unbridled power over policy. He particularly urged that King should meet Lloyd George who, he argued, was still lucid for a few hours each day and "should have been in the Ministry and a help to Churchill in furnishing him some ideas on the side that he, Churchill, was lacking". Astor also pushed the case for Menzies, arguing that someone like Menzies, or Mackenzie King himself, should be included in the War Cabinet to "stand up to Churchill as his colleagues were not inclined to do". He further claimed that the British public would welcome an outsider to reform the War Cabinet. The Canadian was not swayed by the arguments of Astor whom he labelled as "one of the group that have been trying to keep Churchill where he is but get others to work their particular will upon him".[72]

With Mackenzie King now firmly on side, Churchill apparently felt free to become more open in his own attacks on the Australian Premier. During a weekend at Chequers, he revealed the depth of his own bitterness at Menzies' plans. Mackenzie King seemed to have been quite taken aback to hear Churchill speak

> *very strongly against Menzies. Quite differently than he had in*
> *previous conversation when he had alluded more particularly to*
> *Menzies' difficulties and the difficulty that the labour party were*
> *making for him. In speaking strongly, he said he loathes his own*
> *people. He wants to be in England. He says you cannot hope to*
> *be Prime Minister of a people you don't like.*

While Churchill admitted that he had "many enemies in the Tory party", he nevertheless stoutly defended his War Cabinet and resisted any call for change. As he told King: "I know I have the people and I don't much care about anything else".[73]

Over lunch on the following day, Churchill was joined by Beaverbrook, who now joined in being "quite outspoken about Menzies' zeal to get to London instead of staying with his own people". Later that afternoon, Mackenzie King approached Churchill and confided:

> *having heard the way he had spoken the night before of Menzies*
> *and of what he knew of what Menzies had been saying and his*
> *attitude generally, I did not think it would be betraying any trust*
> *but rather doing my duty to the whole situation if I let him see*
> *the reply I had sent to Menzies in answer to his request for my*
> *views on Dominion representation in the Cabinet.*[74]

Churchill cannot have been too surprised at the contents of the cables as he well knew Menzies' views and ambitions. But the disclosure of the cables cemented the alliance between Churchill and Mackenzie King and created a solid wall blocking Menzies' path.

Nevertheless, there were still attempts by Churchill's critics to find a formula to allow Menzies' passage to London. Beaverbrook's associate, Beverley Baxter MP, now proposed a way around the opposition from Mackenzie King and Churchill. In an article in the *Sunday Graphic*, Baxter proposed that Menzies go to London for the duration of the war and, along with other Empire representatives, be appointed as special Ministers of State, answerable only to the King.[75] An alternative solution, proposed by the *Times*, was for Dominion Prime Ministers in London to be *ex officio* members of the War Cabinet, there as a matter of right rather than invitation. Additionally, the paper proposed that the Dominions Secretary be made a member of the War Cabinet.[76] All these suggestions were to come too late for Menzies.

The Australian Prime Minister was already beginning to be written out of contention by the men in London who had rallied around him in earlier days. One such Churchill critic informed Mackenzie King confidentially that he had "begged Menzies not to make the kind of mistake that he was making, to imagine that he was the Messiah...and not to be carried away by the idea that because he could make speeches, he was going to take everything in hand". Mackenzie King reflected sadly that Menzies had now "spoiled his future in Australia" but was happy to note that this would prevent him carving out a position for himself in London.[77] In Mackenzie

King's deeply religious scheme of things, it doubtless smacked of divine intervention, and just retribution for Menzies' pride and ambition, and it also vindicated his own stance against closer Imperial integration.

The way to London was finally barred to Menzies as Prime Minister when, on 26 August, the Labor Party announced it would not take up his offer of a National Government and suggested instead that Menzies resign in favour of a Labor administration. This in turn prompted further dissension within Menzies' UAP, with a growing chorus of his colleagues and members of the Country Party calling for him to step down in favour of Fadden.

On 28 August Menzies announced to the House of Representatives that the Government had decided to dispatch a minister other than the Prime Minister to London as soon as possible. He then adjourned the House for several weeks' recess and proceeded to a meeting of his Cabinet where he announced to his UAP colleagues his intention to resign. Few asked him to reconsider. Within a few hours a joint meeting of UAP and Country Party members had voted to elect Fadden into the Prime Ministerial chair.

It has been widely remarked that Menzies resigned without rancour or bitterness and in a surprisingly cheerful frame of mind. It is difficult to escape the conclusion that he had already arranged with Fadden that he would resign on condition that he (Menzies) be the minister to be dispatched without delay to London. This in fact is the claim made later in a sympathetic biography of Menzies written by one of his close friends.[78] If true, as seems likely, Menzies had failed to allow for Churchill's continuing ability to short-circuit his plans. Then again, Menzies' control of his own destiny was increasingly slipping from his grasp and his resignation was probably a last-ditch attempt to reassert some control over events.

Whatever was in Menzies' mind, Churchill remained determined that the Australian would not rejoin his War Cabinet. He had already advised Menzies that an ordinary minister would not be admitted to its ranks, and he now moved to make this crystal clear.

Mackenzie King was attending the British War Cabinet on the day of Menzies' resignation but before news of it had reached London. He noted in his diary that, when the War Cabinet discussed press speculation about Menzies joining them as a Resident Minister,

Churchill at once said this should be denied by the Ministry of Information and the Dominions Office at once . . . Churchill said

the best thing for Menzies to do, if he is bound to come, was to take Bruce's place, but he was quite determined not to have any Minister other than the Prime Minister in the Cabinet, and said they would have to take up the matter with other Dominions.

. . . It is quite clear that they are all considerably perturbed by the latest word that Menzies may resign, be succeeded by some other person, and he, himself, come over as a Minister. Later, Churchill asked me to have my staff keep his office informed as to my movements as it might be necessary for him to consult with me at any moment.[79]

It would seem that Churchill was going to once again use Mackenzie King to thwart Menzies' ambitions. However, it was no longer necessary. Menzies had largely defeated himself. Later, the Canadian Premier was informed of Churchill's immense pleasure with the way he had "relieved them of the Menzies difficulty".[80]

On 29 August, as Fadden took over as Prime Minister, Churchill dispatched a cable of good wishes for his success and pronounced himself glad to see Menzies serving under Fadden as Minister for Co-ordination of Defence. However, the bulk of the very long cable was devoted to reasons why Churchill could not accept an Australian minister as a "responsible partner in the daily work of our Government". Not only would an Australian minister not be admitted to the War Cabinet, but the question of an Imperial War Cabinet would only be decided with the agreement of all of the Dominions.[81] This cable was obviously designed to rid Menzies of any lingering idea that the door to the British War Cabinet might still be open to him.

However, Menzies seems already to have had second thoughts about going to London as an ordinary minister. In a cable on 29 August, he informed Churchill of his resignation, claiming to "deeply regret the fact that this will mean that I am no longer in contact with you". He admitted that he had "so looked forward to the possibility of a renewed association in London but this now appears most unlikely".[82]

It was Lord Cranborne who best summed up the reaction of the British Cabinet to Menzies' defeat and confirmed how seriously his challenge had been regarded in Downing Street. Writing to a friend and colleague on 31 August, Cranborne complained of having had a "rather hectic time with the miserable Australians" but expressed relief that Menzies' return to London had at last been blocked. In fact, he could hardly believe their good fortune when Menzies was struck down by his own hand after having made "more of a hash of things than one would have thought possible". Though Cranborne could not help feeling sorry for him in his humiliating fall from power, he well realised that Menzies' humiliation would help ensure Churchill's salvation. As he concluded, it was better that Menzies was out of the way as his "intriguing was a constant danger".[83]

The relief in London at Menzies' defeat was profound but proved to be rather premature. Though ousted as Prime Minister, Menzies had not relinquished his desire to sit on the benches at Westminster, nor did his misgivings about the war suddenly abate. Over the next 18 months Menzies continued his attempts to make his mark in British politics. And it was Churchill who repeatedly blocked his every move.

NOTES

1. "NOTES ON MY LIFE" by Lord Alanbrooke, p. 282, 3/A/IV, Alanbrooke Papers: KC
2. In Australia, Curtin concluded that "the most obvious and clearest lesson emerging to-day was that any country, including ourselves, who sought to make peace with an undefeated Germany would make a peace which Germany would not keep...", *Age*, Melbourne, 24 June 1941: KC
3. LETTER, Frances Stevenson to Liddell Hart, 2 July 1941, 1/450, Liddell Hart Papers: KC
4. M. GILBERT, p. 1119
5. *DAFP*, iv, Doc. 522, Cable No. 402, Menzies to Churchill, 28 June 1941
6. *AGE*, Melbourne, 24 June 1941
7. CABLE (DRAFT), Churchill to Mackenzie King, 23 June 1941, PREM 4/43A/12: PRO
8. *AGE*, Melbourne, 25 June 1941
9. *DAILY TELEGRAPH*, London, 25 June 1941
10. *DAFP*, v, Doc. 1, Cable 46/2, Menzies to Smuts and Mackenzie King and repeated to Bruce as No. 3465, 3 July 1941
11. *IBID*.
12. *IBID*.
13. *IBID*.
14. *DAFP*, v, p. 5, fn. 4
15. CABLE (EXTRACT), Mackenzie King to Menzies, 2 August 1941 and repeated to Churchill who initialled it on 7 September 1941, PREM 4/43A/13: PRO
16. MACKENZIE KING DIARY, 14 July, 1941: CUL
17. *IBID*., 1 August 1941
18. M. WARD, "Sir Keith Murdoch: The Flinders Street Broker", B. Litt. thesis (ANU, 1981), MS 6624: NLA
19. *AGE*, Melbourne, 5 July 1941
20. *ECONOMIST*, London, 5 July 1941
21. *AGE*, Melbourne, 8 July 1941

22. AGE, Melbourne, 29 July 1941
23. WESTERN MAIL, 23 July 1941; see also *Public Opinion*, 18 July 1941; *Birmingham Mercury*, 20 July 1941, *Scotsman*, 24 July 1941, *Times*, *Times Literary Supplement*, 26 July 1941, *Observer*, 27 July 1941
24. CHURCH OF ENGLAND NEWSPAPER, 11 August 1941
25. NICOLSON DIARY, 29 July 1941, Sir H. Nicolson (ed.), p. 183
26. CAZALET DIARY, 29 July 1941, R. R. James (ed.), p. 263
27. CAZALET DIARY, 5 August 1941, *ibid.*; see also Letter, Cranborne to P. Emrys-Evans, 31 July 1941, ADD.MS.58240, Emrys-Evans Papers: BL
28. HARVEY DIARY, 3 August 1941, ADD.MS.56398, Harvey Papers: BL
29. M. GILBERT, p. 1143
30. KING DIARY, 7 August 1941, C. King, p. 138
31. COLVILLE DIARY, 18 August 1941, in M. Gilbert, p. 1170
32. CABLE NO. 514, Menzies to Churchill, 7 August 1941, PREM 3/296/13: PRO
33. CABLE 627, Bruce to Menzies, 7 August 1941, CRS M100, "August 1941": AA
34. AGE, Melbourne, 7 August 1941
35. IBID.
36. AGE, Melbourne, 9 August 1941
37. AGE, Melbourne, 11 August 1941
38. P. SPENDER, *Politics and a Man*, Sydney, 1972, p. 161
39. AGE, Melbourne, 13 August 1941
40. DAILY EXPRESS, London, 13 August 1941
41. TIMES, London, 13 August 1941
42. See SCOTSMAN, *Yorkshire Post*, 13 August 1941; *Yorkshire Post*, 14 August 1941; *Observer, Sunday Graphic*, London, 17 August 1941
43. DAILY MIRROR, London, 14 August 1941
44. IBID., 15 August 1941
45. DAFP, v, Doc. 41, Cable, Menzies to Bruce, 13 August 1941
46. IBID.
47. DAFP, v, Doc. 43, Cable No. 2, Bruce to Menzies, 13 August 1941
48. WAR CABINET CONCLUSIONS, 14 August 1941, Cab. 65/19, W.M.82(41): PRO
49. CABLE ABBEY NO. 46, Attlee to Churchill, 14 August 1941, PREM 4/43A/12: PRO
50. CABLE TUDOR NO. 36, Churchill to Attlee, 15 August 1941, PREM 4/43A/12: PRO
51. IBID.
52. HARVEY DIARY, 15 August 1941, ADD.MS.56398, Harvey Papers: BL
53. ADVISORY WAR COUNCIL MINUTES, 14 August 1941, CRS A2682/3/467: AA
54. IBID.
55. AGE, Melbourne, 14 August 1941
56. LETTER, Grigg to his father, 15 August 1941, PJGG 9/6/16, Grigg Papers: CC
57. HARVEY DIARY, 17 August 1941, ADD.MS.56398, Harvey Papers: BL
58. See DAILY MAIL, *Daily Telegraph, Evening News, Daily Express*, London, *Liverpool Post*, 21 August 1941
59. DAFP, v, p. 75, fn. 7
60. CABLE NO. 10, Bruce to Menzies, 19 August 1941, CRS M100, "August 1941": AA
61. IBID.

62. NOTE of meeting with Trevor Smith, 9 August 1941, CRS M100, "August 1941": AA
63. HARVEY DIARY, 20 August 1941, ADD.MS.56398, Harvey Papers: BL
64. CABLE, Churchill to Menzies, 19 August 1941, in W. S. Churchill, iii, p. 365. A slightly different version appears in "The Prime Minister's Personal Telegrams 1941": VI/I, Ismay Papers: KC
65. AGE, Melbourne, 16, 18, 19, 20 and 21 August 1941
66. IBID., 23 August 1941
67. MACKENZIE KING DIARY, 21 August 1941: CUL
68. IBID.
69. AGE, Melbourne, 23 August 1941
70. MACKENZIE KING DIARY, 22 August 1941: CUL
71. V. MASSEY, *What's Past is Prologue*, Toronto, 1963, p. 316
72. MACKENZIE KING DIARY, 22 August 1941: CUL
73. IBID., 23 August 1941
74. IBID., 24 August 1941
75. SUNDAY GRAPHIC, London, 24 August 1941
76. TIMES, London, 25 August 1941
77. MACKENZIE KING DIARY, 25 August 1941: CUL
78. SIR P. JOSKE, *Sir Robert Menzies, 1894–1978*, Sydney, 1978, p. 122
79. MACKENZIE KING DIARY, 28 August 1941: CUL
80. IBID., 16 October 1941
81. DAFP, v, Doc. 53, Cable No. 607, Churchill to Fadden, 29 August 1941
82. CABLE, Menzies to Churchill, 29 August 1941, PREM 4/50/4A: PRO
83. LETTER, Cranborne to P. Emrys-Evans, 31 August 1941, ADD.MS.58240, Emrys-Evans Papers: BL

15

Dénouement

*L*ike some great shooting star, Menzies had flashed across the political skies of the English-speaking world, dazzling onlookers with his brilliance. The waning was now so sudden that people could easily be excused for believing it was an apparition from the first. But Menzies' meteoric rise was not a figment of anyone's imagination.

From his first appearance in Victorian State politics in 1928, Menzies had moved quickly through the ranks of his more mediocre peers and onto the grander stage of Federal politics. In a little more than 10 years he had reached the very pinnacle of power in Australia. Within a further two he was being widely touted as the future leader of the British Empire. Now, barely in his prime, all was lost, or so it would have seemed. The effect on Menzies must have been devastating. Yet he managed to survive his rejection and the lack of public appreciation and acclaim, and draw on his massive inner resources for sustenance during the dark period that now confronted him.

Churchill's early rise had been similarly meteoric and he had also suffered an eclipse that had sent him wandering off into the political wilderness. Like Churchill, Menzies would emerge stronger and wiser for his experience, and indeed go on to dominate Australian politics for a generation. However, all that lay in the future. For the moment things looked very black.

Menzies' resignation as Prime Minister did not remove him from all political posts. Fadden kept him on as Minister for Co-ordination of Defence and he also retained his leadership of the UAP. He had therefore not extinguished his chances of regaining top political office in Australia.

Following his resignation, the question arose as to who was to be appointed to London as Australia's special representative. At least one writer has claimed that Menzies not only wanted this appointment, but that Fadden passed him over out of spite.[1] However, Menzies claimed that he was offered the post but refused it for the very good reason that it would not entail a seat in the War Cabinet and that the minister was simply on a brief mission and would have to return to Australia. Almost as an afterthought, Menzies added that he was now hardly placed to speak with any authority on behalf of Australia.[2] It is not clear whether Menzies' claim was accurate or merely a face-saving explanation to hide his embarrassment at being outwitted by the separate efforts of Fadden and Churchill.

Ironically, the post of Australian ministerial representative would have provided a perfect opportunity for Menzies' ambition to be realised. The man appointed, Sir Earle Page, arrived in London shortly before the Japanese attack on Pearl Harbour. The widening of the war led to Page being retained in London until mid-1942 and being permitted to sit in at meetings of the British War Cabinet. Churchill's popularity at that time was seriously threatened and Menzies, had he been in London, could almost certainly have turned the events to his advantage. Though he could not have known it in September 1941, by passing up the London post—if that's the way it happened—Menzies missed his last real chance for a tilt at Churchill.

Despite the fact that Menzies' plans had been aborted, the talk of his imminent departure for London continued. One of Page's duties was to explore the possibility of boosting Australian representation in London and it was now suggested that Menzies might proceed to London once Page had laid the groundwork for Menzies' entry into the British War Cabinet.[3] It is likely that this was no more than idle speculation by the press. Of more substance, though, was the suggestion that Menzies might go privately to London and take up a seat in the House of Commons. This suggestion arose in London immediately after the announcement of Page's appointment.

Churchill was asked in the House whether he would now consider inviting Menzies and other Dominion statesmen to London for consultation and whether he would establish an Empire War Cabinet. Though he refused to answer the question,[4] the rumours of Menzies' return were given a fillip.[5] From London, the Australian journalist Trevor Smith reported the rumour that Menzies would "seize any opportunity offering here to enter Westminster". Smith claimed that this rumour had its genesis during Menzies' visit to London when it was said that he was "ambitious to become Deputy Prime Minister of Britain" and that the question undoubtedly "entered into private conversations at the time".[6] Though Menzies refused to comment on these rumours apart from disclaiming any knowledge of them, they provided confirmation for him that, even in defeat, his presence would be welcomed in some of London's political circles.[7]

The rumours were given extra life by Menzies' temporary disappearance from public view when he departed to his mountain retreat at Macedon. Bearing in mind that Menzies had so recently claimed the existence of a great emergency in the Pacific and that it was a most vital hour for Australia, it was more than a little incongruous to find him as Minister for Co-ordination of Defence at his Macedon holiday house.[8]

In Britain, though Churchill had a seemingly strong hold on power, there were many critics waiting in the wings. Liddell Hart was still arguing for a negotiated settlement with Germany,[9] while Lloyd George looked to a Russian collapse to produce the necessary political changes that would spell the end of Churchill and his policies.[10] For his part, Beaverbrook had latched on to the Russian cause and was apparently set on using it for his own self-promotion, perhaps even at the expense of Churchill.[11] Eden was still privately critical of Churchill,[12] while Sir James Grigg reported his own growing conviction that the British leader was "showing signs of becoming ga ga".[13]

The climate of public opinion in Britain was such that these criticisms could not be safely aired. Liddell Hart was still having articles published in the press but he had to tailor them to the prevailing view. When he suggested even the possibility of a compromise peace, the heavy hand of the press's self-censorship bore down.[14] As for Churchill, he ensured that such a possibility could never be explored by banning any governmental contact with the purveyors of German peace feelers.[15]

Menzies, one of the men who might have been able to bring such peace feelers to fruition, now made a further bid to reach London. It was made in the context of political turmoil in Australia. After losing the support of the two Independent MPs holding the balance of power, Fadden resigned as Prime Minister in favour of Curtin on 3 October. In the aftermath of Fadden's resignation, the UAP opted to retain Fadden rather than its own leader, Menzies, as leader of the combined Opposition parties. In protest, Menzies resigned the leadership of the UAP. On 9 October, the day after his resignation, the Governor-General of Australia, Lord Gowrie, cabled an urgent appeal to Churchill calling for Menzies to be given a seat in the House of Commons. Gowrie argued that Menzies would "render more useful service there than here, and his wide experience and knowledge of the Australian outlook would be useful both to the United Kingdom and Australia". Gowrie suggested that Churchill issue a suitable invitation as Leader of the Conservative Party that would "facilitate his severance from Australian politics".[16] It is doubtful whether Gowrie's cable could have been dispatched without at least the implicit concurrence of Menzies. In all likelihood it was done at his urgent request.

Churchill, though, still preferred to keep Menzies at arm's length. In his reply to Gowrie, Cranborne reported that he had spoken to Churchill who

> *feels strongly that from the Imperial point of view it would be unwise of Menzies to leave Australia at the present time. Though he will not be in office, he will occupy a unique position in the politics of the Commonwealth. With his outstanding abilities and experience, he will be able to speak in the Australian Parliament with a voice of combined authority and independence which no one else could command. In this way, he may play a far greater part in moulding the future than would be possible for a newcomer to political life here.*[17]

These reasons were, of course, completely spurious. As a lowly backbencher, devoid of party position, Menzies slipped into the political shadows. Though he retained a seat on the Advisory War Council, there was little opportunity for him to mould anything in Australia, at least in the short term.

Over the next few months, various suggestions arose for the employment of Menzies' talent outside of Australia. When they were made at Menzies' suggestion or with his agreement, Churchill firmly countered them by maintaining that Menzies' place was in Australia. However, twice the suggestions were made by Churchill himself with the intention, presumably, of neutralising Menzies as a potential political force in Britain. Churchill's suggestions firmly relegated Menzies to Australian roles only and were obviously designed to occupy Menzies' largely idle talents, stem the calls for his return to London and generally prevent his transfer into British politics.

The fall of Fadden not only pushed Menzies onto the Opposition backbenches, but also closed off one of his possible avenues for reaching London. As part of Earle Page's brief in London, the question of Australian representation in the War Cabinet was to be explored. The Labor Party opposed this idea and, with its accession to power, the question lapsed. Page now let it be known that he had no intention of trying to alter the membership of the British War Cabinet. It was only after the Japanese attack on Malaya in December that pressure again increased for Australian representation in the War Cabinet.

On his way to London, Page called on Mackenzie King in Ottawa where he scathingly criticised Menzies for being out of touch with the Australian people. Page alleged that Menzies had "not unpacked the grip that he had come back from England [with], he was so much in haste to get back to England again".[18] Mackenzie King later cabled to Churchill with the assurance that Page had "no thought of urging any kind of an Imperial War Cabinet or representation of Australia in the British War Cabinet, nor does he himself expect to be invited to attend any meeting of the War Cabinet".[19] Churchill could therefore be confident that Menzies would not be able to use this method of approach to the War Cabinet. For his part, Menzies would be forced into more indirect avenues to his increasingly distant ambition. Even now, there remained some possibilities.

Churchill had dispatched one of his Ministers, Duff Cooper, on a mission to Singapore to recommend measures for the co-ordination of defence in the Far East. As part of his subsequent report, Duff Cooper recommended the appointment of a British Commissioner General in the Far East, based at Singapore. In a letter to Churchill at the end of October, he suggested that Menzies should fill this post. He assured Churchill that Menzies had "no prospects in Australian politics for the next few years" and could be amenable to spending that time in a "big imperial post where he could regain credit on a broad, non-party basis". Duff Cooper was then in Singapore and was due to visit Australia. He informed Churchill that he would put the proposal to Menzies during his visit.[20]

Duff Cooper's proposal was clearly fraught with difficulties for Churchill. Though Menzies would still be far-distant from London, he would be occupying a British position of importance. Such a position would no doubt require consultations in London and might conceivably prove an ideal stepping stone to Westminster. Churchill therefore could not countenance such a possibility and he noted that he was "against Menzies, and think D. C. [Duff Cooper] should be told to stay there and do it himself".[21]

However, for some reason, Churchill did not learn of Duff Cooper's proposal until the end of November. By that time, Duff Cooper had been to Australia and put the plan to Menzies.[22] On 21 November, he cabled back to Churchill that Menzies "definitely welcomed the suggestion and I believe he would accept the post if it were offered him". Moreover, Duff Cooper assured Churchill that politicians from all parties in Australia would be glad for Menzies to be "given work which would occupy his talents while removing him further from the arena".[23] In the absence of Duff Cooper's explanatory letter, this cable had come like a shot out of the blue to Churchill. He immediately minuted to Cranborne: "I have heard nothing of this."[24]

Cranborne replied to Churchill that he also had heard nothing of the idea and that he was "not greatly enamoured" of it. It could, Cranborne claimed, put both Menzies and the British Government in an awkward position if Menzies had to implement instructions to which the Australian Government was opposed. Such an objection, it is worth pointing out, did not later prevent Churchill appointing the Australian diplomat and former politician Richard Casey as British Minister in the Middle East. However, this was Menzies, and Churchill merely noted shortly, "I agree."[25] It was only after this exchange that Duff Cooper's earlier letter came to light.

It seems that Churchill's opposition was never made known to either Menzies or Duff Cooper. The latter noted in his memoirs that events intervened to prevent the plan and no mention was made of the fact that Churchill had vetoed it.[26]

Unaware of the fact, Menzies dispatched a couple of excessively cordial cables on the occasion of Churchill's birthday and at Christmas. On 1 December, in a birthday message, Menzies assured him that their association was a "proud memory and an inspiration for the future".[27] Churchill replied non-committally.[28] If Menzies hoped by his cables to ingratiate himself, he was disappointed.

While these friendly messages flashed across the world, the Japanese armed forces were preparing to deliver messages of their own —to Roosevelt as well as Churchill. In simultaneous attacks on British and American possessions in the Pacific, even more violently than Australia had feared, the Japanese entered the Second World War. Britain's eastern Empire lay practically defenceless before them. If Menzies' failure in London to secure adequate reinforcements for the Far East was now beginning to haunt him, it was producing living nightmares for those forces already in Malaya, including the ill-fated Australian 8th Division. Again, and this time to an appalling degree, Australian troops were to suffer as a result of Menzies' inability to force strategic common sense on Churchill in theatres where Imperial troops were to bear the brunt of the fighting.

With the entry of Japan into the war, Churchill immediately left for Washington to co-ordinate the Allied response to hostilities on two fronts and to ensure that the main American effort was to be directed against Germany rather than Japan. In his absence, his critics re-appeared in force. One MP described the atmosphere in the House of

Commons on 18 December as being similar to that in May 1940 when Chamberlain fell from power.[29] Hugh Dalton confirmed this impression but took solace in the lack of any obvious alternative to Churchill. He claimed that there was "evidence that the old gang of Chamberlainites are fanning up each other's animosities against the Churchill Government". But without an obvious leader they were powerless.[30] While Dalton remained firm in his support for Churchill's leadership, the increasing criticism re-awoke the aspirations of Lloyd George.

With both Russia and America now actively on the same side as Britain, Lloyd George's conditions for a British victory had been fulfilled. He was therefore resigned to the fact that Britain must now see the war through to the end. At the same time, he entertained renewed hope that the rising rebellion in the Commons could still cut back Churchill's power and force his own inclusion in the Government.[31]

It was in this critical political atmosphere that Churchill once again sought to neutralise whatever remaining potential Menzies had for causing him political trouble in Britain. His chance arose when the British Minister to the Middle East, Oliver Lyttelton, demanded that the Australian Army Commander, General Blamey, be removed from the Middle East. Churchill took up this demand but, in a draft cable to Australia's Prime Minister Curtin, he added a suggestion of his own — that Curtin "should send someone with political experience, such as Menzies, to represent you on the Middle East War Council, and generally assist Lyttelton at Cairo".[32]

In the event, Churchill was unable to implement this suggestion, as the removal of Australian troops from the Middle East also caused Blamey's return to Australia and ended the need for an Australian political representative in that theatre. Still, it pointed to the tendentious nature of Churchill's previous claim that Menzies could best serve the Empire by remaining in Australia.

As for Menzies, the diminishing possibility of getting to Westminster still seemed to occupy his mind. He tried to ensure that any British resentment of Australia would not affect his own influence in London. In the absence of promised British assistance, Curtin's government had openly courted the United States with a view to it filling the place that Britain had vacated. This apparent disloyalty had caused intense resentment in certain quarters in Britain and Menzies acted to counter it. Choosing Beaverbrook's *Daily Express* for his message, Menzies explained that Australia now necessarily had to depend on the United States for help against Japan but that this did not denote any reduction in her attachment to Britain.[33]

With Australia now also in the front line of the war, the call for Dominion representation in the War Cabinet was renewed. As before, it arose at the same time as British calls for the reform of the War Cabinet.[34] Churchill tried to parry the call for Dominion representation by demanding that Australia must firstly set up a National Government before such a call could be considered.[35] However, the calls continued. On 19 January, the *Times* praised Menzies and urged on Churchill a war policy which embodied the ''assent of the Empire as a whole, with the Dominions participating continuously in its determination to the extent and under the form of representation that they desire''.[36]

Two days later, the *Times* returned to the attack, this time with an article by Menzies arguing for a permanent Australian representative in the War Cabinet.[37] Menzies' arguments were buttressed again by the *Times* on 24 January when the paper urged the inclusion of the Dominions Secretary in the War Cabinet and, if Australia so demanded, a representative of that Dominion also.[38] The *Spectator* similarly supported Menzies' call and noted that it was ''difficult to see how their request can be denied, or why anyone should wish to deny it''.[39] Churchill, though, was well aware that the call for Dominion representation was but a pretext to achieve the reconstruction of his War Cabinet and he firmly opposed it.

Lloyd George, who had been largely in the shadows ever since his unsuccessful attack on Churchill in May 1941, was now urged to adopt a prominent and critical stance once again. R. R. Stokes, MP, wrote to the ageing statesman on 22 January claiming that there were signs of a rift among the Conservatives and that it was ''of the utmost commonwealth importance that changes should be made *at the head*''. He urged Lloyd George to speak in the Commons and to attend it regularly. ''What is badly needed at the moment,'' Stokes wrote, ''is a 'Queen Bee' on which the Drones can swarm, but they have of course got to get used to the idea first—and they cannot if the 'Q.B.' is never there!''[40] When it came to the test, though, the Drones were found to prefer the Queen already in residence rather than the aged pretender.

Churchill addressed the Commons on 29 January and again managed to persuade his critics to stay their hands.[41] However, the criticisms of Churchill could not be stilled by a single speech. Military events both in Malaya and Libya were running badly against Britain and, with the fall of Singapore in mid-February 1942, Churchill's position was to come under renewed threat.

Demands were again being made for a smaller War Cabinet composed of ministers freed from departmental duties. At the same time the Curtin government was pushing for full membership for an Australian representative in the War Cabinet.[42] Menzies fell in with this move and vigorously argued for its implementation.[43] Whether he still saw it as a possible means for his own advancement in London is not completely clear. But it is clear that he still had his eyes firmly fixed on London. In late January, he pronounced himself very interested in a suggestion by a British MP that he be invited to enter the Commons.[44]

On 2 February, Menzies contributed another article to Beaverbrook's *Daily Express*. With Singapore set to fall, it carried implicit criticism of Churchill's leadership in allowing Australia to be so threatened by the Japanese. Menzies argued strongly that strategic imperatives made the defence of Australia a top priority and he urged that Britain divert one month's aircraft production to the Australian theatre.[45]

The fall of Singapore in mid-February brought everything to a head. In the Middle East, Rommel was again routing the British forces and threatening the security of Egypt. At the same time, the Germans defiantly sent two battle cruisers up the English Channel from Brest to Germany. The press and public were outraged and one observer wrote of the general anger at Churchill which produced "some talk about the formation of a so-called 'Centre Party' composed of Liberals, disgruntled Conservatives, etc., with Beaverbrook at its head".[46] Oliver Harvey also expected a political crisis and wrote to Eden that he had "never been so worried at the situation", that Churchill must "reform his Cabinet including a separate Minister of Defence, or he must be got to go . . . ".[47]

There were now frenetic discussions in London on how to dispose of Churchill. Bruce was actively involved in promoting the political aspirations of the Labour politician Sir Stafford Cripps, who was being widely touted as a likely candidate for the War Cabinet and even as a replacement for Churchill.[48] From Australia, Evatt, now Minister for External Affairs, also threw in his lot with Cripps in any campaign against Churchill.[49] In the Commons on 17 February, Churchill faced a hostile audience and was "obviously disgruntled and shaken by his reception".[50] Lloyd George, who had been invigorated by the upsurge of rebellion, was later seen in the Commons, "stamping up and down calling Churchill 'the old fool', and saying he had burnt all the bridges behind him and stopped up all possible ways of escape".[51] That night

Eden saw Lloyd George and pressed him to approach Churchill with a view to reconstructing the Cabinet. However, Lloyd George foresaw Churchill's imminent demise and again held back.[52]

In the midst of all this turmoil, Menzies saw fit to dispatch a message of encouragement to Churchill. Menzies complained that he was "compelled by political circumstances to be very much of an onlooker" but that he had "watched recent events with clear understanding [of] your problems". He expressed the greatest admiration for Churchill's "sustained and sustaining courage and leadership".[53] In his reply, Churchill claimed that he was indebted to Menzies for "all you are doing for our common cause".[54] The problem was that Menzies was doing little for the common cause. As an Opposition backbencher, there was little scope for his talents in Australia, while Churchill's continuing private resistance made impossible any role for him in London. Perhaps Menzies' cable had again been designed as a conciliatory gesture to prompt some sort of employment proposal from Churchill. It is even possible that Menzies may have foreseen the Cabinet changes being forced on Churchill and entertained wild hopes of his own inclusion. If so, he was again disappointed as Churchill outmanoeuvred his critics once again.

In a reconstruction of his War Cabinet, Churchill brought in Cripps and Lyttelton. The numbers in the Cabinet were reduced by one, from eight to seven, with the resignation of Beaverbrook and his departure for the United States, ostensibly for health reasons. Attlee was also made Deputy Prime Minister to give the appearance of Churchill's power being curbed.

The general reaction was that Churchill had survived by the skin of his teeth and that even these changes might only delay his downfall.[55] Oliver Harvey noted that the wily Churchill was also apparently trying to still the critics by suggesting that, for health reasons, he might soon go under his own volition. In his diary, Harvey predicted that Churchill "cannot last much longer and the present is only a temporary arrangement which can at most go on for two or three months".[56] This was also the view of other Churchill colleagues.[57] It was in the midst of this atmosphere, as he again fought for his political life, that Churchill received another proposal for Menzies' transfer to London.

This time, it came through the British High Commissioner in Canberra, Sir Ronald Cross. Cross had been Churchill's Shipping Minister during Menzies' visit to London and had been dropped from that position to fill the High Commissionership. On 26 February, Cross cabled to Churchill, informing him:

> *Menzies tells me he has no present opportunity of pulling his weight in the war effort and has no prospect of doing so. . . .*
>
> *Lacking opportunity in Australia, Menzies desires experience of membership of the House of Commons, say, for the remainder of the war. I believe he genuinely desires this experience. No doubt he also hopes for promotion so would gladly take his chance of that.*
>
> *Menzies believes that he would be more at home in the House of Commons than he is in the Federal Parliament.*
>
> *. . . Ignorance of your views makes it difficult for me to talk with him and I am now in need of guidance as to the line I should take.*[58]

As the new Dominions Secretary, Attlee advised Churchill to reiterate the view given to Gowrie the previous October. Attlee claimed that Australia was "none too strong in personnel" and argued that "Menzies' duty and utility was there". It did not take much to convince Churchill, and he merely marked on Attlee's note: "I agree: at present".[59] The "at present" part of Churchill's note was perhaps an indication that Churchill already had other plans. For just 13 days later, Churchill suggested to Curtin that Menzies be appointed Australian Minister to Washington.

The chain of events that brought this latest suggestion began with Churchill's Cabinet changes in mid-February 1942. Oliver Lyttelton, Britain's Minister of State in the Middle East, was brought back to London to take over Beaverbrook's Ministry of Production. The Cairo post thus fell vacant and Churchill took some four weeks to find a replacement. Many candidates were considered and rejected by Churchill.[60] According to Eden, Menzies was one of those considered but he was rejected because "he probably would not get on with the people in the Middle East being a somewhat difficult person. . . ".[61]

Eden's rationale for Menzies' rejection does not accord with the fact that Churchill had been prepared to propose Menzies for a Middle East post just two months previously. The difference was that the previous post had had a purely Australian dimension whereas the present one was purely British with, of all things, a seat in the War Cabinet. This Churchill would never accede to Menzies.

The candidate finally settled on by Churchill was Richard Casey, Australia's Minister in Washington! The appointment was made more incredible by the fact that Casey was virtually a complete unknown in Britain, despite this being a time when Churchill needed a person of stature to boost his failing political fortune. What could have caused him to appoint this unknown Dominion diplomat and court the displeasure of the Australian Government? Menzies may well provide the key to this riddle.

In an explanatory cable to Curtin on 13 March, Churchill justified the appointment of Casey by claiming that it "strikes the note of bringing statesmen from all over the Empire to the highest direction of affairs". So to that extent the Casey appointment was designed to allay the calls for greater Dominion representation. Churchill could, as well, now argue that Australia itself had *de facto* representation on the War Cabinet. But the most important aspect of the appointment is probably to be found later in Churchill's cable, where he suggested that Menzies could "fill the gap caused by Casey leaving Washington".[62] With Menzies securely tied to the American post, Churchill could practically write him off as a potential threat to his position. Moreover, with Casey as an Australian in the War Cabinet, proposals for Menzies' appointment could be cunningly rejected as superfluous. Churchill had turned the dissembling tactics adopted by Menzies and his British supporters against them.

Menzies, probably facing up to the inevitable, was willing to take the Washington post and he was widely supported in this by the Australian press.[63] However, he met with determined opposition from within the Labor Government. Though Curtin was willing, Evatt was not. Evatt's arguments won out and Menzies was left frustrated and idle in Australia.

In London, Churchill was still not free from the baying of his critics. He later recalled:

> The Ministerial reconstruction did not give much confidence or enthusiasm and I am ashamed to admit it as a concession or rather submission to Press criticism and public opinion. I believe I was strong enough to spit in all their faces. This was certainly not my Finest Hour.[64]

Though Lloyd George, Beaverbrook and Cripps all separately sought Churchill's political demise, none ever mustered enough strength to effect it. As the American commitment to the Allied cause increased in scale, Churchill's position grew more invulnerable. Even

Rommel's capture of Tobruk in June 1942 failed to rouse Churchill's critics into an effective opposition.[65]

As for Menzies, he bided his time on the backbenches waiting for the changes that could see his return to power and influence. Privately, he was critical of the way the war was going. In April 1942, he admitted to an associate that he had "shock after shock about our Naval position".[66] Publicly Menzies kept up his veneer of being a trenchant supporter of Churchill's policies. In a broadcast in July 1942, he stridently proclaimed that there must be no peace without complete victory and that Germany and Japan must realise the "whole anguish of war and learn the salutary lessons of defeat".[67] It is possible that Menzies may by then have believed what he was propounding. The prospects for a British victory were looking somewhat brighter and the impulse for a compromise peace was more difficult to sustain. But while Menzies' rationale had probably changed, he still retained an ambition to forge his future in Westminster.

By early 1943, an eventual Allied victory seemed even more likely. The limits of Japan's expansion had been set by the US Pacific Fleet, which had secured Australia, while in New Guinea and the Solomons Australian and American forces were steadily chipping away at the edifice of the short-lived Japanese Empire. In the Middle East, Rommel was on the run for the last time and would soon see his battered forces expelled from North Africa. In Russia, the wholesale German advance had been halted. Unable to proceed decisively, and denied by Hitler the chance to retreat, the German Army was in serious trouble. In the west, despite the U-boats, a fleet of ships was providing a virtual bridge across the Atlantic linking Britain and America. Across it flowed the men and *matériel* of war that would allow British troops in 1944 to march again into Europe.

In February 1943, Menzies fell out with most of his Opposition colleagues over a bill to introduce conscription on a limited basis only. On 10 February, Menzies and Percy Spender resigned from their membership of the Opposition's Joint Executive and the following day voted against the bill in the House of Representatives. It was a lonely group of 13 members who made their stand against the Opposition leadership. This has usually been taken as the beginning of Menzies' return from the political wilderness, the stand that was to lead to his eventual re-accession to the Australian Prime Ministership in 1949. In fact, at this stage, he was still looking to London for his political future.

On 11 February, the Australian businessman W. S. Robinson took up Menzies' case. Gowrie, Cross and now Robinson were all used by Menzies as intermediaries to smooth his way with Churchill. Robinson, as has been said, had important business links overseas, especially in London, and was close to both Lyttelton and Churchill's confidant, Brendan Bracken. Since Curtin had come to power in Canberra, Robinson had attached himself to Evatt and had accompanied him on a visit to Washington and London from March to June 1942. In April 1941, Robinson had pointed Menzies towards Lloyd George. Now he tried to overcome Churchill's opposition to Menzies' London transfer.

Robinson wrote to Evatt enclosing a letter to Brendan Bracken which he suggested should be sent via a British intelligence agent to London. In the enclosed letter to Bracken, Robinson wrote:

> There is no future for [Menzies][68] here. He recognises it. He alone is responsible. He is anxious to spy out the land elsewhere, and I feel that it is well that he should.
>
> . . . He recognises the mistakes he made on his last visit and is certain they will never be made again. He would go as an out-and-out supporter of Winston and as a Britisher devoted to Australia and the Empire.
>
> He would not care to go unless he felt he would be reasonably welcome. This is why I write you.[69]

Six days later, Robinson followed this up with another message to Bracken. No record of it seems to have survived, but, in an accompanying note, Robinson gave a good indication of its contents. He informed Bracken that Menzies and Spender had

> cut sorry figures last week. Both want to retire—their departure may make things easier for us all—it certainly does so for their opponents. . .
>
> I hope you are able to satisfactorily respond to the suggestion in the two cables, one through Canberra and one privately. If you are not able to do so, you and we may find ourselves landed with a couple of unutterable and uninteresting bores perfectly useless either to the British Empire in general and Britain and Australia in particular.[70]

These are the only records that have so far surfaced of Menzies' ambition at that time. No record has yet come to light of any reply from Bracken.

Meanwhile, Churchill had recently returned from a conference with Roosevelt at Casablanca that had celebrated the Allied successes in North Africa and had set the course for eventual victory in Europe.

After his arrival in England on 6 February, Churchill fell ill with a cold that developed into pneumonia 10 days later. This kept him in bed and away from most of his work until late February.[71] This may well have prevented Robinson's request from reaching him for some time. In the interim, Menzies dispatched a get-well cable to Churchill on 24 February. A week later, Churchill thanked Menzies for his "kind telegram".[72] As for Menzies' wish to leave for London, there was not a word. This seems to have been the final confirmation for Menzies that his future must lie in Australia, and he set about clawing his way back to political power in Canberra.

In later years, in an attempt to fashion the views of future historians, Menzies was to play down his differences with Churchill during 1941 and deny the existence of any conflict.[73] As a final irony, the siren song from London was to rise again in 1957, during the Suez crisis, when it was again suggested that Menzies could walk into Downing Street unopposed.[74] This time Menzies shut his ears to it and went on to complete his record term of 17 continuous years as Prime Minister of Australia.

NOTES

1. (SIR) P. JOSKE, *Sir Robert Menzies 1894–1978*, Sydney, 1978, pp. 122–3
2. *AGE*, Melbourne, 8 September 1941
3. *COURIER MAIL*, Brisbane, 9 September 1941
4. *STAR*, London, 9 September 1941
5. See *YORKSHIRE POST*, 10 September 1941; *Daily Mirror*, Sydney, 10 September 1941; *Sun*, Sydney, 12 September 1941
6. *SUN*, Sydney, 10 September 1941
7. There was, of course, open hostility from other political circles allied to Churchill. See "Talk with J. Winant", 15 September 1941, M100, "September 1941": AA
8. *DAILY TELEGRAPH*, Sydney, 15 September 1941
9. "TRIAL BY FACTS", note by Liddell Hart, 6 September 1941, 11/1941/62, Liddell Hart Papers: KC
10. LETTER, Frances Stevenson to Liddell Hart, 23 September 1941, 1/450, Liddell Hart Papers: KC; King Diary, 3 October 1941, C. King, pp. 142–3
11. A. J. P. TAYLOR, *Beaverbrook*, London, 1972, p. 492. See also King Diary, 14 and 19 October 1941, C. King, pp. 145–6
12. CAZALET DIARY, 20 September 1941, R. R. James, (ed.) p. 264
13. LETTER, Grigg to his father, 1 October 1941, PJGG 9/6/17, Grigg Papers: CC
14. Liddell Hart complained to Lloyd George that one of his articles had been rejected by the *Daily Mail* because they were "too apprehensive of the '100 per centers' to venture publishing it". Letter, Liddell Hart to Lloyd George, 10 September 1941, 1/450, Liddell Hart Papers: KC

15. DALTON DIARY, 7 September 1941, Dalton Papers: LSE
16. CABLE, Gowrie to Cranborne, 9 October 1941, PREM 4/50/15: PRO
17. CABLE, Cranborne to Gowrie, 13 October 1941, PREM 4/50/15: PRO
18. MACKENZIE KING DIARY, 21 October 1941: CUL
19. CABLE NO. 217, Mackenzie King to Churchill, 25 October 1941, PREM 4/50/5: PRO
20. LETTER, Duff Cooper to Churchill, with note by Churchill, 31 October 1941, PREM 3/155: PRO
21. IBID.
22. It was not after Pearl Harbour, as Hazlehurst suggested, but a few weeks beforehand. C. Hazlehurst, p. 256
23. CABLE T. 845, Duff Cooper to Churchill, 21 November 1941, PREM 3/155: PRO
24. IBID., note by Churchill, 23 November 1941
25. MINUTE, Cranborne to Churchill, 24 November 1941, with note by Churchill, 25 November 1941, PREM 3/155: PRO
26. A. D. COOPER, *Old Men Forget*, London, 1953, p. 298
27. CABLE, Menzies to Churchill, 1 December 1941, MS 4936/1/57, Menzies Papers: NLA
28. CABLES, Churchill to Menzies, 5 December 1941 and 7 January 1942, MS 4936/1/57, Menzies Papers: NLA
29. CHANNON DIARY, 18 December 1941, R. R. James (ed.), p. 315
30. DALTON DIARY, 19 December 1941, Dalton Papers: LSE
31. "SUNDRY NOTES FOR HISTORY", Talk with Lloyd George, 19 December 1941, 11/1941/78, Liddell Hart Papers: KC
32. DRAFT CABLE (NOT SENT), Churchill to Curtin, 27 December 1941, PREM 3/63/3: PRO
33. *DAILY EXPRESS*, London, 6 January 1942
34. CHANNON DIARY, 9 January 1942, R. R. James (ed.), p. 316
35. WAR CABINET CONCLUSIONS, 17 January 1942, Cab. 65/25, W.M.(42)8: PRO
36. *TIMES*, London, 19 January 1942
37. IBID., 21 January 1942
38. IBID., 24 January 1942
39. *SPECTATOR.*, London, 23 January 1942
40. LETTER, Stokes to Lloyd George, 22 January 1942, G/19/3/37, Lloyd George Papers: HLRO
41. CHANNON DIARY, 29 January 1942, R. R. James (ed.), p. 319; see also H. Pelling, *Winston Churchill*, London, 1974, pp. 485–6
42. WAR CABINET CONCLUSIONS, 26 January 1942, Cab. 65/25, W.M.(42)11: PRO
43. *ADVERTISER*, Adelaide, 31 January 1942
44. *AGE*, Melbourne, 29 January 1942
45. *DAILY EXPRESS*, 2 February 1942
46. CHANNON DIARY, 13 February 1942, R. R. James (ed.), p. 321
47. LETTER, Harvey to Eden, 13 February 1942, ADD.MS.56402, Harvey Papers: BL; see also King Diary, 16 February 1942, C. King, p. 158; D. Carlton, *Anthony Eden*, London, 1981, pp. 202–6; R. R. James (ed.), *Cazalet*, p. 273
48. See TALK WITH CRIPPS, 16 February 1942; Talk with Eden, 17 February 1942; Talk with Attlee, 18 February 1942; Cable, Bruce to Curtin, 17 February 1942; all in M100, "February 1942": AA
49. *DAFP*, v, Doc. 335, Cable (draft), Evatt to Cripps, 16 February 1942

50. CHANNON DIARY, 17 February 1942, R. R. James (ed.), p. 322
51. KING DIARY, 18 February 1942, C. King, p. 159
52. SYLVESTER DIARY, 18 February 1942, C. Cross (ed.), p. 301
53. CABLE, Menzies to Churchill, 18 February 1942, MS.4936/1/57, Menzies Papers: NLA
54. CABLE, Churchill to Menzies, 23 February 1942, MS.4936/1/57, Menzies Papers: NLA
55. For various reactions, see KING DIARY, 19 and 25 February 1942, C. King, p. 159; Channon Diary, 20 February 1942, R. R. James (ed.), pp. 322–3; Letter, Tom Jones to his daughter, 19 February 1942, T. Jones, p. 497; Letter, Cazalet to Halifax, 26 February 1942, R. R. James (ed.), p. 273
56. HARVEY DIARY, 27 February 1942, ADD.MS.56398, Harvey Papers: BL
57. DALTON DIARY, 5 March 1942, Dalton Papers: LSE
58. CABLE NO. 177, Cross to Churchill, (received) 26 February 1942, PREM 4/50/15: PRO
59. MINUTE, Attlee to Churchill, 26 February 1942, with note by Churchill, 28 February 1942, PREM 4/50/15: PRO
60. HARVEY DIARY, 16, 20 February, 3, 9 and 14 March 1942, ADD.MS.56398, Harvey Papers: BL
61. TALK WITH EDEN, 19 March 1942, CRS M100, "March 1942": AA
62. *DAFP*, v, Doc. 412, Cable Winch 12, Churchill to Curtin, 13 March 1942
63. LETTER, N. T. Johnson, US Minister to Australia, to Cordell Hull, US Secretary of State, 23 April 1942, P. G. Edwards, *Australia Through American Eyes 1935–1945*, Brisbane, 1979, p. 68
64. "NOTES 1942", paper by Churchill, 12 July 1949 as preparation for his history of the war: II/3/165, Ismay Papers: KC
65. H. PELLING, pp. 492–3
66. LETTER, Menzies to Sir John Latham, 13 April 1942, MS.1009/1/5557, Latham Papers: NLA
67. *SYDNEY MORNING HERALD*, 18 July 1942
68. This quotation was taken from a copy of the letter in Robinson's Papers. Menzies' name was presumably omitted from the typescript for reasons of confidentiality and written into the original letter given to Evatt
69. LETTER, Robinson to Evatt with enclosure to Bracken, 11 February 1943, "Dr. H. V. Evatt" file, Robinson Papers: UMA
70. LETTER, Robinson to Bracken, (wrongly listed as being to Evatt) 17 February 1943, "Dr. H. V. Evatt" file, Robinson Papers: UMA
71. See H. PELLING, p. 501; Lord Moran, *Winston Churchill: The Struggle for Survival 1940–1965*, London, 1968, pp. 108–9
72. CABLES, Menzies to Churchill, 24 February 1943, Churchill to Menzies, 1 March 1943, MS.4936/1/57, Menzies Papers: NLA
73. See LETTERS, Menzies to Churchill, 7 November 1957, and Churchill to Menzies, 14 November 1957, MS.4936/1/58, Menzies Papers: NLA. This exchange of letters concerned the publication of General Kennedy's memoirs which had accurately reported Menzies' criticisms of Churchill. Menzies now claimed not to recall meeting Kennedy
74. LETTER, Eric Harrison, Australian High Commissioner in London, to Menzies, 4 February 1957, MS.4936/1/Personal Correspondence, Harrison, Eric, Sir 1948–1957, Menzies Papers: NLA

Conclusion

Menzies went to London to secure Australia's defence position. In this he was singularly unsuccessful. In material terms, he returned with little to buttress Australia's defences. In London he had too readily accepted British military priorities as his own and had not sufficiently kept Australian needs to the fore. This said, it is also true that there was little chance of extracting very much from an embattled Britain anyway. Churchill's Euro-centric view was firmly opposed to any dissipation of military strength on behalf of the distant Dominions. Still, Menzies' prestige in London was such that it might have effected some improvement for Australia had he been inclined to apply it more strenuously in that direction.

Though Australia remained largely defenceless despite Menzies' four months overseas, there was an important change in the Australian outlook as a result of his experiences. He had confirmed that the Far East came low on the list of British priorities and that Australia could not count on British help in the event of a Japanese attack. Shedden seems to have realised this even more keenly than Menzies and it doubtless allowed Australia to turn with less compunction toward the United States following the events at Pearl Harbour and the fall of Singapore. It emphasised that as far as defence was concerned Australia would have to rely on its own devices to a far greater degree than had ever been anticipated.

Menzies' trip therefore confirmed one of the realities of international relations that nevertheless seems to demand constant repetition for it to be appreciated. It is this, that in the final analysis great states will act only to protect their perceived interests regardless of treaties and understandings with lesser states. Menzies, along with most Australians, had lived confident in the belief that Britain saw Australia as important and that the ties of Empire and blood would impel the "Mother Country" to spring to the defence of her Dominion just as

Australia had previously sprung to Britain's defence. In fact, to Britain in 1941, Australia was a distant charge of doubtful value which could only be defended at great cost to Britain's extra-Imperial interests.

Menzies recognised this unwillingness to divert defence resources to Australia but made the mistake of blaming it all on Churchill. He felt that with Churchill trimmed of his power, or even removed altogether, the British Empire could re-assume its proper coherence and proceed to a bright and peaceful future. However, Churchill was widely supported in Britain for the secondary importance he assigned to Empire. And the first two years of war had done much to confirm his position on this. Neither economically nor militarily was the Empire sufficient to sustain Britain against the might of Germany. It was only with America's economic support and supply of armaments that Britain could be secure. Imperial troops had not even been able to bring the minor Middle East battles to a decisive conclusion.

Menzies certainly acknowledged the weakness of the Empire but saw it as temporary. His view was undoubtedly—he was not alone in this—that there should be a temporary accommodation with Germany and Japan with the option of resuming the struggle when Britain was stronger. He was firmly opposed to Churchill's policy of selling out the Empire to America in order to ensure victory against Germany. Whereas Churchill argued that Britain could only be safe on the edge of Europe under the aegis of America, Menzies retained his faith in the ability of the far-flung Empire to forge itself into a force formidable enough to protect its many parts.

His views were obsolete. The forces of nationalism were already eating away at Imperial links and these were given extra impetus by the war. Even in Australia, the Labor Party was opposed to Australia's involvement in the conflicts of Europe. Empire military arrangements had no attraction whatsoever without the understanding that Britain should spring immediately to Australia's defence in the event of her being threatened. Indeed, there was decreasing inclination for Australia to reciprocate if Britain were threatened. This held true for Britain's other Dominions and colonies.

During the war and in its aftermath Churchill carefully created for himself such a historical presence that his opponents have tended to be lost in his shadow. But there were opponents and Churchill gave them much greater credence at the time than most people have done since. Lloyd George, Beaverbrook, Eden and Cripps were all at some time in determined opposition to him and each was considered at various times as his possible successor. Menzies was also among their number, and while he suffered from the disability of being a Dominion politician, was for a time seen as having more potential than any of them.

Writers who later recognised his British ambition tended to dismiss it as fantasy, as an aberration in the career of an otherwise consummate politician, but the fact that Menzies' attempt never amounted to anything public and has left few obvious traces, does not mean that it had no substance. Of all the contenders for Churchill's position, Menzies probably provided the most serious challenge. Churchill certainly took it seriously. All the others were sectional contenders whose past activities had generated animosity and opposition in rival political circles. Only Menzies could claim the cloak of apparent factional disinterest and have the potential to unite the disaffected British elite behind his banner. This can be seen in the wide range of British newspapers that came out in his support, together with the number of military, political and business leaders who encouraged him to believe that he could transfer his talents to Westminster.

It was on the British Prime Ministership that Menzies had set his sights. He was certainly aware that a political vacuum would follow Churchill's fall and Shedden's diary indicates that Menzies saw himself filling this void. Many observers in London and Canberra clearly recognised the extent of Menzies' ambition and acknowledged it as being within the bounds of possibility. Though Menzies himself realised that he could not expect to depose Churchill immediately, it was his eventual aim. His desperate attempts to call an Imperial Conference and obtain a seat in the War Cabinet reveal the method by which Menzies hoped to secure Churchill's downfall and his own accession to power. Churchill's equally desperate attempts to divert each successive thrust from Menzies indicate more clearly than anything the seriousness with which the British Premier regarded the Australian's challenge.

The question remains as to how realistic was this ambition and Churchill's fear of its success. In a sense the question is irrelevant so long as Menzies and Churchill believed in it themselves and allowed it to guide their actions. This they certainly did. And they were probably both right to do so. After all, it was not a question of Menzies transferring himself overnight from the Lodge in Canberra to 10 Downing Street. The process, rather, was to be step by step; the gaining of a seat in a reformed War Cabinet as Australian Prime Minister, the carving out of a place of prominence within the confines of the Cabinet, and then resignation from the Australian Prime Ministership in order to propel himself into British politics from the already elevated post of

War Cabinet member. Menzies clearly expected that he would rapidly become heir apparent to Churchill, and take over when the war took another turn for the worse, as he clearly expected that it would.

If the peak of Menzies' ambition was to be found in Downing Street and the purpose was to save the British Empire, the means was to be found in a negotiated peace with Germany. In searching for a possible compromise, Menzies had more than a few friends in Britain. Many military, political and business leaders hoped for an end to the war short of Churchill's total victory. Some of them recognised Menzies as an adherent to their cause and as the possible means of achieving it. However, they were never able to achieve the level of cohesion that might have allowed their hopes to meet with success. Nor did they ever manage to elicit a level of popular support serious enough to threaten Churchill's constituency.

Menzies might have been misguided in his prolonged attachment to appeasement and the Empire, and his London activities certainly did little to discharge his responsibility for Australia's defence. But there can be no denying the essential greatness of the man. In a short time in London he cut a wide swathe through British politics and was compared favourably with the best that Britain had to offer. While some of the plaudits were more anti-Churchill than pro-Menzies, most of the admiration that he generated was genuine. Never before or since has an Australian political figure received such widespread acclaim on the world stage.

The irony was that, in his own country, Menzies was a rank failure able only to produce enmity when unity was required. The contrast with his reception in Britain and America magnified the acclaim still further in Menzies' mind and convinced him that he was capable of anything in Britain. So, when the suggestions began to flow in from disaffected British politicians, soldiers and press barons, Menzies too readily gave them a hearing. They seemed to light up the path to Downing Street and, perhaps more importantly, to invest the ambition with a higher and nobler purpose. Imperial salvation and personal elevation were the motives which fuelled Menzies' efforts to topple Churchill. Churchill ensured that he met with defeat on both fronts. And when Churchill and Menzies came to recall for posterity their versions of these events, they were both careful to conceal the depth of their differences in 1941.

Bibliography

1 UNPUBLISHED MATERIAL

(a) Official Documents—Australian Archives, Canberra

AA CP 290/9, Cables to and from Rt Hon. Menzies and party during his visit to London, 21 January–26 May 1941

CRS M100, S. M. Bruce, Monthly War Files

CRS M103, S. M. Bruce, Supplementary War Files

CRS M104, S. M. Bruce, Folders of Annual Correspondence

AA 1970/559, S. M. Bruce, Miscellaneous Papers, 1939–45

CRS A1608, Prime Minister's Department, Correspondence Files, Secret and Confidential War Series (Fourth System) 1939–1945

CRS A2673, War Cabinet Minutes, 1939–1946

CRS A2682, Advisory War Council Minutes, 1940–45

CRS A2697, Cabinet Secretariat, Menzies and Fadden Ministries, minutes and submissions, 1939–41

CRS A3300, Australian Legation to USA, Correspondence Files, 1939–48

CRS A5954, Sir Frederick Shedden, Papers

(b) Official Documents—Public Record Office, London

CAB. 65, War Cabinet Conclusions and Confidential Annexes

CAB. 66, War Cabinet Memoranda

CAB. 69, War Cabinet Defence Committee (Operations), minutes and memoranda

PREM 1, 3, 4, 7, 10, Prime Minister's Papers

(c) Private Papers—Australia

FLINDERS UNIVERSITY LIBRARY, ADELAIDE
Dr H. V. Evatt, Papers

NATIONAL LIBRARY OF AUSTRALIA, CANBERRA
Sir Frederic Eggleston, Papers
Sir John Latham, Papers
Sir Robert Menzies, Papers
Sir Keith Murdoch, Papers
Sir Percy Spender, Papers

UNIVERSITY OF MELBOURNE ARCHIVES
W. S. Robinson, Papers

(d) Private Papers—Great Britain

BRITISH LIBRARY, LONDON
Admiral Sir A. B. Cunningham, Papers
P. Emrys-Evans, Papers
Oliver Harvey, Papers

CAMBRIDGE UNIVERSITY LIBRARY
W. Mackenzie King, Diary (microfiche)
Viscount Templewood, Papers

CHURCHILL COLLEGE ARCHIVES CENTRE, CAMBRIDGE
A. V. Alexander, Papers
Sir Alexander Cadogan, Papers
Lord Caldecote, Diary extracts
Sir Walter Crocker, Memoirs
Admiral Sir A. B. Cunningham, Papers
Admiral Sir William Davis, Memoirs
Sir Percy James Grigg, Papers
Lord Halifax, Papers (microfilm)
Lord Hankey, Papers
Sir Horace Seymour, Papers
Gerald Wilkinson, Papers

HOUSE OF LORDS RECORD OFFICE, LONDON
Lord Beaverbrook, Papers
David Lloyd George, Papers
Lord Wakehurst, Papers

IMPERIAL WAR MUSEUM, LONDON
Vice-Admiral J. W. Durnford, Papers
John Hughes, Papers

KING'S COLLEGE, LONDON
Lord Alanbrooke, Papers
Lord Ismay, Papers
Captain Liddell Hart, Papers

LONDON SCHOOL OF ECONOMICS
Hugh Dalton, Papers

NATIONAL MARITIME MUSEUM, GREENWICH
Admiral Kelly, Papers

READING UNIVERSITY LIBRARY
Nancy Astor, Papers
Waldorf Astor, Papers

SCOTTISH RECORD OFFICE, EDINBURGH
Lord Lothian, Papers

II PUBLISHED OFFICIAL DOCUMENTS

MURRAY, D. R. (ED.), *Documents on Canadian External Relations*, Volumes 7–8, Ottawa, 1974, 1976

NEALE, R. G., *ET AL.* (EDS), *Documents on Australian Foreign Policy 1937–49*, Volumes 1–6, Canberra

III PRESS

(Mainly from Menzies' extensive collection of newspaper cuttings)

(a) Australia

ADELAIDE
Advertiser

BRISBANE
Courier-Mail
Telegraph

MELBOURNE
Age
Argus
Herald
Sun

SYDNEY
Daily News
Daily Telegraph
Smith's Weekly
Sun
Sunday Sun
Sydney Morning Herald

(b) Canada

Amherst News (Novia Scotia)
Edmonton Journal
Evening Citizen (Ottawa)
Farm Journal (Ottawa)
Lethbridge Herald (Alberta)
Ottawa Journal

(c) Great Britain

Birmingham Mercury
Birmingham Post
Church of England Newspaper
Daily Express
Daily Herald
Daily Mail
Daily Mirror
Daily Sketch
Daily Telegraph
Economist
Empire News
Evening News
Evening Standard
Glasgow Bulletin
Glasgow Herald
Imperial Review
Lancashire Daily Post
Liverpool Post
Manchester Dispatch
Manchester Guardian
Morning Advertiser
Newcastle Journal
News Chronicle
News Review
New Statesman
Observer
People
Picture Post
Press News
Public Opinion
Scotsman
Spectator
Star
Sunday Chronicle
Sunday Express
Sunday Graphic
Sunday Mercury
Sunday Pictorial
Sunday Times
Sussex Daily News
Tatler
Times
Times Literary Supplement
Western Mail

Yorkshire Observer
Yorkshire Post

(d) United States

Chicago Tribune
Chicago News
Christian Science Monitor
Daily Mirror (New York)
Daily News (New York)
Examiner (Los Angeles)
Herald-Tribune (New York)
Life
Mirror (New York)
New York Times
News (Chicago)
Register (New Haven, Connecticut)
Star (Indianapolis)
Star (Washington)
Sun (New York)
Time
Tribune (Salt Lake City)
Washington Post

IV MEMOIRS, COLLECTED LETTERS, PUBLISHED DIARIES, SPEECHES, ETC.

(a) Australia

CALWELL, A. A., *Be Just and Fear Not*, Melbourne, 1972

CASEY, M., *Tides and Eddies*, London, 1966

CASEY, R. G., *Personal Experience 1939–46*, London, 1962

FADDEN, A, *They Called Me Artie*, Melbourne, 1969

HOLT, E., *Politics Is People*, Sydney, 1969

MENZIES, R. G., *To the People of Britain at War*, London, 1941

        Speech Is of Time, London, 1958

        Afternoon Light, London, 1967

        The Measure of the Years, London, 1970

PAGE, E., *Truant Surgeon*, Sydney, 1963

SPENDER, P., *Politics and a Man*, Sydney, 1972

WATT, A., *Australian Diplomat*, Sydney, 1972

(b) Canada

MASSEY, V., *What's Past Is Prologue*, Toronto, 1963

PICKERSGILL, J. W. (ED.), *The Mackenzie King Record*, volumes I and II, Toronto, 1960 and 1968

(c) Great Britain

ATTLEE, C., *As It Happened*, London, 1954

AVON, EARL OF, *The Reckoning*, London, 1965

BUTLER, LORD, *The Art of the Possible*, London, 1971

COLVILLE, J., *The Churchillians*, London, 1981

       Footprints in Time, London, 1976

       The Fringes of Power, London, 1985

COOPER, A. D., *Old Men Forget*, London, 1953

CROSS, C. (ED.), *Life with Lloyd George: The Diary of A. J. Sylvester 1931–45*, London, 1975

CUDLIPP, H., *Walking on the Water*, London, 1976

DILKS, D. (ED.), *The Diaries of Sir Alexander Cadogan O.M. 1938–1945*, London, 1971

HALIFAX, LORD, *Fulness of Days*, London, 1957

JAMES, R. R. (ED.), *Chips: The Diaries of Sir Henry Channon*, London, 1967

      Winston Churchill: His Complete Speeches 1897–1963, Volume 6, New York, 1974

      Victor Cazalet, London, 1976

JONES, T., *A Diary with Letters 1931–1950*, London, 1954

KENNEDY, MAJOR-GENERAL SIR J., *The Business of War*, London, 1957

KING, C., *With Malice Toward None*, London, 1970

LONGMORE, SIR A., *From Sea to Sky*, London, 1946

MARTIN, K., *Editor*, London, 1968

MORAN, LORD, *Winston Churchill: The Struggle for Survival 1940–1965*, London, 1968

NICOLSON, SIR H., *Diaries and Letters*, volume 2, London, 1967

ROLPH, C., *The Life, Letters and Diaries of Kingsley Martin*, London, 1973

TAYLOR, A. J. P., *A Personal History*, London, 1983

      (ED.), *My Darling Pussy: The Letters of Lloyd George and Frances Stevenson 1913–41*, London, 1975

YOUNG, K. (ED.), *The Diaries of Sir Robert Bruce Lockhart*, volume 2, London, 1980

(d) United States

EDWARDS, P. G. (ED.), *Australia Through American Eyes 1935–1945*, Brisbane, 1979

SHERWOOD, R., *The White House Papers of Harry L. Hopkins*, volume 1, London, 1948

WELLES, S., *The Time for Decision*, London, 1944

(e) South Africa

VAN DER POEL, J. (ED.), *Selections from the Smuts Papers*, volume 6, Cambridge, 1973

V SECONDARY WORKS

ANDREWS, E. H., *Isolationism and Appeasement in Australia*, Canberra, 1970

BARKER, E., *Churchill and Eden at War*, London, 1978

BEAVERBROOK, LORD, *Men and Power 1917–1918*, London, 1956
         The Decline and Fall of Lloyd George, London, 1966

CARLTON, D., *Anthony Eden*, London, 1981

CHURCHILL, W. S., *The Second World War*, volume 3, Sydney, 1950

COLLIER, R., *1941: Armageddon*, London, 1982

COLLIS, M. S., *Nancy Astor*, London, 1960

EDWARDS, C., *Bruce of Melbourne*, London, 1965

EDWARDS, P. G., *Prime Ministers and Diplomats*, Melbourne, 1983

FITZHARDINGE, L. F., *The Little Digger 1914–1952*, Sydney, 1979

GILBERT, M., *Finest Hour: Winston Churchill 1939–1941*, London, 1983

GRANATSTEIN, J. L., *Canada's War: The Politics of the Mackenzie King Government, 1939–1945*, Toronto, 1975

HAMILL, I., *The Strategic Illusion*, Singapore, 1981

HASLUCK, P., *The Government and the People 1939–42*, Canberra, 1952

HAZLEHURST, C., *Menzies Observed*, Sydney, 1979
         (ED.), *Australian Conservatism*, Canberra, 1979

HINSLEY, F. H., *British Intelligence in the Second World War*, volume 1, London, 1979

HORNER, D., *High Command*, Sydney, 1982

HUDSON, W. (ED.), *Towards a Foreign Policy, 1914–1941*, Melbourne, 1967

JAMES, R. R., *Churchill: A Study in Failure 1900–1939*, London, 1973

JOSKE, P., *Sir Robert Menzies, 1894–1978*, Sydney, 1978

LEE, J. M., *The Churchill Coalition 1940–1945*, London, 1980

LIDDELL HART, B., *History of the Second World War*, London, 1973

LONG, G., *Greece, Crete and Syria*, Canberra, 1953

McCARTHY, J., *Australia and Imperial Defence 1918–39*, Brisbane, 1976

MANSERGH, N., *Survey of British Commonwealth Affairs*, London, 1958

MILLAR, T. B., *Australia in Peace and War*, London, 1978

OVENDALE, R., *Appeasement and the English Speaking World*, Cardiff, 1975

OWEN, F., *Tempestuous Journey: Lloyd George His Life and Times*, London, 1954

PAWLE, G., *The War and Colonel Warden*, London, 1963

PELLING, H., *Winston Churchill*, London, 1974

PERKINS, K., *Menzies: The Last of the Queen's Men*, London, 1968

ROSKILL, S., *Hankey, Man of Secrets*, volume 3, London, 1974
  Churchill and the Admirals, London, 1977

ROSS, L., *John Curtin*, Melbourne, 1977

ROWLAND, P., *Lloyd George*, London, 1975

STIRLING A., *Lord Bruce*, Melbourne, 1974

TAYLOR, A. J. P., *Churchill: Four Faces and the Man*, London, 1969
  Beaverbrook, London, 1972
  (ED.), *Lloyd George: Twelve Essays*, London, 1971

THOMPSON, L., *1940—Year of Legend, Year of History*, London, 1966

WATT, SIR A., *The Evolution of Australian Foreign Policy 1938–1965*, Cambridge, 1967

WOOD, A., *The True History of Lord Beaverbrook*, London, 1965

WRENCH, J. E., *Geoffrey Dawson and Our Times*, London, 1955

WRINCH, P. M., *The Military Strategy of Winston Churchill*, Boston, 1961

YOUNG, K., *Churchill and Beaverbrook*, London, 1966

VI ARTICLES

ANDREWS, E. M., "The Australian Government and Appeasement", *Australian Journal of Politics and History*, April 1967

D'CRUZ, V., "Menzies' Foreign Policy, 1939–41", *Australian Quarterly*, September 1967

EDWARDS, P. G., "R. G. Menzies's Appeals to the United States, May–June 1940", *Australian Outlook*, 1974

"S. M. Bruce, R. G. Menzies and Australia's War Aims and Peace Aims, 1939–40", *Historical Studies*, April 1976

FADDEN, SIR A., "Forty Days and Forty Nights: Memoir of a War-Time Prime Minister", *Australian Outlook*, 1973

HAMILL, I., "An Expeditionary Force Mentality?: the despatch of Australian troops to the Middle East, 1939–1940", *Australian Outlook*, 1977

IRVINE, P. F., "The Implications of Australian War Aims", *Australian Quarterly*, December 1939

McCARTHY, J., "Australia: A View from Whitehall 1939–45", *Australian Outlook*, December 1974

ROBERTSON, J., "Australian War Policy 1939–1945", *Historical Studies*, October 1977

"Australia and the 'Beat Hitler First' Strategy, 1941–42: A Problem in Wartime Consultation", *Journal of Imperial and Commonwealth History*, May 1983

VII UNPUBLISHED PAPERS

HEMMINGS, W. J., "Australia and Britain's Far Eastern Defence Policy, 1937–42", B. Litt. thesis, Oxford, 1972

PRIMROSE, B., "Australian Naval Policy 1919–1942: a case study in Empire relations", Ph.D. thesis, A.N.U., 1974

WARD, M., "Sir Keith Murdoch: The Flinders Street Broker", B. Litt. thesis, A.N.U., 1981

WOODWARD, D. F., "Australian Diplomacy in the Second War—Relations with Britain and the U.S. 1939–41 under the Menzies and Fadden Governments", B.A. (Hons) thesis, Flinders University, 1973

Index